The Complete
Game

The Complete Game

Reflections on Baseball, Pitching, and Life on the Mound

RON DARLING

WITH DANIEL PAISNER

ALFRED A. KNOPF ————————————————————————

NEW YORK

2009

THIS IS A BORZOI BOOK
PUBLISHED BY ALFRED A. KNOPF

www.aaknopf.com

Library of Congress Cataloging-in-Publication Data
Darling, Ron.
The complete game : reflections on baseball, pitching, and life on the mound /
by Ron Darling with Daniel Paisner.
p.   cm.
ISBN 978-0-307-26984-3
1. Darling, Ron.   2. Baseball players—United States—Biography.
3. Pitchers (Baseball)—United States—Biography.   4. Pitching (Baseball)
I. Paisner, Daniel.   II. Title.
GV865.D37A3   2009
796.357092—dc22
[B]
2008055706

Manufactured in the United States of America
First Edition

My life has been punctuated by good times and bad.

My family represents all that is good.

This book is for them.

It breaks your heart. It is designed to break your heart. The game begins in the spring, when everything else begins again, and it blossoms in the summer, filling the afternoons and evenings, and then as soon as the chill rains come, it stops and leaves you to face the fall alone.

— A. BARTLETT GIAMATTI
former president, Yale University
former commissioner, Major League Baseball
from "The Green Fields of the Mind,"
Yale Alumni Magazine (November 1977)

Contents

Contents

The Complete Game

Let's Get It Right Today

"*Give* me the damn ball!"

That's been the rallying cry of major league pitchers since the turn of the last century. The ball. The pill. The rock. Call it what you want, it's the only equipment we need—our badge of honor, our point of pride. It's basic, as weapons go: a rounded piece of cushioned cork layered with a fine coating of rubber cement and wrapped in a tight winding of gray and tan wools and a thin poly-cotton thread. Then, another fine coating of rubber cement and two strips of cowhide, bound together with eighty-eight inches of waxed red thread—hand-sewn in the small farming village of Turrialba, Costa Rica, with 108 stitches.

But, of course, it's not only about the ball. It's about the act and the art of throwing it, and the responsibility that goes with the privilege of doing so for a major league baseball team. For most of us who have taken the pitcher's mound at the professional level, it's the weight of carrying the fortunes of our teammates, the sweet burden of being on point, that sets our role apart. If we don't execute, there's no hiding it out there on that mound.

Everyone who plays a sport likes to think he or she is pivotal, but with pitchers this is not an arrogant or self-aggrandizing view. The game rests on our shoulders. We stand apart from our teammates and set the tone. All eyes are on us. The game is in our hands. The hopes of our teammates are pinned to our chest. Sure, the outcome of any one game might turn on a remarkable effort in the field, a mighty swing of the bat, a gutsy play on the bases, but everything that happens on a ball field—everything!—flows in some way through the pitcher. It has every damn thing to do with us. That's how we feel, and the reason we feel this way is because it's been drummed into us over countless starts, countless innings, countless pitches with the game on the line.

Tom Seaver, one of the greatest pitchers ever to take the mound, and certainly the greatest to do so in a New York Mets uniform, had a cutting way with words. If he liked you, he was one of the most generous souls in the game. If he didn't ... well, not so much. We played together, briefly, in 1983, when I joined the big club for a late-season cameo. It was Tom's second tour with the Mets, and he was cast as a conquering hero, a favorite son turned elder statesman. He had a not-so-flattering nickname for the Mets trainer, "Fifty-Fifty"; I couldn't figure why. After I'd been in the bigs for a couple weeks, I got up the courage to ask Tom how he came up with the name.

"He's not the best trainer, kid," said Tom, who himself was

known as "the Franchise." (How's *that* for a nickname to con-
firm my point?) "And he's not the worst. He doesn't help you,
he doesn't hurt you. Fifty-Fifty."

I've thought about that moniker a lot over the years, and
early on I hoped it would never apply to me as a ballplayer,
affectionately or otherwise. Over time, however, I realized
there was no avoiding the tag. Sometimes you justify the faith
your teammates place in you, and sometimes you don't. If you
come through more often than not, you're doing okay.

And yet, in success and in struggle, getting the ball on
game day has to be the greatest rush in professional sports.
The game acknowledges this, in its own way. There's a certain amount of ceremony to the "anointing" or assigning of
pitching duties, like a transfer of power. It used to be that
pitchers knew they were getting a start only when they
arrived at their locker to find that day's pristine game ball sitting in their glove. The first time I heard about that, I was
already in the bigs, and it struck me as a fitting tradition: you
come to the ballpark; you find the ball in your locker; you
understand it's on you. That particular baseball ritual is gone,
but the symbolism holds. You can see it in the way an entire
team stands back in deference to the particulars of its starting
pitcher. You can see it in the stony silence position players
offer their pitcher while he's throwing a gem—or a dud. You
can see it in the way a manager waits on the mound to place
the ball in the hand of a reliever after a pitching change. He
strips one pitcher of the honor and delivers it to the next,
sending one man to the showers while his successor takes the
hill. The sword is passed, and we're entrusted with the fate of
our franchise—for that one day, or even that one batter, at
least until we fall short.

A starting pitcher, on his day, is a man alone. You're totally
ignored by your teammates. You feel it the moment you get to

the ballpark, and it runs through the entire game. There are exceptions: some pitchers are nervous and like to kid around, to relax; some pitchers reach out to their teammates and engage them in conversation, about the game or something else. But most pitchers are off on their own, lost in thought, making ready. They're looking for that zone, that tunnel, that place of calm and quiet that lets them get their head around the game, while their teammates hang back warily, afraid to encroach.

It's a special, certain thrill to head out to the ballpark knowing the game is yours, to do with what you will. For my family, it was somewhat less thrilling. I'd get a little moody as game day approached. On the morning of a game, it's possible I even lapsed into surliness. I was something of a bear, I was told, and my game-day habits reflected this. I would not be crossed or told what to do. For night games, I took my lunch at noon, because I wanted to be good and hungry and in an even fouler mood when game time rolled around. Lunch was always the same: steak, mashed potatoes, and peas. (Note: try finding good peas in Cincinnati.) All day long, I drank plenty of water—more or less, depending on the weather. (Another note: there wasn't enough water on the planet to keep a pitcher hydrated on the St. Louis turf in the middle of August, when temperatures ran to 130 degrees.) There was also a touch of cold sweats and nausea.

Game days at Shea were a particular adventure. On the road, I could hide in the shadows of the team bus, but at home I was on my own. You'd never know what might set me off. Early on in my career, I was the guy you didn't want to talk to on the 7 train out to Flushing—not quite De Niro in *Taxi Driver,* but close. Later, when the fans started to recognize me and the subway was no longer an option, I was the guy you didn't want to piss off on the Grand Central Parkway—the guy who could claim road rage as an essential occupational tool.

Leave me alone. That's the message I put out to the world on days I was due to pitch. Even to my wife and kids, the message was much the same: leave me alone so I can do my thing and prepare for battle.

People who know me will tell you I'm basically a good person. I'm kind to animals, and kids, and little old ladies. I hold the door open for strangers. But on game day, I was someone else, someone I didn't recognize—someone I didn't even necessarily *like*. Understand, I didn't will myself into a sour, angry mood; it just happened, and it happened for a reason. I was on a knife edge. It all fell to me—that's how I approached my time on the mound, and that approach inevitably colored my personality. I imagined I was a boxer, getting ready to step into the ring. A matador preparing to face down a charging bull. A fighter pilot embarking on a do-or-die mission.

God help the poor manager or pitching coach who had to administer last-minute instructions. Mel Stottlemyre, the Mets pitching coach and a great father figure to all of us young pitchers on those talented Mets teams of the late 1980s, knew how to handle me on game days. He was careful not to set me off, but at the same time there were always a couple things he felt he needed to discuss. I rarely bit Mel's head off, but I don't think I ever really listened to him, either. Despite his best efforts, I never could pay attention. Between starts, sure, I let Mel have his say, and I valued his input. He made me a better pitcher. But just before a start, I didn't want to hear it. I *couldn't* hear it.

Keeping up with Mel and his final analysis was like trying to read the phone book. I couldn't focus on it. Nothing against Mel, but my mind was always someplace else. I was impatient. I hadn't eaten. I'd angered or frustrated or otherwise alienated every poor soul who had crossed my path on the way to the stadium. I was pumped and primed. I needed a baseball in my hand. Enough already with the pregame discussions, I always thought. Enough with the nerves and the nausea. I was a bundle of raw energy, held together by one pleading thought: *Just give me the damn ball. Please.*

It wasn't until I was out in the bullpen going through my pregame warm-up that my pitching brain would click on. I'd ease into my first couple throws, soft tosses to the bullpen catcher, first from thirty or forty feet away, then fifty, and finally from the full pitching distance of sixty feet and six inches. Just a mindless game of catch, the kind I played on a thousand lazy afternoons as a kid, until I forced myself to pay attention to how my arm was feeling. There was no need for any more talk. Was I getting loose or was I in trouble? That's all that mattered here in the bullpen. Was I ready? Was I *on*? I'd be acutely aware of every muscle in my body, every ache and pain, every tic and twitch. I could see and feel everything, and underneath the mindlessness of the routine I'd find time to consider every game-day variable: who was catching me, who was playing behind me in the field, who'd given me trouble in the opposing lineup, what I planned to eat for dinner that night, the weather.

The pitching coach would stand watch. When it was Mel, he'd be motionless and quiet, until the throwing grew more intense. After that, he still didn't say anything, but I could see from the corner of my eye that he was paying careful attention. In just a few minutes, the manager would call down to ask how I was throwing. God bless Mel. I know he must have lied to Davey Johnson on a number of occasions—but there were even more occasions when he didn't have to lie. When my arm felt great. When I finished strong, hitting my spots, making the ball do whatever I wanted. When I felt invincible.

The warm-up over, I'd begin that long, purposeful walk back to the dugout. The walk out to the bullpen may have been slow, but this return trip always had a little more urgency to it. I'd sidle past my bullpen brethren, accepting their claps on the back and their go-get-'ems like I had them coming. (None would admit it, but I'm sure a few of those well-wishers were imploring me to do well so they wouldn't be called on to pitch me out of a jam.) I'd make my way through the bowels of the stadium, my cleats clicking against the cement floor like Morse code, the message a warning to the other team that I was really bringing it or a signal to my own guys to be on their toes. Mel would usually attempt a joke, to ease the tension, but I never thought the tension needed easing. I wanted to be on edge in order to do what I had to do. The security guards would shout out words of encouragement as I passed. (Half of them were Yankee fans, but what the hell.) On to the family room, where the next-of-Met-kin waited out the long stretch between warm-up and first pitch, and I'd chide myself for not knowing the names of my teammates' wives and children.

As I moved toward the mound—my office! my haven!—a voice switched on in my head, guiding me the rest of the way: *No left turn into the clubhouse, you coward. Continue on.* And I would, over the makeshift catwalk of AstroTurf remnants leading down the stairs to the dugout. At the bottom of the stairs, I'd find the other eight starting players, hastily sucking the last drags from their cigarettes. (Sorry, kids, but the players smoked in those days.) I'd ignore their initial looks of *Shit, I can't believe he's here already* and register instead their follow-up looks of *C'mon, Ronnie, we need this one tonight.* I'd walk past the boys and up the five short steps into the Mets dugout. At the other end, I'd spot Mel talking to the manager. I'd hope he didn't have to lie tonight. I'd tell myself I felt pretty good, and then I'd take my seat on the dugout bench and towel off.

This was always the most peaceful time of my pregame ritual. It didn't last all that long, but I would try to lose myself in that brief moment. I'd think back to what baseball had meant to me as a kid. To all those hours playing with my brothers, my friends, my parents. To how lucky I was to wear a major league uniform. To be pitching, in just a few short moments, in front of fifty thousand fans.

Soon the other starting players would join me on the bench, awaiting their cue to take the field. That cue doesn't come from the public address announcer. It doesn't come from one of the coaches or the umpire. It comes from the starting pitcher. Remember, it starts with us, and it ends with us. Every starting pitcher has his own cue, some version of the "Give me the damn ball!" rallying cry that opened these pages. Dwight Gooden, with his eerily quiet confidence, used to nod his head ever so slightly, as if to say, "Let's go!" Sid Fernandez would humbly shrug his burly Hawaiian shoulders and offer a look: *Hey, you want to go?*

When I pitched out in Oakland, I was always struck by the transformation of Dave Stewart before one of his games. Dave was such a fun-loving, gracious person off the field, but he would take on this frightening demeanor when it was his turn to start. He had the most intense glare of any athlete I've ever seen. With most pitchers, players look for that certain cue for when to stand up and take the field. With Dave, it was a much more solemn, subtle gesture. He would sit on the edge of the bench, his shoulders sagging, looking almost defeated. It was as if all the energy had been drained from him, and he hadn't even gotten going. It always reminded me of that famous photograph of a bloodied and beaten Y. A. Tittle, of the New York football Giants, on his knees on the field after a backbreaking loss. That was Dave Stewart right before one of his games. And then, just when you'd catch yourself thinking this guy couldn't possibly rev himself up in time to start the game, he would throw back his shoulders and slowly, purposefully stand. The intensity coursed through him and he was transformed into a no-bullshit warrior. And the team would stand with him, in unison—as if he were a priest, telling his congregation to stand: *All rise!*

My cue wasn't much, but it was mine. A tug of the pants. A positioning of my protective cup. A long, deep breath. A final look, to make sure my teammates were good and ready. Of course they were. They were always ready. They were at the top step of the dugout by this point, poised like greyhounds to start a race. I would look each one of them in the eyes, and at the end of the line I'd quietly say my cue: "Let's get it right today."

THIS BOOK IS NOT a traditional baseball memoir. It's not a wistful reflection on a workmanlike career. I haven't set out to tell the story of my life or my time in the game. Rather, it's an attempt to bring readers inside the mind of a major league pitcher—to break the game of baseball down to its component parts and to offer my take on each piece so that we might better understand the whole. One inning at a time, one pitch at a time—because every pitch is different. Every situation is different. There are autobiographical passages, to be sure, but they are offered only as illustrations to set these situations in context, not to chart the highs and lows of my time on the mound.

Consider: I might have faced the same batter three or four times in the same game, but each time there was some new element to analyze, some new strategy at play. And each succeeding pitch within each of those at-bats carried its own drama as well. That's the beauty of the game of baseball. It's shot through with nuance and context. It never unravels according to plan. And it can spin off in a thousand different directions at any time, in such a way that no one game will ever even remotely resemble another.

And so I've collected several representative innings, from several different games. Some of them are career highlight–type innings from career highlight–type games, and some of them are of the garden variety. Some of them are well remembered, and others have long been forgotten by everyone but me. A couple didn't even involve me at all, except for the coincidental fact that I was up in the broadcast booth offering commentary. There's a chapter dissecting a prototypical first inning—my very first big league inning, in fact. There's a long look at a second inning that offered an important lesson on harnessing my energy and putting it to effective use. There's insight into a deflating third inning and a career-changing sixth inning, and so on, all the way to a ninth-inning clincher to seal the 1988 National League title. There's even an extra inning for good measure, a twelfth-inning disappointment that some folks consider the capper to the greatest college baseball game in history.

All of these innings, taken together, tell the story of what it's like to stand on that hill and stare down your opponent and will your team to victory. Sometimes, as these recountings show, I was able to prevail. Other times, I was not. At all times, though, I was thinking. This last was key, although "thinking" is not an entirely accurate description. To put a fine point on things, what I was really doing was *out*thinking my opponent—attempting to, anyway—because of course he was up there at the plate doing some thinking of his own. This, too, is the beauty of the game: every action has an equal and opposite reaction, every punch a counterpunch, every line of attack a line of defense. In the end, in baseball as in any field of endeavor, the pendulum swings most often in the direction of the guy who's one step ahead of his opponent.

A major league pitching mound can be the loneliest place in all of team sports, and it can be the loftiest. It's up to each pitcher to claim that small piece of real estate and make it his own—no matter the inning, no matter the situation, no matter what.

A Personal Note

Here's something most baseball fans don't realize: pitchers are considered the nonathletes of the game. We're there because we can do one thing well: we can throw the ball hard, or put it where we want to, or present it to a major league hitter in such a way that it appears to do one thing while actually doing another. It doesn't matter if we're overweight or undersized, because for the most part we're not called upon to do anything but throw a baseball.

As a result, pitchers are constantly being second-guessed or grumbled at impatiently by their teammates, and yet you'll never hear someone questioning or criticizing a center fielder if he drops the ball, a speed demon for getting thrown out trying to steal second, a hitter for swinging at a bad pitch. Those guys are athletes, and you can forgive an athlete almost anything as long as he's hustling. Not so for a pitcher. The thinking in the clubhouse when a position player is struggling is that he's giving it his all. Pitchers, on the other hand, are held to an entirely different standard; we might be ballplayers, but we're not necessarily athletes. At least, we're not the same kind of athlete as our position-playing teammates. When we struggle, the perception is that we're doing something wrong. We don't get beat; we beat ourselves.

Remember Terry Forster, the left-handed reliever who pitched successfully for a number of teams in the 1970s and 1980s? He was part of that solid Dodger pitching staff that shut down the Yankees in the 1981 World Series. When I came into the league, he was pitching for the Atlanta Braves and weighing in at about 270 pounds; this was around the time David Letterman famously called him "a fat tub of goo." That got a lot of media attention, but it barely made a ripple in most big league clubhouses, because every team had a couple pitchers built the same way. Terry was a good sport about Letterman's joking disregard, which felt a whole lot like the disregard pitchers had been fielding for generations; the only difference here was that now it was fodder for late-night television.

If it was up to them, most managers would play the game without pitchers. They really would. Sidle up to Lou Piniella and say, "Lou, how about a new game? It's just like baseball only without the pitchers." He'll say, "Perfect." This is not unlike the disregard Hollywood directors have for actors; they'd much rather make a movie without them, but of course they can't. Or the way some politicians dismiss voters as a necessary nuisance. In the clubhouse, most managers seem to resent the fact that the fate of their team rests in the hand (literally!) of just one guy—a guy who might be out of shape, at that.

Position players aren't crazy about it either. They don't like it that starting pitchers, who play every fifth day, make as much money as their teammates who play every day. (This was always the pet peeve of my opinionated teammate Lenny Dykstra—and for all I know he's still railing about it.) They don't like it that a pitcher can be twenty or thirty pounds over-weight as long as he has a strong arm. Perhaps as a result, most position players treat most pitchers a bit like second-class citizens. Between starts they may act as if you're not even there—or as if you don't really belong. On game day, when you've got the ball, you're placed on a kind of temporary pedestal, but after the game you're quickly deposed. If your teammates acknowledge you at all between starts, it's done so grudgingly, with a kind of tacit agreement that position play-ers are better, smarter, and more essential to the ongoing for-tunes of the team than their hard-throwing, hardly used colleagues. Not everyone buys into that, of course, but it's the prevailing sentiment.

Another remark you hear is that it's a good thing pitchers are stupid, because if they were smart it'd be a whole different ball game. I don't know where this thinking originated, but I've never agreed with it. For one thing, pitchers need to out-think the opposing hitter with every throw to the plate. In any case, I didn't pay much attention to the idea of the dumb-pitcher nonathlete as I moved up the ranks into organized ball—maybe in part because I never really thought of myself as a pitcher until I signed my first professional contract. I was a ballplayer; that was my bottom line. I became a pitcher because I could throw hard—and, I guess, because I couldn't field or hit or run the bases well enough to cut it in the bigs.

I'd pitched in Little League, because all the best athletes pitched back in Little League. My dad was my coach, and he knew I'd rather play shortstop, but he threw me out there when he felt he needed to. In high school, I was one of the few guys on our team who could blow a ball past a real hitter, so I would take my turn on the mound without complaint. I was never a full-fledged part of the rotation, but I was a fixture on that mound.

I thought my pitching days were over after high school, but when I got to Yale my head coach told me I had to pitch. I said, "I don't want to pitch." He said, "We've got to work something out, because if you don't pitch, we've got no shot."

I didn't go to Yale just to play baseball. I went to get an education, and to play two sports if I could manage it. Baseball was something to do between football seasons, after classes. I wasn't alone in this. Our roster was filled with football players, basketball players, and hockey players. Players would come out in the spring if they didn't have a big workload. They'd sit out the season if they had an internship or a heavy class schedule. Half the team was pre-med, so they'd miss games and practices when they had a lab or an important exam.

I didn't really know what I was doing at first, but I got college hitters out on sheer competitiveness. I figured it out as I went along. I also figured out that pitching is more of an art than a science. There's a feel to it. The thing for a pitcher is to fool around with your grip until you hit on something that works. You mess around until you find your pitch, or until it finds you. You try a bunch of different deliveries. There's no one *right* way to pitch: there are thirty different pitching coaches working with thirty major league staffs, and each one has a different approach. Sometimes that approach works, and sometimes it doesn't. Usually, though, it works when it's carried out by a pitcher who actually knows what he's doing, who takes what his coaches tell him and develops it into something else. To be successful, a big league pitcher has got to become his own pitching coach at some point in his career. Otherwise, he'll flounder; he'll never have a handle on his game.

It took a while for me to trust my abilities over the insights and observations of some of these veteran coaches who'd been around the game. I had trouble with this, particularly in the beginning. My first pitching coach after college was instructed to teach every young pitcher to throw a good slider. Up and down the Texas Rangers' farm system, young pitchers struggled with the hard slider. That's how it goes sometimes in big league organizations: every pitcher who moves through your system has to learn a certain pitch. In the late 1980s it was the split-finger, thanks to the success of guys like Bruce Sutter. Now it's the changeup. With Texas, in the early 1980s, it was the hard slider, and I just couldn't master it. I couldn't throw a big league changeup either—not for a strike, anyway.

It was the hard slider, though, that nearly did me in. A slider is thrown with a real stiff wrist, almost like you'd throw a football. If you look at the face of a clock, a curveball will break from 12 to 6. A slider will break from 2 to 8 if you're a right-hander, 10 to 4 if you're a left-hander. (Keep in mind, this is from the pitcher's perspective. To the batter, and to the fans watching at home, it's the other way around.) I could never get that stiff wrist action. After a while, it began to hurt my arm. I started feeling an ache I'd never felt before, but I just assumed these guys knew what they were doing, so I kept working on that pitch. I had just signed and I wanted to impress my coaches and I didn't know any better.

The toughest adjustment, other than having to learn a

pitch that was hurting my arm, came off the field. All of a sudden, I was competing with men. I'd gone from playing a game with a bunch of kids, in a sideline sort of way, to pursuing a career with a bunch of twenty-six-, twenty-eight-, even thirty-year-old men. I'd just come from college, where everything was rah-rah. We all pulled for one another to do well. Baseball hadn't been any kind of ticket up and out for any of us. Now everybody was out for themselves. Now baseball was a way of life. These were guys with wives and kids and mortgages. Guys with everything on the line. If you were the new kid, everybody was checking you out. You were competing for the same innings, the same job, the same attention from the organization. There were only so many calls to the bigs, and each new player might intercept a call that was meant for you.

By the time I got to Tidewater, the New York Mets Triple A affiliate, I'd settled onto a mediocre minor league path. I'd been traded to the Mets along with pitcher Walt Terrell for fan favorite Lee Mazzilli following the 1981 season. I was pitching well enough to get promoted, probably even well enough to get a call to the bigs, but I wasn't dominating the way I had back at Yale. I certainly wasn't making a convincing case for any kind of long-term career, and I couldn't shake the thought that if I had been performing at a higher level the Rangers would have never looked to unload me in a trade. True, I could have taken up the converse argument—that the New York Mets must have seen something they liked in my performance, enough to want to trade for me—but young athletes without a lot of confidence tend not to see the bright side in such situations.

Some of my outings were real adventures—and not always in a good way. I was on and off. Nothing special. Until one day in 1983, May or June, when Davey Johnson, the new Tidewater manager, pulled me aside to talk about my game.

I'd been at Tidewater for one full season, and now here we were, just a couple months into my second campaign. I was having a decent enough year. I'd finish up at 10–9, with 107 strikeouts in 159 innings and a 4.02 earned run average. At that point in the season, I was about 6–4. Good, but not great, at a time in my career when good enough was no longer good enough.

Davey could see that something wasn't right. He'd read the scouting reports. He'd seen me make a dozen or so starts. He'd talked to guys who'd seen me pitch in college. Heck, knowing Davey, *he'd* probably seen me pitch in college. In any case, the reports didn't match what I was doing on the mound, and he was determined to help me figure it out. I was throwing on the side one day when he came up to me and said, "You always throw like this?"

I said, "No, not really." I explained how when I got to Texas they wanted me to throw that hard slider, and how before that I'd had more of a three-quarter motion and a killer overhand curveball.

He grabbed a bat and said, "Show me."

Mike Fitzgerald was catching me at the time, and Davey stepped in at the plate in front of him and said, "Throw like you're throwing now."

So I did. Over the top. Hard. On the gun today, it would probably register 92, 93 miles an hour. Straight fastball. Cut slider. Whatever piece-of-shit thing I was throwing at the time. It was mostly just heat—but it was serious heat.

Then Davey said, "Okay, now throw like you did in college."

All of a sudden, there was movement on my ball, and an overhand hook. I dropped down to my accustomed three-quarter delivery and just blew the ball by my new manager.

The heat was still there, but now there was more. Now there was authority and precision and all those good things.

At Yale, I'd had more of an athletic motion. I'd had an idea, intellectually, of how to get hitters out, but I hadn't had the mechanics that you find and refine when you get to the major leagues. I'd had that all-important competitive streak, that fire, but it was pure athleticism. My natural motion was a three-quarters motion, I guess because I grew up playing shortstop, and that was how I threw. That all changed, of course, when the Texas Rangers drafted me as their number one pick. All of a sudden, I had to be a strikeout pitcher. That's not the kind of pitcher I was, but when an organization pins that kind of marquee, big-time label on you, that's the kind of pitcher you're expected to become. I ended up striking out more than fifteen hundred batters in my major league career, but I never thought of myself as a strikeout pitcher. All the same, the Rangers took a cookie-cutter approach, like a lot of organizations do. There were all these expectations on me, which I guess I can understand. When you draft a pitcher with your number one pick, you're telling your fans and the baseball community that this guy's the next Nolan Ryan. But really what you're doing is drafting the most talented amateur pitcher in the country at the time, the kid with the best chance of quickly reaching the bigs.

This session with Davey Johnson was probably the first time I'd been asked as a professional to throw with my natural motion—and it was the most remarkable thing.

After a while Davey stepped out of the box. He said, "That other stuff you're throwing? It's okay. Might even get you to the bigs for a stretch. But what you threw just now? That's nasty. That's big league stuff."

I nodded. I didn't know what to say.

Davey kept talking. (He liked to talk, as I'd learn over the next couple seasons.) He said, "The way you're throwing now, I can hit that. The way you just threw, that I can't hit. You throw like that the rest of the year and you'll be in the big leagues next year with me."

I said, "With you?"

He said, "Yeah, I'll be the Mets' manager next year."

He was a very confident guy, Davey Johnson. There'd been nothing in the papers about his becoming manager, nothing in the air even, the way there sometimes is around an organization about to make a change. But he just knew he'd get the call, and his confidence rubbed off on me. For the rest of that year, I was dominant every time I took the mound. I was a completely different pitcher. I went from the guy occasionally getting embarrassed to the guy doing the embarrassing. All on the back of this one session with a guy who wasn't even my pitching coach. Just a former big leaguer who'd once hit 43 home runs in a season, and who changed my career in about fifteen minutes.

Al Jackson also gets some credit here. He was the pitching coach at Tidewater, and he taught me the split-finger. It came about because I was trying to work on a screwball. I couldn't master a changeup, so I thought a screwball might work for me—especially since Al had thrown a screwball when he'd pitched for the Mets. Somehow, my screwball morphed into a split-finger, which Al helped me turn into a real out pitch. He also taught me how to be a professional. This last was key, and yet it's a piece most coaches leave out of the mix. Al taught me how to think like these twenty-six- and twenty-seven-year-old guys in the locker room. He got me to recognize that baseball might have been a game before, but now it was also my job. And the thing of it is, he said, if you treat it like a job, it'll pay you back. Show up at the ballpark, be professional, get your work in, and prepare yourself for your next start.

Al's biggest lessons were wrapped around his stories. He told wonderful, heartbreaking, uplifting stories of his time in the bigs back in the 1960s, when it was still a struggle for most black ballplayers. I'd always been a fan of the game, so I knew this on some level, but it took hearing it from Al, in an intimate, firsthand way, for the stories to really resonate—and once they did, I had no choice but to take the gift of my situation more seriously. There was no hardship in this game, for me. There was no struggle, other than the challenge to perform and be at my best. I couldn't take anything for granted. Hank Aaron, Willie Mays, Frank Robinson, Al Jackson— they all had those stories, and I needed to hear them. Not being able to travel with the team or stay in the same hotels or eat in the same restaurants. Getting booed heading into the stadium—even their *home* stadium. Hearing all kinds of ugly epithets rain down on their wives and their children. It took the luster off the game for me. In my head, baseball had always been an idyllic, romantic pastime, but Al broke it down for me, and I started to see it as a tough, hard road. The whirlwind of Triple A ball would spit out just a precious few who'd go on to make it in the bigs. The others would go back to their regular lives and wonder what might have been. If I wanted to be one of the guys who made it, I had to recognize the difficulties that lay in wait. Of course, they wouldn't be the same difficulties Al faced as a young black man; they would be my own. And yet it took a guy like Al Jackson to help me see my prospects for what they were: there for the taking but certainly not guaranteed.

I'd listen to Al and look around the locker room, at guys who were just taken off the forty-man roster, at guys who thought they were better than one of their teammates who had just gotten called up to the parent club, at guys who'd been starting pitchers their whole minor league career and were now relegated to the bullpen. Each time one of these things happens it takes a bite out of your dream, and after a while you look up and all these bites have been taken and there's nothing left.

That second year in Tidewater, 1983, Al took me aside at the beginning of the season and said, "You're close, Ronnie, but you're not there yet. You and I are gonna work together this year. You'll hate me by the end of the summer, but you'll be ready."

He ran me into the ground, that guy. Worked me harder than anybody had worked me before. He broke me like a horse, really, until I was open to whatever it was he had to teach me. His physical workouts were draining, but on top of that was the total concentration he demanded of his charges. At the other end, he changed me from a fun-loving kid think-ing, *Great, I'm making money, playing pro ball, traveling around,* to a professional athlete. I resisted him at first, of course. I was young and single, living on the beach in Nor-folk, Virginia. I was content. But Al kept on me. He'd say, "What the hell do you have to be content about? You haven't done anything. You haven't struggled."

One of his favorite drills was a line-to-line exercise. He had us running in the outfield, from foul pole to foul pole. You'd start out jogging, then go into a full sprint, then he'd lead you with a toss like a quarterback's, far enough ahead of you so you had to run all out to get under it, and then you'd drop back down to three-quarter speed and walked the last stretch to the opposite foul pole. Al would drift back and forth between left center and right center, making his killingly perfect soft tosses and literally running us into the ground. Twenty reps and you were done. Usually there'd be four or five of us in on the drill, but Al would always take me aside beforehand and tell me he expected me to work harder than anyone else. I was his project, I guess. And when you do these running drills, it's just like life: some people dog it, and some go after it. There would be no dogging it with Al—not for me, anyway.

The four days between starts, I'd always just rested my arm and done some light workouts. Now, under Al's tutelage, I learned that every single day I spent on the bench was a learning opportunity. He forced me to sit with him during games when I wasn't pitching. Most pitchers don't do that. They horse around; they disappear into the clubhouse. But I sat with Al and learned the game. We talked about situations. We talked about fielding your position, backing up the right base on this or that play. We talked about the best way to approach certain batters in certain situations. We talked about how the game presents each pitcher with five or six or seven critical junctures each time out, and how the way each pitcher gets past these crisis points will stamp his career.

Over the course of a long minor league season, you can cover a lot of ground. One of the most important things Al taught me was to think about each outing as having a beginning and an end. There's no starting slow, or ending slow. There's only starting out at full force and finishing strong. That's the ultimate for a starting pitcher, right? To end the game. With a flourish if you can. Well, according to Al, starting the game is a process, but once the game begins there's no easing into it. It's full-on, right from the first pitch.

Al Jackson turned out to be one of my biggest supporters. He was right there, standing and watching, during that sideline session with Davey, and he was blown away. He'd never known I could throw like that. The whole time, I could see

Al from the corner of my eye, nodding. He didn't say a lot while I was working; that wasn't his nature. But at the end of the session he couldn't stop talking. He kept saying, "You got something now, Ronnie! You got something to work with now!"

And, sure enough, I did. The footnote to my relationship with Al was that we each ended our Met careers with the same number of complete-game shutouts: ten. I always thought there was a nice symmetry in that.

THAT 1983 TIDEWATER TEAM PLAYED for the International League championship, but I didn't stick around for our final push. Davey Johnson called me into his office one afternoon toward the end of August and said, "You got the call, kid." Wasn't a whole lot of ceremony to it. Next thing I knew, I was shuffling through the Shea Stadium clubhouse, collecting my gear. I was given a uniform with the number 44 on the back. That was just the number on the uniform at the top of the pile when I arrived, and it would never have occurred to me in a million years to ask for a different one.

Man, I loved that first uniform! I was so proud, so thrilled, the first time I put it on. I remember that it fit perfectly. It was amazing, how well it fit. I actually looked at myself in the mirror and thought, How could they know my size? It was like it had been spun by some fairy godmother. Along with the uniform came a brand-new pair of shiny spikes. I got all kinds of other gear, too. I couldn't believe my good fortune.

It was September 1, 1983, but because the Tides were still making a run at the championship and because the Mets were so far out of contention that they didn't exactly need reinforcements at the big league level, not a lot of my other teammates had gotten the call along with me. In any case, no one else joined the big club on the same day. Clint Hurdle came the following week, along with Mike Fitzgerald, but for the time being I didn't really know anybody. I kept to myself; I remember that. And I was careful not to say or do anything too stupid or rookie-like; I remember that most of all.

My keep-a-low-profile strategy didn't prevent me from standing out. On my very first day with the team, I put on my crisp, clean new uniform and made my way to the Mets dugout, about thirty minutes before anybody else. I wanted to soak it all in. It was a warm, sultry night. After a while, my new teammates started to trickle in. I'd been to spring training that year, so I knew some of the guys, but I wasn't about to say a word. I wanted to stay out of everybody's way, that's all. I sat by myself on the bench, but no one else was sitting. Guys were fooling around, roughhousing, talking about their postseason plans. I hardly noticed, to tell the truth. I was just so excited. I must have looked like such a rube, sitting there on the end of the bench in my too white uniform, too chickenshit to talk to anyone, but I didn't care. I was just happy to be there. Finally, Ron Hodges headed in my direction. He'd been a catcher for the Mets for years and years—since the team's "You Gotta Believe!" 1973 season, when they nearly won the World Series. He wasn't in the lineup, but he'd just finished warming up the pitcher and he'd come back to the dugout to stow some of his gear. He looked at me; for a beat or two I thought he might come over and introduce himself, maybe welcome me to the team.

Sure enough, he did walk over, but he didn't introduce himself. Or maybe he did, only not in the way I was expecting. He just gave me a sidelong look and spit a thick wad of tobacco juice onto my clean white pant leg. He didn't say anything. He just spit, and the tobacco juice left a huge, ugly brown stain. Then he walked to the other end of the bench and continued to put his equipment away.

I wanted to crawl under the dugout bench and die.

Today's ballplayers are issued two or three sets of pants with each uniform, but I had only that one pair. I couldn't go back to my locker and change. I had to sit there, all through my first game as a professional baseball player, with my jacket draped over my pants to hide the stain. It would have been funny if there had been a couple other veterans around to take in the scene—a textbook example of rookie hazing. At least I would have had a chance to be a good sport about it. I might have even understood it if Ron had said something to me afterward. I could have shrugged it off, like it was nothing at all. But I don't think anyone else was watching, and Ron didn't say anything either, so it was just a weirdly mortifying, humiliating moment. It put me in my place—to be taken down a couple notches for no good reason but the perverse pleasure of it. It seemed so cruel, so arbitrary. But that's baseball, I guess. It builds you up like nothing else, and then it knocks you right back down again.

There was another humiliating moment that week I was called up, before I made my first start. Fortunately, I wasn't the victim here, but it shook me up just the same. The Mets had a talented rookie shortstop that year named José Oquendo, who has lately toiled as Tony La Russa's third-base coach with the St. Louis Cardinals. José had come up earlier in the season. He was barely twenty years old, and he couldn't really find his way at the plate that year. He'd go on to have a fine major league career, but it took him a while to get his stroke, and unfortunately Mets manager Frank Howard wasn't the most patient guy in the game. Frank was a hard charger; he didn't go out of his way to coddle his players, even the younger players, who surely could have used some coddling.

It was a Sunday afternoon game at Shea, bottom of the third inning. We were playing the Padres, who, like the Mets, were finishing out the string. José Oquendo was hitting eighth. He'd struck out looking his first time up, with runners on second and third and nobody out, and now the Mets had another rally going. They (*we,* actually, even though I didn't really think of myself as part of the team just yet) loaded the bases with one out; then a sacrifice fly scored the runner from third. José was about to step in with runners on first and second and two outs, but he never got out of the on-deck circle. Frank Howard called him back and sent in Rusty Staub to pinch-hit.

Now, it doesn't usually happen that a manager pinch-hits for his number eight hitter that early in the game, no matter what the circumstance, but I didn't know this at the time. I didn't know that Frank Howard wasn't keenly attuned to a young player's fragile emotional state. I didn't know that other managers didn't show up their rookie hitters by calling them back to the dugout and pulling them for a pinch hitter—for no good reason but the hell of it.

Rusty popped out to second to end the inning, and I thought, Man, this is a tough league. You can't even get up to bat in the third inning of a nothing game: two teams under .500, on a Sunday in September, in front of a crowd of less than ten thousand. It was a meaningless substitution in a meaningless game—and yet all of it was powerfully meaningful to me, as I tried to find a place for myself among these big league ballplayers.

I looked down the bench and saw José Oquendo fighting back tears. The poor kid was completely devastated, and my heart nearly broke for him. What really got me, though, was that nobody moved to tell him that the manager was an ass-hole, or that it didn't usually happen this way, or that he'd get his shot. There was none of that. I hadn't been around long enough to say anything, so I just sat in scared silence, hoping like hell I wouldn't find myself in my own devastation any-time soon.

Gradually, I began to fit myself in and to separate out the routine rookie hazing from the aberrant and illogical behav-ior of guys like Frank Howard. My best buddy from Tide-water, a pitcher named Tim Leary, was called up after the minor league playoffs, so he and I roomed together the rest of the season. He'd been to the bigs before, in 1981, so I caught myself leaning on him and picking his brain. Anyway, it helped to have a pal going through some of the same motions. It helped, for example, when a clubhouse icon like Tom Seaver intercepted my first paycheck and held it out to my new teammates for inspection. He walked it over to me and said, "Maybe you want me to look at it for you, make sure they're not taking out too much for taxes."

I thought, Tom Seaver! Talking to me! Offering to help! I had no idea he was setting me up, so I went along. I told him to take a look at the check and let me know what he thought, so he tore open the envelope and started laughing uncontrol-lably. Then he held up my paycheck and walked it around the clubhouse. His point, of course, was that it was for such a measly amount, and everyone had a good laugh. I could see my good friend Tim Leary laughing over by his locker, so I laughed, too. I knew enough at this point to understand that this was probably something the veteran players did to all rookies.

After a while, Seaver walked the check back over to me and gave me a hug. He said, "I'm only kidding." But, of course, he wasn't quite done. He reached into his pocket and said, "Do you want me to cash it for you? I think I have enough."

I was embarrassed, but it wasn't so bad. I thought, At least he's not spitting tobacco juice on my pants.

I had another run-in with Tom Seaver that first week, only this time he wasn't out to taunt me. I thought he might be at first, because of that razzing over my measly paycheck, and because of everything else that went on in the clubhouse between the veteran players and the September call-ups, so I had my guard up. He walked over to me one day and asked where I went to school. My first thought was that he was up to something, because surely he must have known. After all, I'd come over to the organization in an unpopular trade for one of the most popular players in Mets history—Lee Mazzilli. It was reported in all the papers, and most accounts mentioned where I went to school. A guy like Seaver had to know the answer to his own question, I assumed, but here he was, asking. Naturally, I was wary.

I never liked to tell other ballplayers that I'd gone to Yale. I'd always take a lot of shit for it. Or sometimes it'd turn out that they'd never heard of it, and that would be a whole other hassle. Once, when I was still with Texas, and was playing Double A ball in Tulsa, I was talking to one of my teammates and his wife at a team gathering. They asked where I'd gone to school, and I told them. The wife said, "Wow, that's pretty good. You didn't have to go too far, then."

I had no idea what she was talking about, but then it became clear. She'd never heard of Yale University, but she knew that Tulsa's stadium was on Yale Avenue, so she quite reasonably figured Yale was somewhere on that street.

Usually, though, I'd just get grief for it. Guys would treat me like I was full of myself, or they'd find ways to keep telling me I wasn't as smart as I thought I was—which was certainly true—so I tried to avoid the conversation. But there was no avoiding it with Tom Seaver.

I said, "A small school in Connecticut."

He said, "Where, exactly? I live in Connecticut, you know. Maybe I've heard of it." He was really stringing me along.

I said, "Just up I-95, about an hour or so over the bridge."

He said, "Yeah, but what's the name of the school?"

I was certain he already knew the answer, but he was Tom Seaver and I was just a nothing rookie, so I finally caved. When I said, "Yale," Seaver just nodded, and then he stepped away, toward his locker, apparently to get something. He came back a beat or two later with a copy of the *New York Times,* folded and quartered in the manner of an experienced New Yorker. He handed it to me, and I could see it was open to the crossword puzzle. He said, "Finish this."

I'd never done the *New York Times* crossword puzzle in my life, but someone must have been smiling down on me that day because I finished it straightaway. Some people have an aptitude for crossword puzzles. Some people don't. Happily, it turned out, it came easily to me, so I left the completed puzzle on the chair in front of Seaver's locker and waited for whatever would come next. I figured there'd be some punch line to the exchange, and this would stand as another in a string of *Let's make fun of Darling* moments he had planned for my first week. But there was no punch line—at least, none that I could see. I waited and waited for a response, but there was nothing.

The next day, I arrived at my locker to find a fresh copy of that day's *New York Times,* again open to the crossword. Every day for the rest of the season, that's how it went, and every day I sat down and dutifully completed the puzzle. Every now and then, Seaver would wander over and peek at my efforts. Or he'd ask something like "What'd you get for 35 down?"

There was no Internet then, and you couldn't just look something up with a couple of quick strokes on a keyboard, so I was like his crossword genie. It became our thing. Keith Hernandez, too. He'd joined the Mets earlier that summer in a trade, and like Tom Seaver, he was one of the more cerebral players in our clubhouse. Before long, these great veterans seemed to accept me. Not because I could pitch, but because I could do the *New York Times* crossword puzzle.

This, too, was baseball. It wasn't just what you put out on the field that counted with your teammates. It was how you carried yourself, how you stood up to the razzing. It was whether or not you knew a six-letter word for *arrogance*. (See if *hubris* fits.) It was in these clubhouse-related ways that you earned your stripes as a ballplayer. The stuff on the field came later.

A BIG PART OF PITCHING is getting comfortable. That means getting comfortable on the mound, as well as in the clubhouse and all around. It's tough enough making the adjustment from minor league ball to the bigs, but to do so in a city like New York can be doubly intimidating. For me, it wasn't enough to have a little bit of success in my first few starts; it took me a while longer to feel like I truly belonged. In fact, that feeling of belonging didn't really find me until that first off-season. Like a lot of young players at the time, I looked to supplement my income however I could. The minimum salary in 1983 was $35,000; it was due to go up to $40,000 in 1984. This was a lot of money to a young, single guy, but it was nothing compared to the seven-figure salaries a lot of my teammates were making. I had some signing-bonus money in the bank, but I couldn't keep up with a lot of these guys in terms of spending power, and I was still uncertain about my job security going forward, so I grabbed at every opportunity I could find.

I decided to stay in New York that first off-season. I wanted to experience the city, the neighborhoods, the people, without the distractions of baseball. I rented a sixth-floor walk-up apartment on East Fifty-third Street, too green to realize what a pain in the ass walking up and down so many flights of stairs would be. I worked out every day at the Downtown Athletic Club. I rode the subways. I learned my way around. But money was tight, so when I started getting requests from the Mets front office to appear at this or that event, I jumped. Little League banquets, bar mitzvahs, chamber of commerce dinners—whatever they had. The going rate was $500 for an appearance, and I could do two or three in a weekend. My rent was $700, so I could take care of that on one good Saturday.

The routine was I'd make a three-minute speech, then sign a bunch of stuff—baseballs, bats, posters. It was a curious bargain—after all, what did I have to talk about? I'd been in the majors for one month. (Looking back, I have to think, *That's* hubris!) But it turned out I was a good ambassador for the Mets and for myself. I represented the future of the organization. I talked about how I couldn't wait for the 1984 season to start, how the Mets were a team on the rise, how the folks should come out to watch us. I'd been a Red Sox fan my entire life, but now I bled blue and orange. And the fans just ate it up. The kids, especially. These people were hungry for a winning baseball team, and for some reason they saw me as playing a part in that. Who was I to argue?

I didn't have a car, so the people who hired me usually sent a driver to pick me up, and in this way I got to see pretty much all of Long Island, Westchester, and northern New Jersey. I

went to Brooklyn, Staten Island, the Bronx. I went to Connecticut. I went to Harlem. There was even a surreal outing
to one of the old Borscht Belt hotels up in the Catskills, for a
bar mitzvah celebration for a kid who loved baseball, football,
and the zoo. I rode up there with New York Giants quarterback Phil Simms, and when we arrived at the hotel there was
one grand ballroom filled with giraffes, elephants, and mon-
keys and another grand ballroom filled with baseball and
football stuff and a dozen or so New York sports legends.
(Okay, so I wasn't exactly a New York sports legend, but what
do you expect for $500?)

Make no mistake: I did these personal appearances for the
money. That was my motivation. But in making so many of
them, back-to-back-to-back, I felt like I was making a real
connection and cementing my place on the team. I was getting comfortable. I fell in love with the city, and by the time
the 1984 season rolled around, the Mets had a completely different look. We had a new manager in Davey Johnson. (Son
of a gun, the guy had been right!) We had a new pitching
coach in Mel Stottlemyre. We had a solid core of exciting
young players, like Dwight Gooden, Darryl Strawberry, and
Sid Fernandez. Some of our veterans were gone, including
Tom Seaver, but Keith Hernandez had just re-signed with
the club because he liked our prospects, and George Foster
looked like he still had some pop in his bat.

The Mets were clearly a team in transition, and I allowed
myself to think I'd be a part of that transition. I wouldn't be
the main part, not by any stretch, but the message I took in
over that whirlwind off-season was that both the organization
and the fans expected me to do well. This, too, was me getting
comfortable. This was me getting ready. Now all I had to do
was figure out how to pitch at the major league level.

Getting Started

September 6, 1983
Philadelphia Phillies vs. New York Mets
Shea Stadium, New York
Attendance: 8,863

No major league pitcher forgets his first start. I don't care what you accomplish in your career or what you make of yourself when you leave the game behind, that first outing is elemental.

The night before mine, I stayed in a crap hotel by LaGuardia Airport. The place has changed hands so many times over the years the name has all but washed away. What stays with me, though, is the noise. The room pretty much rattled every time a plane passed overhead. I'd never slept so close to a runway before, although to suggest that I actually got any sleep is to overstate it. Probably, I wouldn't have slept anyway, even without the planes. I was too wired to sleep, too stressed, too everything.

It was a Tuesday, the second game of a nothing series against the Phillies—nothing to the Mets, that is. To me, it was everything. To the Phillies, too. They were battling for the top spot in the NL East, locked in a four-way scrum for first with Pittsburgh, Montreal, and St. Louis, trailing the Pirates and the Expos by only a half game. And they were reeling. The Mets had just knocked them down in the first game of our series in a backbreaker, with a walk-off home run by George Foster. One out in the bottom of the ninth, Philadelphia up 5–3, and runners on first and third, Foster sent one into the night sky that put the Phillies on their heels.

Nobody called it a "walk-off" home run back then, but that's what it was. (The phrase actually originated with my Oakland teammate Dennis Eckersley, who had a particular way with words.) Our guys walked off jubilant, and the Phillies walked off dejected. The few Met fans who'd stuck it out walked off on a cloud. Me, I just walked off. I was psyched that we'd gotten the win, but a part of me thought, Great, just what I need: to get these guys mad.

Like a lot of young ballplayers, I had a kind of tunnel vision when it came to the game and my fledgling career. I cared about making my mark more than anything else. All my life, I'd been a baseball fan, but I hadn't really followed major league baseball since I'd started college. It became less important from a fanatic, rooting perspective as it loomed larger as a real opportunity. I knew my baseball history, but I fell short on my baseball present. I kept up on the big-picture stuff—the league leaders, the postseason, the comings and goings of guys I'd played with in my short time in the minors—but the rest was no longer relevant to me. That is, until it was. I didn't even know Joe Morgan was playing for the Phillies until he stepped to the plate to lead off the series opener. How about that for a head-in-the-sand moment? I saw his name in the lineup and thought, *That* Joe Morgan? The guy from the Reds who got that bloop hit to center against the Red Sox in the '75 World Series? That guy? And Pete Rose? I knew he was on the team, at least, but I'd just assumed he'd be leading off, like he had for most of his career.

Remember, this was 1983. We had scouting reports, but there were no printouts and stat sheets updated every at-bat, or endless highlights played on *SportsCenter.* I couldn't hop online and see how some guy hit in day games, leading off an inning, with his team trailing by two runs or less. Even the newspapers didn't run the elaborate box scores they have now, listing current batting averages and ERAs and total pitches and so on.

I'd known all along I was scheduled to start against the Phillies, but I hadn't looked much past that news itself. It didn't occur to me to study the Philadelphia lineup, to worry over specific hitters or situations. Honestly, I'd never studied a lineup before game day in the minors or in college. You got by on your stuff. At least that was my approach. And I was green enough to think the bigs would be no different.

But, of course, everything was different. We tried to develop a feel for an opposing lineup, to figure out some sort of game plan. It wasn't terribly specific. We didn't look at how a certain hitter performed when he was behind in the count with runners on base and less than two outs. We looked at tendencies. We used certain buzzwords: *free swinger, climb the ladder, first-pitch-fastball hitter.* I used to hear this last one and think, Come on, everyone's a first-pitch-fastball hitter. One of the things I was taught early in my career was that if the guy was a first-pitch-fastball hitter who liked the ball down, you'd do well to go a little lower. Pitch into his strength. Use it against him. If he wants it there, go ahead and give it to him there—only *not* there.

This was my first start, so I don't think the Mets wanted to overwhelm me with information. The big thing with Mets pitching coach Bill Monbouquette was to throw to quadrants. He wasn't about pitching to spots, like some pitching coaches. He broke it into parts. This way, I didn't have to be so precise. He wanted me to think that whatever I brought with me from Triple A would be enough to see me through. I was washed and dried, fluffed and folded, good and ready. That's what Monbouquette was reinforcing with this approach, I think. I could pitch to spots if I got ahead in the count, but we would ease into that. To start, he just wanted me to work in this or that general area. It would be more of a small hop from what I'd been doing in Tidewater, instead of a giant leap.

A good deal of the pregame preparations falls to the pitcher and the catcher. There's a give-and-take between these two guys that no one else can really grasp. They're in the trenches together on game day, and in the heat of battle the catcher is like the pitcher's shrink back there. One of the best illustrations of this is that picture of Yogi Berra jumping into the arms of Don Larsen after Larsen's complete game in the 1956 World Series against the Brooklyn Dodgers. That's such a classic image, and I have to think that one of the reasons it endures is the way it depicts that special bond between a pitcher and a catcher when everything comes together. There's a love there, a trust, a mutual respect.

It doesn't always go that way. I worked with a lot of catchers over the years who never seemed to *get* me. I didn't like the way they threw the ball back to the mound. I didn't like the way they called the game. I didn't like the uncertain rhythms they'd fall into between pitches. Gary "Kid" Carter had the habit, whenever he didn't like what I was throwing, of gunning the ball back to me, and it would really piss me off. But guess what? That anger got my attention, and I was able to be a little more fine with the next pitch. That's how it often happened with Kid, by the way: he'd go about his game a certain way, and it might set you off at first, but he knew exactly what he was doing; he helped me lift my game. Kid wasn't the prototypical catcher; he didn't exactly collaborate with his pitchers. But he had such a deep, encyclopedic knowledge of the league—including every hitter, every tendency, every conceivable situation—that you'd be foolish not to fall in line and follow his lead.

This first start against the Phillies didn't exactly sneak up on me. The day they called me up, Bill Monbouquette pulled me aside and told me how it would go. He said I'd get the ball for the second game of the Philadelphia series; then I'd take my regular turns after that. That would give me five starts by the end of the season. Five chances to show the Mets and the New York fans—and, I suppose, myself—what I could do.

I listened to Bill Monbouquette lay things out for me, how I'd have four or five days to get ready, and underneath all I could think was, Hey, this guy won twenty games for the Sox back in the sixties. That was a little before my time as a serious Red Sox fan, but when you grow up in New England, this stuff is drilled into you at an early age, especially since the Sox didn't have many twenty-game winners. So I only half-listened to what Bill said about the Phillies and the schedule he wanted me to follow leading up to my first game. There was that tunnel vision again. I took in what I thought was relevant and let the rest fall away. I figured I'd worry about the Phillies on the day of the game. Now that the day was upon me, however, worrying was pretty much all I could do. It surprised me, this worry; it wasn't like me. But I couldn't shake it.

Joe Morgan ... Pete Rose ... Mike Schmidt ... I wrote their names on a pad I found by the phone in my hotel room, and then I looked at those names until they were a part of me. I actually said them out loud, over and over: "Morgan, Rose, Schmidt." It became like a mantra. A chilling, haunting mantra. I thought, Who the hell makes his major league debut against that kind of killer lineup?

Three future Hall of Famers. (Sorry, Pete—that's how it looked at the time.) Back-to-back-to-back.

Damn.

I'VE NEVER BEEN A GREAT SLEEPER, but I really tossed and turned that night. Sometime after that game, I fell into the habit of going through the opposing lineup as I drifted off to sleep the night before a start. In fact, I'd fall asleep thinking of my next start as soon as I finished my last one. If I pitched a game against the Montreal Expos, say, I'd go to bed that night knowing who my next opponent was, what their lineup looked like, whether it was a day game or a night game, if it was a day game after a night game, in which case I might get the B lineup instead of the A lineup. I ran through everything. The opposing starter: that mattered, not in a head-to-head, showdown sort of way, but you'd rather go up against a number five pitcher than a number one, to give your guys a better shot. Here I was facing another rookie pitcher, Tony Ghelfi, making his second big league start, and knowing that helped to level the playing field in my mind before the game got under way. It meant our team had a shot. It meant the Mets might be able to absorb a couple of my mistakes.

I'm one of those guys who starts his dreams before he falls asleep. I write a little script. Back then, I would write out my perfect start. I'd retire the side in order, first three innings, with the pitcher striking out on a pitch out of the strike zone. If I still hadn't fallen asleep, I'd go through scenarios. For this Phillies game, perhaps, I might think about how I'd pitch to Pete Rose if there were runners on second and third with Mike Schmidt on deck. If I got ahead of Rose, how would I strike him out? I'd think it all the way through. If our defense was playing away because I'd be pitching him away, that meant I couldn't give him anything soft and in, because anything soft and in would allow a good hitter like Rose to go against the defensive alignment we'd set up for him.

TRY AS I MIGHT, I couldn't get a good night's sleep before that first start. It was the weight of those names. It was the pressure of my first big league start. It was the noise from LaGuardia, on top of everything else. Finally, I spilled out of bed and made for the hotel lobby. I had no idea where I was. I knew I was near the stadium—that's all. New York was like a great sprawling foreign city to me. I didn't know anyone. I didn't know about the five boroughs. I didn't know the subways. I didn't know shit. I asked some guy in the lobby to recommend a place to eat, and he sent me to a Greek diner on Astoria Boulevard. I walked. I didn't know there was a Greek diner on every corner. I don't even know if I ended up at the diner this guy recommended or simply stumbled into the first one in my path. Anyway, I ordered. Breakfast? Lunch? I wish I could remember. It was just a meal, something to settle my nerves.

We were only a couple miles from Shea, where I'd be pitching in just a few hours, and nobody knew who I was. Nobody cared. It would have never occurred to me that this would be one of the last meals I'd eat in a New York City restaurant in relative peace and anonymity—and, even if it had, I'm not so sure I would have thought relative peace and anonymity such a welcome condition.

From the diner, I hailed a cab and went to the stadium. It was way early for a night game, but I knew the clubhouse had to be a nicer place to twiddle my thumbs than my miserable hotel room. Plus, there was stuff to do when I got there. Detail-type stuff. Ticket requests, mostly. One of the toughest parts about joining the team as a September call-up was that I didn't know anybody. And not just my teammates or the coaches—I didn't know anyone in town. I didn't know any of the people in the Mets front office, and I hated having to ask people I didn't know for favors, but there was no way I could cobble together enough tickets for my friends and family without an assist from at least a couple folks. Each player got a certain number of tickets for each game, and the guys were always trading tickets among themselves, but I didn't know anybody well enough to ask them for their tickets. Luckily, the Mets gave me an extra batch, because they knew it was my debut and that I had a lot of people who wanted to come out to the stadium. Still, there was a lot of busywork involving tickets. There were no cell phones. There was no e-mail. It was difficult to keep track of it all, and to tell everyone where to go, and when.

In a way, the ticket grab was a good distraction. It kept my mind off facing all those legends in the Philadelphia lineup and occupied me with something else, and if I had to do it all over again I'd go at it the same way. Let the game sneak up on you, I say. Don't overthink the situation. Do your homework, of course, but don't overdo it. Just get out there and pitch. After a while, I looked at a clock and realized it had been a couple hours since I'd thought of Morgan, Rose, and Schmidt, and I took that as a good sign. All night long, and all that morning, the clock had been moving at a slow crawl, and here, with all this running back and forth, it had skipped a couple of beats. The rest of my life was that much closer.

LET ME TELL YOU, walking through the bowels of a mostly empty major league stadium is a thrill. I was a little too tightly wound to fully appreciate it just then, but it's really something. Think of all the history that's gone down in almost any ballpark: all those great players, all those great moments . . . it's overwhelming. Uplifting, even. Maybe even a little eerie.

Beneath a big stadium like Shea was a labyrinth of old, decaying cement walkways, with open ceilings leading to an exposed network of pipes and wires and gas lines. Here and there a pipe would jut out from the wall at a strange, abrupt angle. It was like walking through an old submarine, and I clambered around, trying to get the lay of the land.

I was a four- or five-day veteran by this point, but I knew enough to wander over to the list they kept for batting practice, the one that tells you which group you're hitting with. I'd always thought of myself as a good hitter; my bat would never have taken me to a professional career, but I could take my cuts. We pitchers usually hit in the first group during batting practice. That is, we *starting* pitchers usually hit in the first group. The relievers and the guys who weren't starting didn't usually bother. I hadn't hit in the longest time, so I was excited. They use a designated hitter in the minor leagues, so this would be my first chance in a long while to be a part of the whole game, to stand once again as a fully formed, well-rounded ballplayer. I couldn't wait to get a bat in my hands. Other than a lone minor league pinch-hitting appearance against Donnie Moore, I hadn't swung a bat since college— and even here all I could manage was a whiff.

As the game drew near, I started to think about heading

out to the bullpen to begin my warm-up. Trouble was, I didn't know whether to walk to the pen via some complicated route beneath the stadium or to just make a beeline across the field. I didn't know anyone to ask, and no one seemed inclined to seek me out and tell me what was expected. So I leaned against the peeling paint of one of the cement walls like I was waiting for a bus, and then I fumbled around until I saw a couple pitchers and catchers taking the underground route. I hung back for a bit before I followed, so it was just me, alone, trudging down this long, empty walkway. Now I tell people it was a real *Goodfellas* moment, because years later, when I saw the Martin Scorsese movie, there was a scene where the camera follows Ray Liotta and his date into the back entrance of some nightclub, through the kitchen, up and down a bunch of narrow hallways, and finally into the main room of the club. That walk took me right back to the bowels of Shea Stadium and my behind-the-scenes march to the place where my career was waiting for me.

I passed a bunch of people who clapped me on the back and wished me well. I didn't know who half of them were. The other half I had just met. Then I passed the family room, where my parents and brothers had holed up before the game, and I thought, Do I stop? Do I have time? Will they think I'm rude if I don't? Will the Mets think I lack focus if I do? All these crazy thoughts, all these crazy worries bounced around my head, and only a few of them had anything to do with the Phillies. Mostly, it was just me, trying to take everything in and make sense of it all. I walked on a film of pure joy. Nerves, too, but my overwhelming mood was one of sheer happiness. I thought about the first time I put on a uniform, back in Little League, and how, like most kids, I dreamed of someday making it to the majors. That's the rallying cry of every young athlete: *Someday, someday* . . . Well, my someday was here.

Eventually, I made my way out to the bullpen. Ron Hodges was the catcher assigned to warm me up. Junior Ortiz would be my catcher during the game, and the drill in the bigs is that the backup catcher gets you warm and the game-day catcher steps in for the last five minutes or so to check out your stuff. Junior was a great defensive catcher with a tremendous arm, but his English wasn't that great, and whatever words and phrases he did manage came out with a serious stutter. I always felt so bad for the guy; his eyes would get all wide whenever he tried to speak and it was the goofiest thing. We gave him a hard time about it. A good-natured hard time, but a hard time just the same. He'd come out to the mound to offer a piece of advice or to calm me down, and it would take just about forever, until finally I'd have to throw up my hands and say, "Junior, just fucking spit it out, will ya?" That would always make him laugh, and once he loosened up he was able to speak.

Here's where I allowed my mind to go, as I tried to get warm out in the bullpen: I thought how I'd have all of September to show the Mets what I could do. Those five promised starts were both a blessing and a curse: a blessing because they freed me from thinking I had to do too much in this first outing; a curse because they kept me from focusing on this first outing with the intensity it deserved. I told myself I had these five starts in my pocket, and that if I messed up on opening night it wasn't like the curtain would come down on the rest of my career.

At the time, I had no idea that New York Mets fans were long-suffering dreamers, accustomed to losing. I just knew the Mets were a pathetic team. Even as I was preparing to make my first start for the Mets, I didn't know a whole lot about my new teammates or the team's recent history. My National League team was the Dodgers, because they were always on the *Game of the Week*. That was where I wanted to play, in Dodger Stadium, where the sun was always shining and Sandy Koufax would show up for games and pretty blond actresses would fill the box seats behind home plate. The Mets? Nobody dreamed of playing for the Mets, unless you'd grown up in the outer boroughs and had decided that the pennant-rich history of the crosstown Yankees just wasn't for you.

There was some providence to the fact that my first big league game was against Philadelphia, because the Phillies had been owned by Ruly Carpenter, a fellow Yalie. Carpenter had sold the team to Bill Giles the previous year, but our Yale team used to go down to Clearwater, Florida, for preseason training at the Phillies' complex, and the Carpenters had made it a special point to welcome the Yale players. The kick here was that we got to see great Philadelphia players like Mike Schmidt and Greg Luzinski—not quite up close, but close enough. In some ways, I felt a deeper link to the Phillies than to the Mets because of all those spring-training trips, but it wasn't until I started throwing that I made the connection to those preseason sessions. It's like my brain finally switched on: *Oh, yeah. The Phillies. From Clearwater.*

I quickly fell into a nice, easy rhythm with Ron Hodges. I started out soft-tossing him the ball, and he just flipped it back to me; then when I added some pace to my pitches, he added the same kind of pace to his throws back to the mound. It's like he was egging me on, encouraging me to bring it, telling me he was ready for whatever I had. Back and forth. Over and over. I didn't realize it just then, but we had lapsed into the familiar choreography of the pregame warm-up, a reassuring routine I would experience 370 times more (including seven postseason starts) before my career was through.

When you're going good, there's a kind of tacit agreement between pitcher and catcher to leave each other alone during a warm-up. Your body language does the talking. If there's something to really talk about, something *off,* it will be quickly apparent. Usually, there's a pitching coach nearby, and if all is right with the world he'll just offer a slight nod of approval. I came to look forward to those moments out there in the bullpen before each start, but here before this first start I didn't know what to make of it. I found myself thinking that if the Mets really cared about this first start, there'd be more coaches out here, watching me warm up, telling me what to do. I wondered why Ron Hodges wasn't saying anything. I wasn't even hearing anything from the fans, who had started to spill into the stadium. I had all kinds of similarly deflating thoughts. I tried to block them out, but they kept clawing through. I noticed that this was the first time I'd had a fear of failure comparable to my drive to succeed. I'd always been an *I'm better than you; let's go!* kind of pitcher. I'd put my stuff up against anyone's. But a certain hesitancy catches up to you when you get the call in the bigs; it's a quantum leap from everything you've experienced. You start to think you have to be exponentially better than you ever were. That's not true, of course, but you don't know that yet. All you know is that Mike Schmidt will be staring you down in an hour or so and you had better be ready.

Here's the thing: you're either brought up at the right time, in such a way that the move from Triple A to the majors is a kind of slow, vertical move, or you're rushed in such a way that it's a leap. That's the nut of it. I'd just won ten games at Tidewater, the Mets' Triple A affiliate, and in those days Triple A was really good baseball. Most of the talented young ballplayers back then were in Triple A ball, so mine was more of a slow, vertical step. I was pitching for a last-place team.

There was no pressure on me, other than the pressure I placed on myself. Contrast that with the situation thrust on a kid like Mike Pelfrey, who struggled mightily in his first stops and starts with the big club. He went from having no substantive minor league experience when he was called up in 2007 to being asked to fill one-fifth of a rotation on a team that saw itself as championship caliber. Nothing against Mike, but that's a tremendous leap—and a whole lot of pressure. Yet to his great credit, he put it all together in 2008 and fulfilled the promise he'd shown as a prospect.

I was brought up at just the right time, but a part of me must have been at least a little nervous, because I looked up at one point and realized I was running out to the mound. A lot of pitchers, you see them sprint to the mound from the pen or the dugout and you think, That guy's pumped. Or: He's a real hard charger. Or maybe you think he's putting out a little too much effort, trying to impress. But that wasn't me. I'd never run to the mound before, at any level. But here I was, running. I didn't think about it. I just ran, and as I was running I actually stepped outside myself and thought, Why the hell am I running? My head was telling my feet to walk, but they were like Fred Flinstone's feet, shuffling as fast as they could go. I couldn't wait to get out there, I guess. That, or I couldn't wait to see myself safely to the other side of whatever was about to happen.

Once I got to the mound, I took a good look around. My first thought was, Man, this thing is high. Really, it felt about a foot higher than minor league mounds—a foot higher than the bullpen mound, even. In the minors, you'd scratch at the dirt in front of the pitching rubber and whole chunks would come loose, but here I started to scratch at the dirt to get a feel for it and I could barely make a dent. It was perfect red clay, pounded hard and fine.

Whenever I went to prepare the mound around the rubber, I always thought of Gerry Cheevers, the great Boston Bruins goalie of the late 1960s and early 1970s—one of the leaders of the Bruins' 1970 and 1972 Stanley Cup championship runs. Bobby Orr was my hero, but every time I took the mound in college or in the minors it put me in mind of the way Cheevers used to take care of the crease in front of the goal before each period. He had this special routine, scratching at the ice with the blades of his skates, sliding his foot back and forth, trying to get the surface just how he wanted it, and I patterned my pregame moves on the mound after Cheevers's moves in the crease. I did a more thorough, more Cheevers-like job of it as I moved up to each new level. A part of me always thought the crease in hockey was the closest thing to the mound in baseball, a private spot on a shared field that was a kind of hallowed ground. I dug and kicked the dirt with my cleats, as if they were skates. I slid my feet back and forth in front of the rubber, trying to get it just right. I marked my territory, the same way Cheevers used to mark his, and then I ran a line down the center of the mound to remind myself of where I wanted to step.

A word or two on the pitching rubber, as long as I'm on it. Every pitcher has a different part of the rubber he likes to use. Mine was basically in the middle. If I went up against a guy who wanted to throw from there, too, I had to be conscious of that. It's like sharing a desk with some guy at work, on different shifts. You get to know the other guy's shoe size. You get to know which guys are heavy on their feet. Who scratches at the mound. Who leaves the mound dirty. I was one of those guys who always brushed off the rubber and kept it clean. I had to *see* it. I think that comes from being a young kid playing on so many crappy fields, but I'm also kind of compulsive about cleanliness. In any case, my mound had to be clean. I couldn't work with mud on the rubber or with the resin bag at the front of the mound. It used to irritate the hell out of me when I had to share the hill with some slob who, to make matters worse, liked to use the same middle territory as I did. When that happened, I'd slide over a couple inches to avoid my opponent's mess. I'd find a spot just to the right or the left, because I wanted a clean, small indent, an indent I could control. I always felt I could make whatever small adjustments I needed to in order to account for the slight lateral shift; it was the landing that had me worried.

I don't always buy it when I hear a pitcher complaining about having to move a few inches to the left or the right to accommodate his opposite number on the mound. To my thinking, the impact of such a slight shift is minimal at best. Sure, the angles are important, but they're not all-important, and they're certainly not as important as the landing.

When I finally had the rubber tidied just right that Tuesday night, I went into my on-field warm-up. The very first pitch I threw from that worked-over mound was ridiculous. Sick. The ball fairly flew from my hands, and as it barreled into Junior Ortiz's glove I thought, Oh my God, I've never thrown a ball that hard! There were no radar guns, there was no way to validate my thought, but the ball popped with tremendous velocity, with *purpose*. It was only one pitch, but it was right and true, and it left me thinking I was on my game. It's hard to believe that one pitch can instill such confidence in a young pitcher, but that's how this first pitch from the real Shea mound left me feeling. The second pitch was much the same. And the best part was that Junior had one of those nice new gloves that give off a resounding clap whenever a fastball thumps into the pocket, so it sounded great on that crisp September night. In those days, a lot of the younger catchers liked those stiff new gloves, and I loved them for the sound they gave off. In my head, everyone in the ballpark could hear that clap—and I suppose it helped that there were only about nine thousand fans that day.

My breaking ball felt great, too. There was a nice snap to it, and I had good location. The more I threw, the more I believed I was going to pitch well. My confidence grew with each pitch. I started to get into the sweet pantomime that goes on between pitcher and catcher. Thrusting the glove to signal a fastball. Flipping the glove to announce a curve. Pulling back on the glove to let the catcher know a changeup is coming. It's like choreography (not quite the step-ball-change of a Bob Fosse, but close), I realized. I'd done all these little baseball things a thousand times before this night, but I'd never thought about them.

I swatted at the back of my shoulder with my glove, to indicate to Junior that it was my last pitch. As I wrote earlier, Junior had a great arm. People in baseball don't really talk about him much anymore, but he threw ropes. I'd seen him throw from the bench before, but never from the mound, and as I stepped out of the way to watch his throw down to second to complete the warm-up, I thought, Okay, Ronnie, these guys are pretty good up here. The infielders tossed the ball around the horn until it got to Hubie Brooks at third, who walked it over to the mound to me. Then he patted me on the rump and said, "Have a good one."

I thought that was cool. I'd hardly said a dozen words to Hubie since I'd been called up, but he knew this was my first start. He knew what it meant. For Hubie especially, baseball had meant a great deal. He'd grown up in Compton, one of the tougher neighborhoods in Los Angeles, so the game was a real agent of change for him. He never took it for granted. Hubie wasn't alone in his goodwill toward me; most ballplayers tend to want to make things easier for their rookie teammates—other than Ron Hodges, I guess. They remember how it was for them. It's only after the game that they look to razz them, because they remember that, too. (Not incidentally, I never did talk about my tobacco-juice razzing with Hodges; we got along well enough when we were teammates, but this degrading moment just kind of hung between us, like something to get past.)

That pat on the rump from Hubie is probably my last specific memory of my first pregame warm-up. The first inning itself is a bit of a blur. Joe Morgan was announced; he looked a little odd to me in that Phillies away uniform, but as soon as he dug in at the batter's box there was no mistaking him, with that little flap thing he used to do with his left arm as he waited on the pitch. Keep the ball down, I told myself as I went into my windup. The first pitch was a fastball away for a called strike. I heard the call and thought, Okay, Ronnie. That's out of the way. You're a big leaguer now. And you're ahead in the count.

Morgan was hanging over the plate, so I wanted to push him back a bit, to bust him inside with another fastball. A purpose pitch, right at that flapping elbow, to make him dance away from that inside corner. But once I got two strikes on him, my thinking changed—I began thinking like a minor leaguer. Down on the farm, trying to make an impression, most pitchers think about padding their stats. You catch yourself deciding that a strikeout looks a whole lot better to the guys up north than a groundout. So there was some of that, but there was also arrogance, confidence, bluster. I'd talked myself into believing I was ready for the big leagues. I'd pumped myself up, and after that easy, solid warm-up this mind-set really took hold. It got to where it wasn't enough just to get Joe Morgan out; I had to strike him out. Anything less would have been a disappointment—and, sure enough, I got him swinging. Fastball, down and away, on a 1–2 count.

Rose was next. My first thought here was, I can't strike this guy out. My next thought was, I can't let him reach. Then: Throw strikes, Ronnie. Make him put it in play. The word on Rose was he didn't take any strikes, so I had to go after him. Hard. He was one of those hitters, like Wade Boggs and Barry Bonds, known to have a good eye for the strike zone. The umpires weren't about to call anything if he didn't swing at it, so here again I didn't think I could catch a break on something just off the plate. But I did: I worked the count to 2–2, and then I threw him another fastball, down and away, that caught the outside corner. Almost a carbon copy of the pitch I'd thrown to Joe Morgan to strike him out, and I thought, Damn, Ronnie, you've got it going on.

As Mike Schmidt strode to the batter's box I allowed myself to think I might just strike out the side. How about that? I mused. First big league inning. Against these big-time hitters. I recalled a line I'd heard somewhere along the way: Great athletes have a flair for the dramatic and deliver; good athletes have a flair for the dramatic and deliver . . . sometimes. I didn't know where I fit just yet, but I wanted to deliver. Here. Now.

Then Schmidt dug in and my thinking turned. I felt a rush of fear. It was almost primal. Schmidt wasn't that big a guy. He had those great, meaty forearms, but other than that he wasn't the most dominating physical presence. And yet, with a bat in his hands, he was like the Incredible Hulk. I couldn't start him with a get-me-over fastball, because he would just crush it. He could swat at it like he was brushing away a fly and send it over the right-field wall—that's how strong this guy was. Junior Ortiz signaled for a curveball, and

I thought that was a good call. I remembered looking forward to working with my first big league catcher and trusting him to help me call my first big league game, and here I caught myself thinking, Okay, this guy knows what he's doing back there. But as I went into my windup I thought, Better be a strike, Ronnie. Can't afford to get behind on this batter. Keep it inside. Don't let him extend those arms.

Looking back, I see that I had a bit of an edge that first inning. Those great hitters didn't know the first thing about me. They didn't know my strengths. They didn't know my tendencies. They just knew I was some kid pitcher. If I'd have thought about that at the time, it would have been a tremendous advantage, but I didn't know enough to think that way. All I could think was how cool it would be to strike out the side. Not just any side. *That* side. Morgan, Rose, Schmidt. It was a rookie approach, but so far it was working. For two batters, it was working.

Here against Schmidt, however, I should have been thinking like more of a veteran. It should have been more about the moment. To a good pitcher, strikeouts mean nothing. They're just outs. A good, experienced pitcher is not about to let a strikeout determine how he approaches the next hitter. In the long history of the game, there are maybe a dozen guys who stand as the exception, including Nolan Ryan, Bob Gibson, Walter Johnson, Sandy Koufax, and Tom Seaver. I'm nowhere close to the men on that list, and yet this *strike 'em out* mind-set had gotten me through Morgan and Rose, and ultimately to two strikes on Schmidt before it caught up to me. The rookie in me was thinking, Okay, I've got the first two batters; now I'll go after this guy and strike him out, too. A veteran would have been thinking, Okay, Mike Schmidt is up—what do I have to execute on this pitch?

I might have believed I had an edge, after striking out Morgan and Rose to lead off the inning, but that was just a fantasy. I should have known exactly what I wanted to do with a hitter like Schmidt, no matter what had transpired with Morgan and Rose. Typically, in the first inning of a scoreless game, bases empty, I'd pitch Schmidt a lot differently than I might later on, in another situation. I would have an idea of the pitch I would throw if I needed to get this guy out in a key spot— say, with two runners on in the seventh, in a close game. Whatever that pitch might be, wherever I might have located it, I would not want to reveal it here in the first inning.

I came late to this type of thinking as a pitcher, but eventually I learned that you don't have to show your hand against every hitter, in each at-bat. You don't have to be so eager in every spot. This was just the first inning. Two outs. Nobody on. I could throw a fastball down and away, and the worst Schmidt could do was hit a single to right field. Of course, I could miss, and he could hit a home run, but I could miss with any pitch. Still, with experience, I wouldn't want him to see the changeup here. Why? Because if he came up in a key spot later on I didn't want him to have a backlog of information on me.

Each pitch determines the next one. That's how it goes. I didn't know this quite yet, but that's how it should go. Back in college, back in the minors, you could get by on good stuff. You could reach back and throw and get hitters out, as long as you had good command of your pitches. But at the major league level, I realized soon enough, it's not about overpowering the opposing batter. It's not about the strikeout. It's about keeping the hitter off balance, guessing. It's about bringing your best stuff—but not *all* of your best stuff, because you want to keep something in reserve. A smart, experienced pitcher looks to establish a fine balance at the front end of a game: you want to mix it up, but not so much that you reveal every weapon.

Of course, if Morgan and Rose had reached base and I had been facing Schmidt with two runners on and nobody out, it would have been an entirely different story. Then it's the seventh inning already. Then it's a critical situation. But that's not where we were. We were in good shape, so I came back at Mike with the most hellacious hook I had ever thrown. My thinking here—and Junior's, too, I guess—was that I didn't have to throw the hook for a strike in this situation, and that as long as I didn't hang it up in the strike zone I'd be okay. I could miss with it outside the strike zone and still get another shot. But how I reached back and found *that* pitch, I'll never know. The ball seemed to break from the top of Schmidt's head to the top of his ankles. Just a wicked, wicked pitch— one of the best I'd ever thrown. And what did Schmidt do? He smoked a ball down to third, a vicious one-hopper that Hubie Brooks managed to snare and send on to first in time for the putout. It went down in the box score as a groundout to third, but that was no simple groundout. That was a bullet shot, and as Hubie made the throw across the infield, I thought, Damn, that was my best curveball. And Schmidt just pounded it. I don't know how Hubie even made the play, but he did. Thank God he did.

I came off the mound to a standing ovation, which strikes me now as funny, maybe even telling. Now that I've come to know and love the city and the New York Mets fans, it was an interesting reception. Of course, it had more to do with the pent-up frustrations of the past several seasons and the bottled-up excitement Mets fans were starting to feel for the young talent the front office was bringing on board than it did with any kind of stellar performance on my part.

Yeah, I retired the side in order, but that was my job. I was a professional ballplayer now. That's what I was supposed to do. Even if this particular side was Joe Morgan, Pete Rose, and Mike Schmidt—three guys who seemed headed for Cooperstown.

SOME FINAL THOUGHTS on that inaugural game: first, as I walked back to the dugout, for some strange reason I noticed an inordinate number of dark-haired people in the stands. I wasn't looking directly at any one section or at any one group of fans, just vaguely and generally toward the sea of Mets jerseys and hats and all the people screaming and yelling in the boxes along the first-base side of the field. It's an odd thing to notice, at such a heady moment, don't you think? It was such a random thought, but I guess I was still that kid who grew up wanting to pitch for the Los Angeles Dodgers, in front of all those blondes.

I strode off the mound after that first inning with a real sense of purpose. It wasn't cake, this big league pitching stuff. Even then, I knew I'd hit some trouble spots, somewhere, and possibly soon. But if any inning could tell you that you belonged in the major leagues, this was my inning, and I knew I'd never throw another pitch in the minor leagues again. Deep down, I knew. This was where I'd be, for the next while.

My teammates and coaches didn't say all that much to me when I sat back down in the dugout. I got a couple high fives, a couple nods of congratulations, but that was about it. In those days, ballplayers didn't talk much to pitchers in the middle of a game, so I sat by myself at the end of the bench and tried to soak it all in. At some point, Junior Ortiz wandered over. He said, "Way to go, Papi." It took him a beat or two to get the words out, with his stutter and his broken English, but I could tell from his smile and his big fluttering eyes that he was happy for me. It was the first time I'd heard one of the Latin players address someone with the familiar "Papi." I thought that was funny, too.

Another funny footnote: though I struck out in my first big league at-bat, I did manage a single to left field off the Phillies' starter, Tony Ghelfi, in my next turn. This alone was no laughing matter, but offered another opportunity for my new teammates to put me through the wringer. Someone chased down the ball and sent it into the Mets dugout, where another someone presented it to me at the end of the inning. I handed it to the trainer for safekeeping, at the same time regretting that no one had thought to retrieve the ball from the first inning, after Hubie made that sweet pick on Schmidt's shot to third. It would have been nice to have that ball as my first keepsake, but I was happy to have this one. That is, I was happy until the game ended, and I got to my locker and found a ball that looked like it had been left out in the rain and mud and chewed by a dog. On it, someone had written "Ron Darling's First Hit," in the kind of handwriting you might find on a kindergarten wall. My heart sank when I saw it, although I had already figured out that rookies have to take a lot of shit. (I got the *real* ball later, by the way.)

On the not-so-funny front, we ended up losing the game. I gave up a run in the fourth, after retiring the side in order in the first three innings. Nine up, nine down. Just like I'd pictured it in my pregame fantasies. But there were some bumps in my second time through the order. I walked Morgan to start the fourth, and he crossed to second on a Rose grounder to third. Then I balked Morgan over to third, with Schmidt at the plate. Then I balked again, allowing Morgan to score. The

Mets bullpen gave up another run in the eighth inning, but it didn't matter. We couldn't get anything going against this kid Ghelfi, although he struggled at the game's midpoint and never made it out of the fifth inning. The Phillies ended up winning anyway, 2–0.

Not exactly the most auspicious performance in the history of major league baseball—but it would have to do. Until I could follow up with something better.

INNING SUMMARY

JOE MORGAN: strikeout, swinging
PETE ROSE: strikeout, looking
MIKE SCHMIDT: groundout to third base

Finding My Way

October 22, 1986
Game 4, World Series
New York Mets vs. Boston Red Sox
Fenway Park, Boston
Attendance: 33,920

Game 4 of the 1986 World Series. A meaningful game on a big-time stage in front of—for me—a hometown crowd. As moments go, it was grand. As a lesson in preparedness, it was unnerving. As a homecoming, it was a little distracting. For a time in there, I thought the moment might be too big for me; and then, for another time, I thought I might have a handle on it. But that handle would slip away once or twice before I could get a good grip.

As it happened, there was a whole lot of backstory to this

game. Tension, too. It took me a while to get to what I've come to see as the game's turning point, in the bottom of the second, so stay with me on this one. A big part of that backstory was my start in Game 1, at home at Shea—a game we ended up losing 1–0. The one run scored on an error. I'd pitched about as well as I could have pitched, until I walked Jim Rice to start the seventh inning. Then: a wild pitch to the next batter, Dwight "Dewey" Evans, allowing Rice to advance to second. I got Evans on a comebacker to the mound, which brought Red Sox catcher Rich Gedman to the plate with one out and a man on second. Gedman grounded to Tim Teufel, our usually reliable second baseman, but the ball skipped under Timmy's glove and Rice came barreling around to score.

That's not all: there was a freakish collision behind home plate just as Rice crossed with the lone run. Rice hadn't been running all that hard when Gedman tapped the ball to second because it had initially looked like a routine grounder. Dave Henderson, the on-deck batter, wasn't moving toward home from the on-deck circle on the third-base side of the field, at least not in any kind of hurry, because there was no reason to think there'd be a play at the plate. And I had started out toward first, as I'd been trained to do ever since I started pitching, whenever a ball was hit on the ground to my left. All three of us kicked it up a couple notches the moment the ball skittered past Teufel: Rice turned it on as he rounded third; Henderson sprinted to the first-base side of the plate to signal for Rice to stand or slide, and I cut hard toward home to back up the catcher. I've since looked at tape of the game, and I don't think I've ever seen three players move in such an all-out way toward the same spot on the field. We were flying. Sure enough, I collided headlong with Henderson, and we both crumpled to the ground behind home plate like we'd been hit by snipers. That's the lasting image I carry of that game, probably the most important professional game of my life to that point: me splayed out on the field as Rice came home with the only run of the contest.

The postscript to that Game 1 crash was that I ended up playing with Dave Henderson in Oakland a few years later, and we would kid each other about it. He'd say, "I knocked you down pretty good." And I'd say, "Yeah, but I got up first." Dave Henderson was a big, powerful guy, all muscle, and running into him was like running into a retaining wall. I was tall but fairly skinny, and Henderson got the better of the bounce, no question. I was shaken up, but I stumbled back to the mound looking like my teammate Lenny Dykstra, my uniform all dirty and disheveled. Somehow, I got Henderson to fly to right. Then I walked Spike Owen intentionally to get to the pitcher's spot, and struck out Bruce Hurst swinging. Davey Johnson lifted me for a pinch hitter in the bottom of the seventh, and that was that. So much for Game 1.

ADDING TO THE BUILDUP and the grand sense of moment of Game 4 was the bizarre homecoming aspect. I'd grown up just outside Worcester, Massachusetts ("Wustah!" to a real New Englander), about a half hour from Fenway Park. I was a major Red Sox fan as a kid. Yastrzemski, Conigliaro, Lonborg, Petrocelli, Boomer—those were my guys. In fact, Fenway was the only big league stadium I'd been to before I actually put on a big league uniform. Now here I was, pitching in Game 4 of the World Series for the hated New York Mets, trailing the team of my youth 2–1, in the storied shadow of the Green Monster, which had been so much a part of my boyhood baseball fantasies.

The game was like a homecoming in every other respect,

too. I must have known about five hundred people in attendance that night. I ran down the left-field line during batting practice, and every step I'd hear, "Hey, Ronnie Dahling," in a thick Boston accent. I'd turn and see a familiar face: someone I went to high school with, someone from the neighborhood, a family friend. They were Red Sox fans, to the core, but they wished me well—to a degree. The best-case scenario for these lifelong Sox fans would have been a repeat of Game 1, where I pitched great and Boston won.

Down the right-field line it was much the same. "Hey, Ronnie Dahling!" "Hey, Ronnie!" "Good to see ya, Ronnie Dahling!" "Remembah me?"

Up and down the baselines, like music.

Ever since Davey Johnson had announced the rotation for the series, I'd been worried about this trip to Fenway. It played with my head, a little bit. It wasn't just a big game—it was bigger than that. The distraction of going home is the last thing a pitcher needs heading into a meaningful game. The mixed emotions of having all those good people rooting for me but not too hard, the tug and pull of those wistful childhood memories, it all got wearying after a while. I stayed at the hotel with the team, of course, at the Westin in Copley Square, and I tried to keep away from friends and family and focus on my start.

By this stage in my career, I'd had a lot of practice tuning out these external factors. Like most starting pitchers, I had my pregame rituals scripted all the way to the national anthem, although I've never met a starting pitcher who approached his turn in quite the same way. I did a lot of chair-facing-into-the-locker time, as I recall. Most pitchers had their own version of this, trying to block out whatever external factors managed to find their way into the clubhouse. There was a lot of history to consider, too, and you had to reach back and reflect on how you'd fared in previous matchups against the players you were about to face. You know them. They know you. They know you know them. And you know they know you. There are no surprises, but you've still got to work it through, and in so doing find a way to clear your thoughts of any bad history. I needed to know it and file it away, so I could start fresh. The good history I kept, front and center. The bad history I tossed. Yes, that bad history can be instructive, but I was one of those guys who wanted only positive reinforcement. It's like standing on a tee box and seeing only pond. I would not see the pond, only the green; that's how I approached the game. It was all good, only good.

Was I deluding myself with these head-in-the-locker reflections that focused only on the positive? I don't think so. I knew full well that every pitcher makes mistakes. And I knew it was more than likely I'd make a couple in the game I was about to start. But mistakes are mistakes, and it wouldn't help to think about them before they happened. Plus, mistakes can be a good thing, in the long run, for what they can teach you about the various adversities that find you on that mound. In the short run, though, there's never a way to justify them or learn from them or explain them away.

My big pregame thing was to take a nap. Really. In all my years in baseball, I've never heard of any pitcher scheduling a nap into his routine, but I started doing it my second year in the bigs, in Montreal. At the time, I was in the rookie habit of drinking a cup of coffee an hour or so before game time, to shake off the doldrums I inevitably experienced as I looked ahead to my first pitch. I'd never felt sluggish before a game in the minors or in college, but the weight of each professional start got a little heavier as it approached. I felt like I was dragging. And so this would be my major league routine, I'd decided: coffee before each start. But then we got to Montreal and the clubhouse guy didn't have any coffee. This was a bit of a surprise, especially in a city like Montreal. Instead, he had some weird type of Canadian soda, which he tried to pass off as a caffeine substitute, and I thought, I'm not trying that, not for the first time just before a start. Instead, I walked around the clubhouse, trying to still my jitters and rev myself up and shake that pregame weight from my shoulders.

Next thing I knew, I'd fallen asleep. I was wired so tight, I shut down. The trainer woke me up about twenty minutes later. He said, "Ronnie, it's a quarter to seven. You got a game." (Start times for night games were at seven-thirty back then.)

I was in a fog. There was heat and haste and activity all around, and there I was, coming out of a deep, satisfying sleep in the middle of all that commotion. It was weird, but I felt good. Refreshed. That weight I'd been carrying, the way I had before every big league start? Gone. That feeling like I was dragging? Gone. I went out that night and pitched a great game. Another 1–0 loss, but a great game. Mitch Webster notched a triple off me to lead off and ended up scoring on a groundout, though I allowed only one more hit the rest of the way. A complete-game two-hitter. Our guys just couldn't get anything started at the plate, but in every other respect it was a decent outing. I looked past the loss and thought, Gee, maybe there's something to this napping. I never took coffee after that; I just went to sleep, usually curled up on a trainer's table that was barely five feet long. For me, at six foot four, it couldn't have been all that comfortable, but I never noticed—or, if I did, I never minded. First couple of times, the trainer had to wake me up. But after that my body clock kicked in, and I always managed to shake myself awake, usually after twenty minutes or so. It was very strange. After a while, at Shea, I started ducking into one of the back rooms, a small doctor's office they had set up, just to grab an extra bit of privacy and avoid the weird stares of my team-mates and the clubhouse personnel.

So that's what I did in Fenway. First I sat, still and quiet, on the chair in front of my locker, facing in. I pulled the chair into the cubby as far as it would go and tried to clear my mind of every nonbaseball thought, every negative thought, every doubt and uncertainty. I'd just come off a big year for the Mets. I was confident, strong. I had made thirty-five starts that season, including the postseason, and the Mets had won twenty-seven of them—so I was clearly on my game. Early in my career, I'd spent a lot of time thinking about how to pitch away from the strength of my opponents, but now my take was that I would dictate the flow of the game. I still studied the lineups and scouting reports, but if I read that someone hit the inside fastball really well I didn't necessarily think, Okay, Ronnie, gotta stay away from the inside fastball. I thought, Let's see him hit *my* inside fastball. It wasn't arrogance or cockiness. It was confidence, a belief in my ability. My own game plan would stamp the game, not the tendencies of this or that hitter.

I pictured each at-bat. I considered pitch counts, and sequences, and whatever slim history I had with each batter. It's like meditating, I guess. You work your way through the lineup and everything else falls away. In my head, of course, I always faced the minimum. First three innings: nine up, nine down. But then I broke it down from there. I imagined a first-pitch fastball, away, to start the game. Wade Boggs was due to lead off, and I'd gotten the best of our matchup in Game 1, retiring him all three times—two groundouts wrapped around a called third strike. Naturally, I couldn't get too full of myself here, because Boggs was one of the best hitters in the history of the game, but I told myself he had nothing on me.

If that first pitch was a strike, I planned to pound one inside to move him off the plate, then come back with another fastball, away. If I missed with the first pitch, I'd come back with another fastball away, thinking Boggs would probably be taking.

After just a single batter, it became a web of tangled *if . . . then* scenarios. I think most starting pitchers do a version of the same thing before each game. They work through the whole damn lineup, making room for every contingency. The cross-sport equivalent would be the way the late, great NFL coach Bill Walsh used to script the first twenty or so plays of each game, then have his quarterback run them in sequence. It didn't matter what down it was; it didn't matter where the 49ers were on the field or on the scoreboard. That's how I felt. It didn't matter what the count was. There was always a pitch I could make to counter any situation.

After I worked my way through the Red Sox lineup, I lay down on the trainer's table, in uniform, and went to sleep. But as I woke up and finished getting dressed, I realized I didn't feel quite right. I was nowhere close to refreshed, nowhere close to game-ready, and I started to worry. I was always a little sluggish on game day, a little bone weary, but the nap usually took care of that. Yet tonight there was something *off*. At this point in my pregame routine, I should have been good to go, but I was far from ready. I was listless. My limbs felt heavy. I ached in places I shouldn't have.

Obviously, I'd pitched in pressure situations before, but this was different. For a beat or two I thought maybe I was still feeling the effects of that dustup with Henderson behind home plate in Game 1, but deep down I knew it wasn't that. Physically, I felt fine. Emotionally, that's where I was falling short. You'd think maybe I'd have felt the same kind of pressure before Game 1, but that wasn't the same kind of must-win this game was turning out to be. Now we were down two games to one. We'd been swept at home. It was up to me to either get us back to even or sink us into an even deeper hole, and this was a different animal, in terms of pressure. On top of that, it was a bitterly cold October night in New England. It was so cold I had to put on a turtleneck under my uniform, for the first time in my career; I started to think maybe it was the weather that was dragging me down. But then I realized, Hey, I grew up with this weather. Advantage: me.

Whatever it was, it was something. Still, I went through my pregame motions like everything was fine, like I would power my way through it. That's all. I found Mel Stottlemyre, our pitching coach, and we walked from the third-base dugout to right field, to warm up. Mel had a special relationship with each pitcher on his staff. He knew how to get the best out of each of us, how to approach his pitchers on game day, when to push, when to hang back. With me, he was mostly quiet. He knew to leave me to my thoughts. He'd check in, take my measure, and then let me do my thing. He said, "How do you feel, Ronnie?"

I said, "All right, all right."

Right there, Mel knew. When I felt great, I said I felt great. When I didn't feel great, I was just all right. That was my tell.

The Fenway Park bullpen is a special kind of hell for visiting pitchers—even visiting pitchers who happened to grow up in the vicinity and once counted themselves as die-hard Sox fans. You're right in front of the bleachers. The two bullpens share a wall, so the opposing bullpen catchers are back-to-back during warm-ups. On one side, the home side, the fans are positive and encouraging; on the other, the visitors' side, they're vicious. The pitchers are right in the middle of this heated back-and-forth. Since my prenap visit to the field during batting practice, the ballpark had filled, and now there was a whole different tone to the shouts that came my way. In the belly of the Fenway bleachers, I was getting it good. The fans out here didn't care that I was some hometown boy. They cared only that I pitched for the Mets. I was the enemy. "Dahling, you suck!" was the prevailing sentiment.

I tuned out the taunts and tried to focus on my warm-up, which wasn't all that promising. I just didn't have it. After the first pitch, I could tell. It was the opposite of the feeling I'd had before my first big league game, against the Phillies, when the ball had left my hand with pop and sizzle. Here, the ball seemed to leave my hand in slow motion. My breaking ball could only tumble, if anything. When it didn't bounce in the dirt in front of the catcher, it slapped the cement wall behind him. I couldn't hit my spots. I thought, This is what it's like to be laboring. That was the word that popped into my head: *laboring*. It was the worst warm-up I'd ever had, before any game, ever—and ever after—and with each ball in the dirt the fans in the bleachers gave it to me a little bit more, a little bit harder.

Normally, I'd throw fifty pitches in a warm-up. It would take roughly twenty minutes—about the same time as my nap. But I saw no reason to prolong my misery that day. I was loose. I wasn't hurting. It wasn't anything physical. The only thing to do was shut it down and hope I could find my way back to whole before Boggs stepped to the plate to lead off the bottom of the first.

I turned to Mel and said, "I'm done. I can't keep throwing like this." I wasn't counting, but I'd probably thrown only thirty pitches, and I was all over the place.

He asked if I was sure.

I said, "I'm sure."

He said, "You okay?"

I said, "Yeah, I'm okay."

He said, "Okay."

My plan was to head to the clubhouse and grab a glass of milk before the game started, thinking it would calm me down. A lot of ballplayers reached for a glass of milk to chase the jitters. I don't know if it worked or if it was just an old wives' tale, but it was something to try—only I never made it all the way back to the clubhouse. I'd completely forgotten one of the key homecoming aspects of this particular game: my father was due to represent the Air Force Reserves on the field as a member of the color guard during the national anthem. I don't know if he got the nod because his son happened to be pitching in the game, or because it was his turn, or what, but it was a huge honor. I'd been thrilled for him when he first told me about it, but I'd put it out of my head as the game approached. There just wasn't any room for any non-baseball stuff in there—until I started walking toward the clubhouse with Mel and heard my dad's familiar voice.

He said, "Hey." That's all. Just "Hey."

There was no mistaking that voice. My father spoke with a thick, drill sergeant–type voice. I still hear that voice in my dreams. I turned and saw him standing out there in right field, in full dress uniform, holding an Air Force flag, looking as proud as could be. It took me completely by surprise, seeing my dad out there on the field like that, but then I thought, Oh, yeah, *right*.

All of a sudden, there was no place in the world I would rather have been than standing alongside my dad on the outfield grass at Fenway Park, before the start of one of the most consequential games of my professional career. It wasn't really a serendipitous encounter, but it felt that way to me just then, and now, as I look back on it, the moment seems almost inevitable, preordained.

I turned to Mel and said, "I'm just gonna stay here for the anthem."

Mel nodded. He didn't continue on to the dugout but stepped back a couple paces to give my dad and me some room. And we just stood there, father and son, shoulder to shoulder, as they got ready for the national anthem. It was such a beautiful, simple, surprising moment, and it turned me completely around. In my head, at least, I was transformed. I went from someone who couldn't throw a strike to someone who would not be denied, all in the space of a pregame ritual. It wasn't just any ritual, of course, and it wasn't just any game, and underneath it all I kept thinking, This is the man who taught me how to play baseball. This is the man who took me to my first big league ball game. This is the man who told me I could do anything, be anything, overcome anything.

When the anthem was about to begin, my father turned to me and said, "Go get 'em, Ronnie." Then he shook my hand, and in that one brief exchange there was the stuff of a lifetime. It was such a powerful, meaningful moment, and as I stepped away from it I felt like an animal being let out of a cage.

I walked over to where Mel was standing and said, "I got it, Mel. I'm good. I'm ready." I was buoyed by this pregame moment with my dad—enough to erase the thought of what my arm might have been telling me out in the bullpen.

And Mel, bless him, didn't say a thing. We walked across the infield in silence, and it felt to me like I'd just had the best damn warm-up of my career. Yeah, I couldn't throw for shit. And yeah, the fans in the bleachers had been tough. But now, out of nowhere, a switch had been flipped.

IT'D BE NICE TO write here that I mowed down the Red Sox lineup with the same effortless precision I'd imagined back in the clubhouse with my head buried in my locker, but that's not quite how it happened. What I hadn't counted on—what you never count on, really—was that these opposing batters had their own pregame rituals, their own ways of pumping themselves up before a game. They, too, would not be denied, and that first inning was a struggle. Some of that struggle was me trying to get out of my own way. I got Boggs to ground back to the box for the first out, but then Marty Barrett stroked a line-drive double to left center. Right away, I was in a hole. Then Bill Buckner grounded to Keith Hernandez at first as Barrett crossed to third. I thought, Okay, I can still get out of this. Remember, this was my game to stamp. But then I walked Jim Rice on five pitches and Don Baylor on six, loading the bases.

Whatever confidence I'd taken from that wonderful "chance" encounter with my dad before the game was still with me in force, but it wasn't getting the job done. It had been everything to me when I was in its middle, but now it wasn't enough. I reminded myself that confidence doesn't mean squat if you can't find the plate, and as Dewey Evans stepped up to hit with the bases loaded I walked off the mound to clear my head and take in the scene. I was never one to talk to myself during a game, but I might have mumbled something just then: "Relax" or "Focus" or "Just pitch." Some piece of sports psychobabble to calm me down and return me to my game.

You see that a lot, pitchers mumbling to themselves. I didn't do it terribly often, but I did it here. My pitch count was getting away from me. I tended not to think about such things in those days, and organizations certainly didn't place the same emphasis on pitch counts that they do today, but a starting pitcher never likes to cross that twenty-pitch threshold in the first inning. It's a big round number, and it hangs out there like a harbinger of things to come. It was by no means a giant red flag, but I was sure my teammates and my coaches and those knowledgeable Red Sox fans in the bleachers were taking note.

LOOKING BACK, that rising pitch count gets me thinking about what coaches mean when they talk about a tough at-bat. This was shaping up as a tough inning, and certainly you can't strain through a tough inning without a few tough at-bats. You hear the phrase used all the time for a hitter, when a guy hangs in there and runs the count full, then fouls off pitch after pitch. Even if he ends up making an out, he gets a pat on the back for not giving in, for forcing the pitcher to work, for allowing his teammates to see the opposing pitcher's complete stash of pitches. But you rarely hear it about the pitcher who does the flip-side job, hanging in against a tough batter—and, when you do, it probably doesn't have a positive connotation. It's almost like a backhanded compliment, and underneath it is the suggestion that you just barely survived.

Those long battles between a tough pitcher and a tough hitter are one of the great things about the game of baseball. You're in a stretched-out, tension-filled moment where the balance of power can tilt either way. I've often wondered if other pitchers ever felt like giving in to a batter and just allowing a base on balls. In certain situations, I suppose it might make sense, for tactical baseball reasons. Maybe the bases are empty and there are two outs and the next guy in the lineup is struggling. Or maybe the battling hitter is lacing the ball so hard down the line that you can't help but think he'll do some serious damage when he straightens one out. But I never caught myself thinking this way. Every batter was a base runner to be avoided, and I never gave in to a hitter in one of these tough spots—at least, not intentionally.

Once, later in my career, when I was pitching for the Oakland A's, I started a game in Milwaukee that would have put us in scoreboard-watching position to clinch the division if the second-place Twins lost that day. The first at-bat of the game, I faced Pat Listach, who ended up being the Rookie of the Year that season. Listach worked me to about twenty pitches—*to start the game.* He ended up hitting a single, and I probably would have been better off walking him on four pitches, but that would have been like admitting defeat. In all, I was pleased with that at-bat. I wasn't happy with the result, of course, but I could count the confrontation a small victory because I'd managed to keep throwing strikes. And not just strikes—pitches that the batter was not able to center. Time and time again.

Those battles can be so revealing, because all of a sudden you find yourself in a situation with a 3–2 count, game on the line, and there's a clear sense of moment. It's all led to this one showdown. The event. The time. The score. Maybe it's the seventh inning. Maybe you're facing a good, capable hitter. Not a home-run hitter, but a battler. All of these factors have spilled into a kind of funnel, and at the other end you have only one option: fastball. The hitter knows it. You know it. And it's down to you and him. You're only going to throw one pitch, and he's only going to see one pitch. Who's going to win that contest?

BACK IN FENWAY PARK on that bitterly cold October night, I worried about Evans. The inning was about to unravel on me, and Dewey was a dangerous hitter. He was especially dangerous at home, with that short porch and Pesky's Pole down the line in right and the looming Green Monster in left. He could send the ball either way. The Red Sox had a tough lineup, top to bottom, but Evans was about the last guy I wanted to face with the bases loaded, bottom of the first. I hated the way he crouched in the batter's box, so low I always felt he cheated me out of some of my strike zone. The Fenway faithful just loved this guy. He didn't have the reputation of Rice or Baylor or Boggs, but he could put the game away with one swing before it was even under way. So I breathed in a couple deep gasps of the cold night air and told myself to just go after him, hard, to trust my stuff over his.

Evans grounded to Rafael Santana at short, who flipped the ball to Wally Backman at second for the force to end the inning. I walked off the mound to shouts of "Hey, Dahling, you suck!" and thought, Here we go.

IT'S NEVER JUST ONE THING for a pitcher. We don't play the game in a vacuum. We don't just step on the rubber and have at it. There's a lot of stuff to slog through on the way to the mound before that first pitch, and in the postseason, when you're an interloper at home, pitching for the other guys, with your dad standing with the color guard in the outfield grass, there's more stuff than usual. Good stuff, not-so-good stuff, and everything in between.

We couldn't get anything going in our first turns at bat. Keith Hernandez reached on a walk in the top of the first, but Gary Carter was caught looking to end the inning. Ray Knight pushed a ground-ball single between short and third with one out in the top of the second, but he was erased on a double-play ball to end the inning. I went back out to the mound for the bottom of the second inning with this tremendous feeling of having to get the job done for my team. There was that weight again, pressing down on me in full force. We desperately needed this win, and I desperately needed to keep the Red Sox off the scoreboard until my guys had a chance to get started.

Trudging back out to the mound for the bottom of the second, I found that my mind-set had turned. I'd had that lousy warm-up. I'd been buoyed by that meeting with my dad in the outfield. I'd pitched out of trouble in the first. My team-mates had been scratching, to no good result as yet. So here it fell to me to keep the Red Sox in check. I was like a tennis player determined to hold serve and wait for a chance to break my opponent. That was my goal in this second inning: to power through the bottom of the opponent's batting order and set right the pendulum of a game that might or might not be swinging away from me.

The second inning can be a real trouble spot for a starting pitcher. In the first, for most of us, there's always an adrena-line rush, an extra push we take to the hill to jump-start our efforts. The drop-off from that, from the first inning to the second, can be huge. It was always one of the biggest hurdles I had to face in my career, finding a way to harness some other source of energy to approximate the rush I'd felt before I threw my first pitch. It's a *Let's see what I really got* kind of moment. *Let's start this walk up this hill.* In the first inning, you've donned your gear and begun your trek, but the second inning is when the climb starts—and here I started mine.

Rich Gedman stepped to the plate to lead off the bottom of the second. I had a history with this guy. We'd gone to rival high schools—me, to St. John's in Shrewsbury; Rich, to St. Peter's in Worcester. These schools had been at each other's throats for over a hundred years, and Rich always took it to me. He hit me hard, but he didn't do a whole lot of damage—

at least not when we played against him in Worcester. Down the right-field line at St. Peter's, the fence was only 250 feet from home plate, which was just a short poke to a high school player; the fence got farther away as it wrapped around a playground and reached toward center. As a result, the ground rules were a little peculiar. Officials had drawn a line on the outfield fence and determined that balls hit over the fence to the right of the line would be considered ground-rule doubles, while balls hit to the left would be home runs. It was a quirky phenomenon of New England schoolboy baseball, and the joke here was that Rich Gedman was such a demon left-handed hitter that he would power the ball four houses past the fence in right field and it would still count as just a double. He took me deep a bunch of times, but I'd pitch him so that he could only pull the ball, and in this weird way I managed to hold him to a bunch of doubles.

Here at Fenway, another field with quirky dimensions, it appeared that Gedman still had my number. On the second pitch he lashed a double down the right-field line, and just like that I was back in the same hole I'd dug for myself in the first inning—only this time there was no one out—and as he pulled into second it seemed like we were back in high school.

Dave Henderson was next. He was hitting in the eighth spot in the order, but he was not your typical number eight hitter. In a National League lineup, he'd bat in the fat middle of the order. He had good power, good speed, good presence at the plate. I knew he liked the ball up and in. He'd just hit that famous home run off Donnie Moore to help knock the California Angels from the playoffs—and that's just where Donnie had put it. I told myself I needed to keep the ball down and away, but my control was still a bit off. As good as I'd felt after the pregame lift I'd gotten in the outfield with my dad, I was obviously still trying to work my way into the rhythm of this game, so I started Henderson out with a fork-ball down. I didn't think he could hurt me with that, and with any luck he'd go fishing for it and I'd be ahead in the count.

Just then my thinking was, If I can get past Henderson to Spike Owen, at the bottom of the order, I'll be in good shape. Owen, the shortstop, was probably the weakest hitter in the Red Sox lineup, and I looked over at him in the on-deck circle like he was some kind of oasis. This was probably a mistake, but I was a young pitcher in a big spot.

As a kid, I'd always hated reading those sports biographies where it said this or that athlete put a little extra something into his or her game to get the job done, because they left me thinking that a little extra something was always on the table, there for the taking. It's not. You might think it's there, and you might keep reaching for it and coming back empty. Or maybe you think you can get by without it, so you don't bother. However it happens, however it doesn't, the game doesn't always play out the way you imagine it. Rather, it moves along on its own momentum, and it falls to you to find ways to control that momentum to advantage. So that extra something all athletes reach for can't always make the difference. In fact, it rarely does, and here I'd loaded the bases in the first and put the leadoff man on second base to start the second, and it appeared that momentum was running away from me.

I thought, This is not good. So what did I do? I somehow found the confidence and brio and *stuff* that had apparently eluded me in the bottom of the first. I fell into the rhythm of the game—at last!—and matched what I had to work with physically to what the game was presenting. I got two strikes on Henderson, and then I managed to locate a fastball down and away to get him swinging for the first out of the inning. It's not like I finally decided to reach back for something I hadn't bothered to go looking for in that difficult first inning. Not at all. I'd been looking for a pitch like that all along. It's just that here I finally found it, at a time when it was exactly right. That's the way it goes sometimes. If you're patient, if you persevere, the pitch you need to get a guy out might just find you, like an old friend. It sounds corny, I realize, but that's how a pitcher knows he's on his game.

Next, Spike Owen dug in, and I went from thinking he'd be an easy out to thinking he'd be trouble. He wasn't trouble in the same way Boggs or Baylor or Gedman could be trouble; he certainly had the weakest résumé of any hitter in that lineup. That's not to diminish his abilities, but the rest of the lineup was extremely talented. Home-run champions. Batting champions. MVPs. The problem, though, if you take hitters like Spike Owen too lightly, is that you end up getting beat by guys like Spike—or Marty Barrett, Boston's relatively light-hitting second baseman, who ended up hitting over .400 against us in that series. (Or, for Met fans, Al Weis, who lit it up in the 1969 World Series.) There are players like that lurking everywhere, players who don't have that Hall of Fame pedigree yet end up being the World Series MVP. The reason you see that so often? There's pressure on the big guys. Great pitching can always neutralize great hitting. So it's the little guys who can chip away, get a base hit here, move a base runner over. They continue to play their game, no matter what. Did I take Owen lightly? Not at all. Spike Owen was the kind of guy who found a way to help his team win every time out, and here I thought the best way to approach him was to go at him hard. With certain hitters, you don't try to counter their strength or their approach. You go at them with your best stuff and challenge them. That was the plan here, and it paid off: Spike grounded to Wally Backman, advancing Gedman to third.

Boggs stepped to the plate, and once again I thought, This

is not good. He was already 0 for 4 against me in the series, and if you paid attention to things like statistics and tendencies you might have said he was due. He'd grounded back to the box to lead off the first, but it was no simple comebacker. It was a shot up the middle that I'd happened to snare. He'd won the at-bat, but I'd still set him down, and I desperately didn't want him to win this one, too. To me, Wade Boggs was the key to the whole Red Sox lineup. Going into that series, I believed he was the guy I had to keep off the bases. He wasn't a prototypical leadoff hitter, because he couldn't really run, but he was one of the best hitters in the game, and his on-base percentage was off the charts. He had a great eye, and he didn't swing and miss very often, so the strategy against Boggs was to get him out with as few pitches as possible. Make him put it in play and hope it finds our gloves.

How can one guy be the key to his team's success? Every great team has a great hitter you want to keep under wraps. Whoever that guy is, you don't want to let him get on one of those streaks where he goes 8 for 11 or something ridiculous. It's not just that this one guy can beat you; it's that hitting can be contagious, and you certainly don't want the rest of the opposing lineup to get too confident or comfortable on the back of one hot hand. Wade Boggs was that kind of hitter, and before the series started our goal as a pitching staff was to keep him off the bases, in whatever ways we could.

When a good hitter leads off, he does something as soon as he makes an out, or gets a hit, or scores a run in the first inning and goes back to the bench: he gives everyone the scouting report. *This guy sucks,* he might say. *This guy's meat.* The mood of that bench can tilt, just on the basis of one of these tossed-off comments. Guys who might have been tentative about their at-bats can all of a sudden become confident. That batter will never come back to the bench and say, *He's unhittable.* But there are certain catchphrases you'll hear. *Sneaky:* that usually means the pitcher has a good fastball. *Tough:* self-explanatory. *He's got a good downer:* there's a good break on his curveball. *You can hit this guy:* mostly off-speed stuff. *His ball doesn't move:* again, self-explanatory. As a pitcher, you start to think about it as if you're launching a marketing campaign for a new product: your stuff. You want it to announce itself and create a certain first impression. You want to engender just the right buzz in that opposing dugout to ensure that no hitter gets too comfortable.

Leadoff hitters can spread the word more effectively than most, because they're coming back to their teammates with the first bulletin from the front, and Boggs was certainly one of the best in my day, just in terms of on-base percentage and kick-starting an inning. Rickey Henderson was another. But there are different kinds of hitters. The key guy that day might be lurking somewhere in the middle of the order. The idea that there's one important hitter who you're not going to let beat you is a very important realization for a starting pitcher. You look up and down that lineup, and it probably pops right out at you. If you were facing the Mets in 1999, for example, there was no way you could let Mike Piazza beat you. He was just too good. That was one of the reasons why Edgardo Alfonzo, Robin Ventura, and John Olerud had such awesome years around then. Nobody wanted to pitch to Piazza with runners on base, so the guys ahead of him in the lineup always had something to hit. And, at the back end, if a pitcher worked around Piazza, the guys hitting behind him would get to see a few more fat fastballs than usual, because pitchers would be careful not to walk another batter. In my day, the key middle-of-the-order guys in the National League were Mike Schmidt, Pedro Guerrero, and Jack Clark. There were others, of course, but these hitters stood out. You looked at their team, and they were the roadblocks.

Key batter or not, Boggs seemed to have me figured out on this trip, but he got himself out anyway. He hit a hard, sinking liner to the center fielder, Lenny Dykstra, who strode under it to make the catch to end the inning. As I walked off the mound with the game still scoreless I allowed myself to think, Okay, Ronnie. You're still in the game.

That's the great thing about pitching and hitting. Both sides are trying. Both sides are locked in. Both sides are bringing it. This was a World Series game, to be sure, but in one respect it was like any other game: you can do everything right and still get smacked around. Or you can do everything wrong and somehow come out on top. That's baseball. You're going to get hit, sometimes hard. You're going to miss your spots. You're going to step inside a moment that might be too big for you at first, but then maybe you'll find a way to bring it down to size.

The great lesson of this inning, for me, was to never again judge how I was going to pitch by how I warmed up. You just never know. You might *think* you know, but you've got no clue. You'll either have it or you won't, and so for me the warm-up became all about getting loose and taking my temperature. Physically, you couldn't deny it if you felt good or if you felt lousy. But I never again came out of that bullpen thinking, *Man, my curveball is going to be awesome today, I'm going with that,* because you never knew what the other guy was thinking until he stepped to the plate. You never knew if he was seeing the ball particularly well or if the hot hand of momentum had shifted in his favor. This is the tone and tempo of the game, and it never presents itself until you're in its middle.

That's where I was in this game, two innings in: in its middle, and finally feeling like I had some kind of command. I hadn't really been ready to meet the particular challenges of this particular game when I threw my first pitch, but somehow I'd managed to skate through the Boston lineup and back around to Boggs without allowing a run. Yeah, the moment was big, but now it was manageable. Now I had held it and worked it and started to get a good feel for it, and as I stepped back into the visitors' dugout at Fenway Park, the stadium of my growing up, I thought, Enough of this shit; this game is mine.

And it was.

INNING SUMMARY
_____

RICH GEDMAN: line-drive double to right field
DAVE HENDERSON: strikeout, swinging
SPIKE OWEN: groundout to second baseman
Gedman advances to third
WADE BOGGS: flyout to center field

Dealing with Adversity

April 22, 1984
New York Mets vs. Philadelphia Phillies
Veterans Stadium, Philadelphia
Attendance: 20,348

A *lot* of young pitchers never get to taste failure or struggle until they make it to the bigs. Then they look up one day and their out pitches are being hit out of the park. The fastball they could blow by minor league hitters can't quite sneak past guys at the bottom of a major league lineup. A mistake pitch to the leadoff batter in the first can careen into a couple more mistakes before the inning is over. There's a whole lot of stuff that can go all the way wrong, but it's how you navigate these initial rough patches that determines the course of your career. That's what I learned here in Philadelphia—even though my first instinct was to bail on myself and my team-mates as soon as I got into trouble.

Let me back up and set the scene. Somehow, I managed to make my first few major league starts to close out the 1983 season without too much difficulty. True, I finished with a nothing-special 1–3 record, but I never felt overmatched, and I wound up with a respectable 2.80 earned run average to show for it. All of my outings were solid: a good start, another good start, a not-so-great start against Chicago at home, another good start, and finally a great start to finish off the season, a complete-game 4–2 victory at Pittsburgh for my first big league win.

I looked ahead to the 1984 season with tremendous excite-ment and confidence—as did the New York Met fans, who were led by the organization and the local media to believe that they'd finally have a decent team to root for after nearly ten years of miserable baseball. This wasn't just hype or hot air. We were a good young team, with a solid young pitching staff—some of the best young arms in baseball. There was every reason to be hopeful. On a personal level, too, there were positive signs all around. I'd pitched well enough in spring training to earn a spot in the rotation to start the sea-son, and for a beat or two it appeared I might continue my rookie success as we turned the corner into 1984.

I opened the season with a 2–0 victory over the Cincinnati Reds, going six scoreless innings. The speed bump here was that I allowed six walks, but I shrugged them off to early-season rust and inexperience. (There's always an excuse, right?) My second start was okay, too. I got a no-decision against the Atlanta Braves, giving up two runs and another bunch of walks in six innings before the Mets edged out a 4–2 win. All in all, not too bad, although the high ratio of walks to innings pitched might have given me pause—that is, if I'd stopped to think about it. All I cared about, really, was that we'd gone 2–0 in my first two starts and I was getting the ball every fifth day. But then my third start rolled around, against the Montreal Expos, and those guys really pounded me. We ended up losing 10–0; I lasted just four innings, allowing four more walks and six runs, including a grand slam to my future battery-mate Gary Carter.

A Met fan threw a grapefruit onto the field that day as I walked off the mound and headed for the showers. It was the first time in my young career that I'd been booed at Shea Stadium, and for whatever reason, the booing was accompanied by this grapefruit, which I guess was meant to suggest that I should still be down in spring training, learning how to pitch. One of the reporters asked me about it after the game. He said, "What did you think about the grapefruit, Ronnie?"

I said, "Thank God the Mets don't play in the Cactus League."

That game against Montreal yielded the ugliest line on my stat sheet to date, and here again I might have worried (or come up with a couple more excuses), but I was too young and cocky to dwell on one lousy outing. Anyway, it was just one start—certainly nothing to knock me off my game. I figured I'd dust myself off and come back fighting the next time out, which was scheduled for Philadelphia.

The 1984 Phillies had a decidedly different look at the top of their order than the 1983 team. Joe Morgan and Pete Rose were gone, but Mike Schmidt was still hitting third and looming large as the "key" guy I talked about in the last chapter. The new leadoff hitter was second baseman Juan Samuel, another late-season 1983 call-up, who had quickly become one of the most exciting young players in the league. (He'd go on to lead the league in triples in 1984, with nineteen, and finish second in steals to Tim Raines, with seventy-two—not bad for a rookie.) On paper, at least, the 1984 Phillies were a mediocre team. There were some holes in their lineup I hoped to exploit, but at the same time there were a couple of dangerous hitters to complement Schmidt and Samuel, guys like Von Hayes and Glenn Wilson, who I knew could give me trouble.

There were some changes to the 1984 Mets, too. Davey Johnson's prediction that he would be managing the big club at the start of the season turned out to be dead-on. He replaced Frank Howard at the end of the 1983 season, and right away he seemed to make his young pitchers a priority. I knew his eye for detail when it came to his pitching staff, and I welcomed his patience and his game-won insights, but I imagine his emphasis on pitching must have surprised some people. After all, he'd been a position player. I guess he'd spent so much time in the field at second base, behind all those great Oriole pitchers—like Jim Palmer, Mike Cuellar, Pat Dobson, and Dave McNally—that he must have picked up a thing or two.

Another surprise: Tom Seaver was gone. The Mets left him unprotected in the free agent draft, thinking no other club would be interested in taking him on at a high salary, but the White Sox swept in and claimed him and left us young Met pitchers without our mentor. (*Tormentor* might be a better word, since Seaver always liked to put us rookies in our place.) Mike Torrez, who had been another veteran presence in the rotation, was still with us at the start of the season, but he would be released by June, as the organization made way for young guns like myself, Dwight Gooden, Walt Terrell, and Sid Fernandez.

Perhaps the biggest surprise was that we were playing good baseball. It was still early in the season, but our hitters were hitting, and we were sharp defensively and on the mound. We got off to a 9–5 start, heading into this game at

Veterans Stadium, and it fell to me to stop the bleeding after a 12–2 loss to these same Phillies the day before. I'd made only nine big league starts, so it's not saying all that much to call this the biggest game of my career to that point. Granted, it's tough to call a mid-April contest between division rivals a meaningful game, but there's no denying that the tone and mood of our clubhouse was a whole lot different than the first time I faced Philadelphia. That game hadn't really meant anything to anyone but me. The 1983 Mets were a lousy team, going through the motions at the end of a lousy season. These Mets, though, were expecting to win. These early games were important because they would put a mark on our season going forward. It's essential for every team to get off to a good start, and this is especially true for a young team. There was an energy to these 1984 Mets, an excitement, and while I wouldn't go so far as to suggest that there was pressure on us young pitchers to keep our team in the game each time out, there was a certain expectation. If there was pressure, we put it on ourselves—and, I suppose, on one another. We were a competitive bunch.

All of which takes me to the mound at Veterans Stadium, where all I was thinking about was trying to show the Mets that they could count on me to make thirty-three or thirty-four starts for them this season, and that I could bounce back from a rough outing. I wanted to win the ball game, make no mistake, but at just that moment I wanted more than anything to show that I belonged. That, and to give the guys out in the bullpen a bit of a breather after the shelling we had taken the day before. These were my bottom lines: pitch well enough to give my team a chance to win, well enough to justify the faith my coaches and teammates had placed in me, and well enough to give our relievers a little bit of rest. After that, the game could take care of itself—or not.

Unfortunately, Juan Samuel had his own agenda. I left a

fastball out over the plate, and Juan crushed it for a home run to start the game. We'd gone down one, two, three in the top of the first, so here we were, down a run before I even had a chance to settle in. I tried not to look at Juan as he rounded the bases, because I always hated the smug, self-satisfied look you'd usually see on the faces of hitters when they took you deep. Guys I'd played with would tell me how pumped they'd get whenever they hit one out, and you could see it in the way they trotted around the bases. Most guys would keep their heads down, but it always felt to me like they were biting back a smile. This is nothing against Juan Samuel, who would become a teammate and a friend; I felt this way about every opposing batter who hit a home run off me. Whatever they were doing, I told myself, I didn't have to watch it, so I stepped off the mound and looked to the sky.

The idea was to settle in and shake it off. I'd never given up a leadoff home run in my brief major league career. In the minors, sure, it happened from time to time, but I was supremely confident in my ability to get hitters out, so I always dismissed these early long balls as a fluke. Here, though, coming off a bad outing against the Expos, I got rattled by Samuel's poke—so much so that I proceeded to walk the next hitter, first baseman Len Matuszek. It felt to me like I was headed for trouble. Mike Schmidt was strolling to the plate, and he was about the last guy I wanted to see in that spot. For the first time in my big league career, I felt like I didn't have a good handle on the situation. I wasn't exactly *scared,* but I had no idea how to get this guy out. Not a clue. To be sure, I'd been in trouble before, but maybe I'd been too arrogant or too green to recognize it. Here, though, it was staring me full in the face: top of the first, nobody out, one run in, a runner on first, and one of the most feared hitters in the game stepping into the batter's box—in a game where I needed to go deep.

Like a lot of young pitchers, I had a difficult time of it early in my career whenever I found myself in a tough spot. Over time, you learn to trust your stuff and your teammates and the law of averages, and start to recognize that whatever tough spot you're in will soon pass. It's like turning into a spin when you lose control of your car. Eventually, the car will come to a stop, and you just hope that you don't hit anything before it does. Even an ineffective pitcher can get guys out from time to time. You might understand this on some level, when you first make it to the bigs, but it's not a part of you yet. You need to live through it a time or two to really believe it, and for me this was one of those times.

I thought back to the few times I'd faced Schmidt in my first start, the previous September. He managed a single off me in three trips, but he hit the ball hard each time up. I hadn't *solved* him, not by any stretch. My idea was to pitch him down and away and hopefully get him to ground into a double play; but then I caught myself and thought, Just get one out, Ronnie. There was no reason to think I could get Mike Schmidt to ground into a double play, but maybe I could get him out anyway. The one out was a hard-hit fly to Darryl Strawberry in right, and after that I got clean-up hitter Joe Lefebvre on a comebacker to the box. (I made a nice play, spinning toward second and forcing the lead runner.) Then Glenn Wilson grounded to Hubie Brooks at third, and Hubie gunned the ball to Wally Backman at second for the force to retire the side.

I was still somewhat rattled by that leadoff home run when I got back into the dugout, but nobody seemed to notice. Or maybe they did and decided to leave me alone anyway. Back then, it was like the pitcher was tucked away in some cocoon. Now you've got the pitching coach in his ear, the manager, the catcher, but during my career the convention was to give the pitcher his space, and that was just fine with me. I caught myself hoping our guys would get something going in our half of the second, so they'd reach down to me in the order and I could get a bat in my hand and try to forget about the Samuel home run.

I got as far as the on-deck circle. George Foster flied out to right to start the inning, but then Strawberry got a single and promptly stole second. (Goodness, he could run!) Mookie Wilson filled the empty base at first with a walk, but then Phillies pitcher Charlie Hudson managed to get first Hubie Brooks, then catcher John Gibbons to fly out to center to end the rally, leaving me stranded in the on-deck circle.

The bottom of the first had been a struggle, but the bottom of the second was even worse. Von Hayes led off with a single. I was so flustered by how the game was going that I balked him over to second. (In my sheepish defense, these major league umpires were far more particular about balks than their minor league colleagues.) Then I walked Phillies catcher Ozzie Virgil to fill the open base behind Hayes. After that, the wheels came off: a double off the bat of Ivan DeJesus, scoring Hayes. Another double, off the bat of Charlie Hudson (the pitcher!), scoring Virgil and DeJesus. A Samuel single, scoring Hudson.

Two singles, a walk, and two doubles (with a balk thrown in for good measure), and I still hadn't gotten anybody out in the inning. I'd been smacked around before, but I'd never struggled like this, and the deeper the hole I dug for myself, the more I started to think I would never manage to climb out.

At some point during this massacre, I looked over to the Mets bullpen. It was a bush league move. I did it without thinking about it, but it was a sign of desperation and inexperience. I was dejected, beaten. My manager and my pitching coach must have seen me as half-expecting to be pulled from the game. I'm sure I had that bewildered, deer-in-the-head-lights look. It was the first and only time in my career that I turned toward the bullpen like that, hoping someone would be throwing, getting ready to rescue me from a mess of my own making.

It may have been a quick, nothing glance toward the out-field, but Davey Johnson must have noticed it, and you can bet he read something into it, because he sprinted out to the mound. My first thought was, Gee, Davey doesn't run that well anymore. My second thought was, Why is Davey coming out, instead of Mel Stottlemyre? Usually, with most teams, the pitching coach makes the first visit out to the mound. If there's a pitching change required, it's typically the manager who makes the trip. The routine varies somewhat, from club to club, but you know you're in trouble when the manager is coming out to see you—and if he's sprinting, then you're *really* in trouble.

I knew from my peek toward the bullpen that no one was throwing, so Davey wasn't coming out with a hook. He was coming to talk to me—and at that moment I couldn't decide which was worse, being yanked from the game with no outs in the second inning or being on the receiving end of a public dressing down on the Veterans Stadium mound. Davey liked to think he had a way with us pitchers—and, in truth, he did. He made an effort to understand us, to get inside our heads. Mel did all the mentoring and coaching between starts, but when our turn came around in the rotation, we belonged to Davey. He knew what it was for one of his guys to get knocked around. He knew what it was to stand out there on that small patch of dirt, elevated above everyone else, exposed for all to see. He knew it could be a humiliating experience, even if he'd never been on the receiving end of such humilia-tion. And he knew how fragile our young psyches could be.

As a pitcher, you don't know where to turn, where to look, when your middle-aged manager is sprinting out to the mound to talk to you and you've been unable to put the ball over the plate or get anyone out. My heart was racing. I was furious, too, but a lot of times that anger gets misplaced. You put it on your teammates if someone made a bad play to prolong the inning. You put it on the weather if the conditions weren't ideal. You put it on an opposing batter for getting lucky at the plate and making matters worse. But here there was nothing else to put it on. It was all on me.

Let me tell you, that pitcher's mound can be the loneliest, most vulnerable place on earth while you're out there waiting for your manager or coach to arrive. It's certainly the loneliest, most vulnerable place in team sports. You're left to stand and wait, nakedly disgraced by whatever inability you have just demonstrated. You're exposed, in every sense of the word, and on top of that you're stressed and sapped and pissed. The best managers and pitching coaches find a way to defuse those emotions and get you back into your game. Once, when I was grinding through some trouble or other for the Oakland A's, Dave Duncan came out to try to settle me down. As a former catcher, he was cut a little differently than most pitching coaches. He knew his stuff, but he wasn't quite a brother-in-arms. He was more like a cousin. He could empathize with his pitchers, but he wouldn't sympathize. He was one of the best at trying to lighten a dark mood, and on this trip he flashed me an earnest look and said, "R.J."—that's what they called me on these Oakland A's teams—"you ever get one out in a row?"

The question threw me. I said, "What?"

He said, "One out in a row. You ever manage that?"

I shrugged my shoulders and said, "Yeah."

He held my gaze and said, "This would be a good time to do it again."

A lot of times, a trip to the mound is nothing more than a time-buying move to allow a reliever to get loose in the bullpen—and on those occasions, no manager or pitching coach likes to come out to the mound to spin his pitcher's wheels. In Oakland, Tony La Russa and Dave Duncan hated it so much that they had our third baseman, Carney Lansford, come over instead. (Carney hated the assignment even more, I'm afraid.) He'd get the signal from the bench and trudge over to the mound, knowing I wouldn't be very happy to see him.

"They tell you to come over?" I'd usually say.

He'd just nod and apologize and ask me how I was doing.

"Really fucking great," I'd say.

Of course, that was much later in my career, when outs seemed a whole lot harder to come by, and yet I had enough experience to know that they would eventually come. Here, early in my career, I knew no such thing. By the time Davey reached the mound during this second inning against the Phillies, I'd imagined a dozen different ways our conversation could go. What I hadn't imagined was the gentle, fatherly tone of his voice. He wasn't mad. He said, "Listen to me, Ron. It's a long season. Let's take a deep breath here." Then he told me what he thought I was doing wrong, how he wanted me to approach each hitter. "No more of this caveman baseball," he said. That was one of his expressions, *caveman baseball*. It meant: Don't just rear back and grunt and throw the ball. It meant: Don't always try to overpower the hitter. It meant: Start to trust your breaking ball, and some of your other pitches.

"You're a smart guy," he said. (I always hated that line of

approach, but I guess when you go to Yale you're bound to hear it.) "You've got to think. You've got to have some type of game plan."

I nodded, hoping Davey was nearly through, but he had one more point he wanted to make. "And just to be clear," he said, "you're not coming out of this game. We've got bullpen issues, but it's not just about the bullpen. You need to learn how to pitch your way out of this shit. I don't care how many runs you give up. I don't care how hard these guys hit you. I suggest you start getting some outs so you don't ruin the back of your baseball card."

That was another one of Davey's favorite lines. This was the first I'd heard it, but I took his point. He knew ballplayers paid attention to their stats. He knew what a start like this could mean to my earned run average. He knew the game was probably lost. About the best he could hope for was for me to take my lumps and spare our bullpen and find a way to get my stat line under some kind of control. The silver lining would be if I could somehow settle down and pitch my way into the middle innings without causing any more damage.

With this, Davey turned and jogged back to the dugout, leaving me and catcher John Gibbons on the mound to sort through what he'd just said. We looked at each other for a long beat, not really knowing what to say. Finally, I said, "Okay, Gibbie, let's change it up."

I struck out the next hitter, Len Matuszek, for the first out of the inning. Mike Schmidt stroked a double, scoring Samuel. Then I got Jim Lefebvre on a fly ball to left. Glenn Wilson walked. And finally, Von Hayes grounded to Wally Backman at second to put me out of my misery.

I walked back to the dugout feeling like complete shit—like a boxer who'd been knocked to the canvas a couple times before staggering to his corner at the bell. I'd just pitched the

worst inning of my career. I couldn't hit my spots. My breaking ball wasn't breaking. My fastball was flat. I'd given up six
earned runs in just two innings, on six hits and three walks.
Physically, I felt fine. It would have been easy to assign all my
troubles to some ailment or other, but I was just plain terrible.
Worst of all, I felt like I'd let my team down. But I took
Davey's words very much to heart, and I sought out a spot at
the end of the bench to gather my thoughts.

I didn't stay there too terribly long. Remember, I'd ended
our last inning at the plate in the on-deck circle, so I couldn't
exactly sit and brood over what had just transpired. I had to
grab a bat and take my licks, so I waited for Charlie Hudson
to finish his warm-up before stepping out of the dugout and
heading for the batter's box. It wasn't much of an at-bat, I'll
say that. We were down 6–0, top of the third, and it would
have been nice to get on base for the top of our order, maybe
start to peck away at that lead. But all I could manage was a
weak grounder to Juan Samuel at second for the first out.

My teammates gave me a wide berth as I stepped back into
the dugout. They must have known what I was going through.
They left me alone at the end of the bench, to continue with
my sitting and stewing. Mercifully, Davey left me alone, too.
I'm sure he thought about sidling up to me, to put a kind of
exclamation point on our conversation on the mound, but he
knew I'd heard him. He knew he didn't need to browbeat
me on this. I played his words over and over in my head. *No
caveman baseball. Think. Trust your breaking ball. Forget about
the score. Change it up. And don't even think about coming out of
the game.*

This last was the key point in Davey's pep talk. (Some
"pep" talk, right?) It took away the one crutch most pitchers
in my circumstance might reach for in an outing like this—to
be so god-awful they get taken out of the game. It meant I'd

have to pitch my way out of it, and I tried to wrap my head around this as my teammates tried to get something going at the plate.

Though we got a couple runners on, we couldn't push anything across. Still, when I stepped back to the mound for the bottom of the third, I was a different pitcher. (At least, I told myself I was a different pitcher.) I knew I'd be facing the bottom of the Phillies order, but I couldn't take these guys for granted. They were major league hitters, after all. Even Charlie Hudson, the pitcher, could put a good swing on the ball, as he had shown with his double in the second, so I looked at them as three tough outs. They loomed as a real hurdle for me. If I could get past them, I told myself, I'd be okay. And it wasn't just this one game that had me worried. It was my entire season—my career, even. I set it up in my head like the most meaningful inning of my baseball life. That was my approach—and, I now realized, that was the approach I should have taken all along. At this level, every inning was the most meaningful inning. Every batter. Every pitch. That's what makes us professionals. That's what separates us from cavemen ballplayers, to borrow Davey's expression.

This was a whole different method, and it had come to me on the back of that one dreadful inning. I'd allowed that lead-off home run by Juan Samuel to shake me from my game plan, and my season to nearly shatter in the bottom of the second, but Davey must have known what he was doing. He understood that in order for me to grow into a bona fide major league starter, I'd have to find a way to pitch through adversity. I'd have to get people out when I didn't think I had it in me.

And I proceeded to do just that. Ozzie Virgil. Ivan DeJesus. Charlie Hudson. Fly ball. Groundout. Fly ball. One, two, three. With one trip to the mound, Davey had lifted the weight of result from my sagging shoulders. He'd gotten me to realize that the outcome of the game no longer mattered. The stat line that would emerge from this abysmal outing no longer mattered. What mattered was that I could pitch through to the other side, because it was in the residue of this struggle that I would find my way. The lesson, that's what mattered. The memory.

Ozzie Virgil, I recalled, had hit a home run off me in spring training by taking a couple shuffle-steps back in the box before swinging. He liked the ball inside, because he could use that little step-back motion to keep the ball right down the middle of his hitting zone. Today, I put this piece of information to use. I kept the ball a little farther away from him this time, knowing that he, too, would remember that spring training at-bat. True to form, he stepped back again here, but my fastball was just beyond the fat part of his bat and he could only drive the ball harmlessly to left. Ivan DeJesus was a notorious first-pitch-fastball hitter, so I first-pitch-fastballed him into tapping a routine grounder to short; he just couldn't catch up to my heat, and I kept it low for good measure. And Charlie Hudson was just a pitcher, after all. I overpowered him with fastballs, and he managed only a weak fly to right.

This was how I should have pitched these guys the first time through, only I hadn't been thinking with my back against the wall then. True, it was the bottom of the order, but I didn't even consider that at the time. And it didn't end there. I got through the fourth and fifth innings without giving up another run. In the top of the fifth, Darryl Strawberry hit a three-run homer to make the game 6–3, and when Davey finally pulled me in the sixth for a pinch hitter I contented myself with the knowledge that what had started out as a

laugher was now a ball game. It was a victory, of sorts. A turning point. We ended up losing 12–5, but I'd kept us in the
game. I'd fought back. I'd been down, but I would not be
counted out.

INNING SUMMARY

OZZIE VIRGIL: flyout to left field
IVAN DEJESUS: groundout to shortstop
CHARLIE HUDSON: flyout to right field

On the Defensive

April 1, 2008
New York Mets vs. Florida Marlins
Dolphin Stadium; Miami, Florida
Attendance: 15,117

$Damage$ control. It's what you seek as a starting pitcher when you give up an early lead. The idea is to keep the game from getting away from you and at the same time send a message to opposing batters that the runs they managed to score the first time around were an aberration and you are once again in command. This is especially so at the front end of a season, when you're looking to establish that command in the eyes of your teammates and coaches as well, and to set a tone for the long road ahead.

How a pitcher manages a difficult inning can be one of the

biggest determining factors in his makeup. It's not just about *stuff*. It's about what you do with that stuff when the other team seems to have you figured out, or when the bad breaks have lined up against you. This is not a fourth-inning observation any more than it's a first- or second- or third-inning observation. It's a learned truth from my time on the mound: there are rough patches all around. It's just that your ability to pitch through them carries more weight at certain points in the game.

For example, I used to tell myself not to get too greedy when I was in a tough spot, to concede a run every once in a while if it meant avoiding a big inning. *Give up one run instead of two*—that's a phrase you hear a lot around pitchers, and it means that if a hitter's trying to hit a ground ball to the right side to score that runner from third, allow him to do so, especially if it's early in a close game, when that one run might not mean as much as it may later on. You have a guy on third base, one out, the infield's back, and you know a right-handed batter is trying to hit the ball on the ground, away, so make sure you play into that as a pitcher. Use your sinker, and keep it down and away. If you get greedy and try to strike this guy out from the start, you might get yourself into trouble. Maybe you'll get behind in the count. Instead, just let him hit the ground ball. If he swings and misses twice and you get two strikes on him, then you can change it up.

Eliminate base runners from your thoughts. That's another thing you hear, and when you're trying to avoid a big inning it's especially important. Yeah, I know, it runs a little bit counter to the point I'll make elsewhere in these pages, about developing a feel as a pitcher for the other team's running game, but sometimes where you are in the lineup or in the game itself will determine how much attention you have to pay to a base runner—or if you have to pay any attention at all. There are no hard-and-fast rules here. It's mostly about *feel,* a pick-your-spots approach to the game. If there's one out and a runner on second, say, and you know that runner is likely to score on a base hit, you can put him out of your mind if there's a weak-hitting, eight-hole hitter at the plate. Concentrate on just the hitter. Sure, you can go through the motions of keeping the runner close, but you don't really have to worry about him darting off second and messing up your timing. If a guy's coming up who's got no power at all, you're not afraid of facing him in that spot with a runner on third, because the chances of his driving a ball deep enough to score the run are not very good. So if that's the case, what's the difference if that base runner is on second or third? A base hit scores him either way, but a runner on third, with fewer than two outs, becomes less of a threat when you're facing a guy without sac-fly power.

You'll often see veteran pitchers struggle in the first inning, putting them in one of these tough spots right away. It's difficult for an older pitcher to know when he's loose. When you're younger, you warm up and you're good to go. It's automatic. When you're older, you don't always trust what your body is telling you—you can't always know if it's telling you the truth. If it took you ten minutes to get loose as a younger pitcher, it might take you fifteen or twenty later on in your career. That can mean that an older pitcher might not *really* be ready to start a game until ten or fifteen pitches into the first inning. Also, it takes a while to decipher what's working for you on a given night. A younger pitcher might have three pitches to worry about—fastball, breaking ball, change—but older pitchers have probably had to add a pitch along the way, so there's more room for inconsistency. Those three pitches might have expanded to six: slow curve, hard curve, split-finger fastball, the changeup you turn over that becomes a screwball, sinker, cutter, whatever. All of this stuff can take time, and you're not allowed that luxury in the first inning.

Get a feel for your secondary pitches. This, too, takes time— more and more as you move on in your career. If you're an older pitcher, you don't have that many bullets left, so it's not like you can work through your repertoire out in the bullpen; more often, you have to try out this stuff while you're on the mound, when it counts. A secondary pitch, to me, is different than an out pitch. It's not your second-best pitch, or any of your subsequent pitches; it's whatever you throw *off* your fastball. I don't care if you're Nolan Ryan or a journeyman whose best fastball is barely 80 miles an hour—almost every pitcher uses a fastball as his base of operations. That's where it starts, for most of us, and whatever else we throw—our *secondary* pitches—are thrown in relation to that foundation. An out pitch is your best pitch to get a swing and miss. For most pitchers, that's just one pitch.

How do you counter all of these drags on your performance as an older pitcher? What worked for me was to change the way I warmed up before a start. I started layering a cool-down into my warm-up. I'd go hard for about half or three-quarters of the time I used to throw; then I'd sit down. And wait. Ten, fifteen minutes, whatever I thought would approximate the amount of time I could be sitting in the dugout while my teammates took their first turns at bat. I used that time to cool down, and then I popped back up and started throwing again.

A great many of these factors came into play during Pedro Martinez's first start of the 2008 season, in Miami. I was up in the booth, broadcasting the game for SNY with my partners Gary Cohen and Keith Hernandez, fresh off the Mets' Opening Day win the previous afternoon against the Florida Marlins. There was the usual excitement and anticipation that comes at the start of a new baseball season, but those emotions were quickly dampened by Pedro's difficulties in the first inning. He hit Hanley Ramirez, the first batter he faced, and then promptly gave up a two-run homer to the Marlins' second baseman, Dan Uggla, digging a hole for himself and his teammates and reigniting speculation that Pedro Martinez might never again be the dominant, go-to pitcher the Mets acquired before the 2005 season.

I don't have any firsthand knowledge or explanation for Martinez's first-inning snags, but they were certainly consistent with the problems most veteran pitchers face getting off to a good start. In Martinez's case, there might have been some further trouble brewing. He didn't fare much better in the bottom of the second, yielding a leadoff home run to deep left center off the bat of veteran left fielder Luis Gonzalez and allowing another run on a two-out triple by Ramirez. In a blink, the Mets were down 4–0, and their prospects for a 2–0 start to the season had been put on dim. Nevertheless, Pedro came back to retire the side in order in the bottom of the third, and then the Mets got to Marlins starter Rick VandenHurk in the fourth, bringing the score to 4–3. So when Pedro took the hill in the bottom of the inning the complexion of the contest had been completely changed. The game had gone from a laugher to a battle in the space of four straight singles, and now it fell to Pedro to settle into his rhythm and allow his teammates to continue their momentum push over the middle innings.

This situation put me in mind of another strategy pitchers can use to keep a game manageable—namely, to think in differentials. A starting pitcher who gets tagged early can take himself out of the game psychologically. Here, Pedro was now in position to think of the game in an entirely different way. He'd just gone from giving up four runs, and looking at a dreadful outing, to seeing his teammates close the gap to 4–3. If he'd been down 1–0 at this point of the game, he wouldn't have been so hard on himself. He'd be thinking, Okay, we're still in good shape here. If you can play those mental games with yourself, and think in terms of that run differential rather than total runs given up, you can take away a little bit of the edge the other team might have gained by getting to you in those first few innings.

Pedro retired Marlins catcher Matt Treanor on a weak grounder to third, and for a moment it looked like he might work his way through the bottom third of the Florida lineup without incident. But he came up lame on his final pitch to Treanor. He limped off the mound, signaling to the bench, and before any of us in the booth could figure out what was wrong, Pedro was out of the game. (It turned out he had strained his left hamstring; he was shelved for the next two months.)

Here, again, Pedro's misfortune is instructive. A leg injury like this is very common for a pitcher after surgery. Pedro had had shoulder surgery in the off-season, and during his rehabilitation he undoubtedly did a lot of work on his legs. With all that time in the weight room, building up his legs, running, riding the bicycle, he changed his body. He became strong and muscular, and along the way he lost some of that suppleness you also need, and that can cause pulled muscles. Some of these guys go six months without picking up a baseball, but they're athletes, so they keep training and working out; only now they're developing the lower part of their body. They run the risk of overcompensating, and it's this different kind of body that can end up failing them.

Mets manager Willie Randolph summoned long reliever Jorge Sosa in the bullpen, and right away my thoughts turned to the tough spot Sosa now faced. Understand, it's impossibly hard for a pitcher to jump into a game on the fly. Obviously, you're allowed all the time you need to warm up when you're entering the game following an injury, but you want to be sure you don't hurry the process. There's a tendency in this situation to rush the tempo a bit. When you're warming up in the bullpen, nobody's watching you. Nobody cares how long it takes for you to get ready—except maybe your manager and your pitching coach. When you're thrust into the spotlight the way Sosa was on this night, there are thousands of people watching you. And what do they want you to do? Hurry up. They want to get back to watching the game, but you have to counter that. The best way to do that is to think back to the last start of your college or high school career, or to your last start as a professional. Most long relievers have at least some experience as a starter, so it makes sense for them to mimic the approach they used to take when this was a matter of routine. The idea is to defuse some of the heat and urgency from the situation, and to reach for the familiar in an unfamiliar setting.

Coming in as a reliever requires more than being physically ready; you've got to be mentally ready as well. Pedro had struggled during the first couple innings, so a guy like Jorge Sosa might have been preparing himself to step into the game at any point. Only the situation had recently tilted, and I'm sure Sosa's thoughts had tilted along with it, to where he had started thinking he would sit this one out. That's one of the hardest parts of a reliever's job—keeping your head in the game when the rest of you is out in the bullpen sucking back sunflower seeds—and this is especially so for a long reliever. If you're able to stay focused in such a way that you might anticipate a call to action, you'll be better prepared to meet that call when it finally arrives.

Under normal circumstances, the fourth inning is a point

of no return for a pitcher and his manager. Get past it in relatively good shape, and you can put your team in a good position to win the game. Get turned back by it, and you might never again get close enough to have a real shot. But the circumstances in this game were a little out of the ordinary. You never expect your pitcher to pull up lame like that, with no warning. It happens, but you never expect it, and when it does you still have that point of no return hanging out there, only now it's a team worry. Now it falls on the bullpen and the rest of the guys in the field to send the game back into your own dugout and push across another couple runs.

If you're a manager, you want to reach for a veteran pitcher here, someone with experience as a starter, someone who can give you length out of the bullpen, someone with a rubber arm. It's also a good idea to tag a guy who can handle the bat. He doesn't have to be a .250 hitter, but he needs to have some idea up there; he needs to be able to get down a bunt, because you don't want to have to pinch-hit for him as soon as his turn in the order comes around. Sosa fit the bill on all fronts, so he was an obvious choice, and initially his job was to keep it simple until he had time to get his head all the way around the game and the moment.

Joe Torre says he judges his relievers by their ability to retire the first batter they face. He's right: the percentage of first hitters retired by relief pitchers with runners on base is one of the most important stats in the game. Few people, however, pay attention to it. Sosa couldn't have asked for a better guy to go after than the Marlins' light-hitting center fielder, Alfredo Amezaga, who hit behind Treanor in the eighth spot in the order. Amezaga, for his part, knew Sosa was coming on in a difficult situation, so he very smartly took the first few pitches, hoping Sosa might be a bit rattled. It was like a head game between the two of them: each guy knew what the other had in mind, but each also thought he could outthink his opponent. Sure enough, Sosa had a little trouble finding the plate and judging the umpire's strike zone, and he quickly fell to a 3–1 count, which meant the next pitch would likely be a fastball right over the plate. Amezaga was thinking the same thing, and he pounced on the pitch and drove it deep to right center, where it hopped over the wall on one bounce for a ground-rule double.

With one out and a runner on second and the pitcher's spot due up in the order, the game changed once again—only here it took a turn I didn't see coming. A situation such as this is not a textbook sacrifice situation—not even close. You don't really gain any kind of edge, pushing that runner over to third and giving up an out at the plate. You've still got a runner in scoring position, but now you've got two outs—and one less way to bring that runner home, because of course you can no longer tag and advance on a fly ball. Yet for some reason Marlins manager Fredi Gonzalez put on the sacrifice here. The better move, to my thinking, would have been a straight steal. In any case, Marlins pitcher Renyel Pinto, who had come on for VandenHurk in the top of the inning, squared to bunt on the very next pitch. I couldn't understand it, but I guessed that probably Gonzalez had forgotten that Pedro Martinez had retired Matt Treanor for the first out of the inning. That happens sometimes when you're in the middle of an unexpected and prolonged stoppage in play. It shouldn't happen, but it does. It's possible Gonzalez registered Jorge Sosa taking all those warm-up pitches and on some level thought he was starting the inning, although the more reasonable explanation is that it was just a bad decision. You can't always assume, when you look into the opposing dugout, that the manager will play the game exactly the same way you would. Even smart, lifelong baseball people take a different approach from time to time, and here I didn't agree with Gonzalez's strategy. It made no sense to me, but there it was.

Pinto squared early, so the Mets had a chance to respond. David Wright was able to charge in from third on the pitch, and Jorge Sosa was able to adjust as well. Mets catcher Brian Schneider had called for a first-pitch fastball, thinking the pitcher was going to come out swinging and that it made sense to give him a quality pitch. It was a good call—the only call, really—and now that Pinto had given himself up and announced his intentions, Sosa was in a good spot to follow through on it.

There are a number of ways to defend against a sacrifice bunt. I had the good fortune to play alongside Keith Hernandez, certainly the best defensive first baseman of his generation. He was what I call an *offensive* defensive player. He'd charge the plate on a bunt, effectively taking away the right side of the infield. My role there was to fall off the mound toward the third-base side, to give Keith the room he needed to cut down the lead runner at second or third.

Here's how Keith used to get such a great jump off first base in an obvious bunt situation: with runners on first and second, he would come to the mound and say, "Ronnie, step off once, throw over once, and on your third pitch go to the plate." Now, a lot of pitchers are taught to throw the ball out of the strike zone when the hitter squares to bunt, hoping to get him to pop it up. That's not a bad play, if you can make it work. But Keith Hernandez was so effective in this spot that we were taught to throw a strike. He was coming in, and he was going to make a play. So we threw a strike right down the middle, and we took a little something off it, like a dad throwing batting practice to his kid, wanting him to hit it hard. *Step off. Throw over once. And on the third pitch, go.* It was in that brief delay before the third pitch that Keith would start his sprint toward home, and he'd have about a two-step jump.

In this way, and in so many others, Keith didn't wait for the game to come to him when he was in the field; he brought himself to the game, and did what he could to bend the situation to his advantage. So that's one way to respond. More often than not, you see the ball bunted toward the third-base side, and in this case the third baseman scoops it up and makes the play at first, with the second baseman covering. This was the more likely outcome here, in the bottom of the fourth. Late in a close game, you might use a version of the wheel play, wherein the pitcher releases the ball and comes in, the corner infielders charge the plate on the throw, and the shortstop moves to cover third. What you're trying to do there is to get your third baseman to field the ball in time to spin and throw to the shortstop covering third, but you need a pretty fast shortstop to make it work. On those great Met teams, we weren't blessed with a lot of speed at the shortstop position, but it didn't matter because Keith covered so much ground on the first-base side of the mound that the pitcher was able to fall to the third-base side and cover that side of the infield, where the speedy shortstop was supposed to be.

Of course, the surest way to defend against the bunt is in your pitch selection. I always thought a fastball straight down the middle was the best response to a pitcher who had squared to bunt. The thinking here was that the guy wasn't used to handling a bat, and I wanted him to put it in play in such a way that we'd have an easy chance in the field—and here in Florida, at the front end of the Mets' 2008 season, that's just what happened. Pinto pushed the ball weakly toward Wright, who gunned it across the diamond to Luis

Castillo, who was covering first, to retire the batter, while Amezaga crossed to third—a solid baseball play by the Mets' talented third baseman.

Now there were two outs, with a runner on third and Hanley Ramirez coming to the plate. Ramirez was one of the best young hitters in the game, a preeminent talent, but realistically he was no more likely to drive in that runner from third with two outs than he would have been bringing him home from second. Either way, he was a threat at the plate, and Sosa wasn't about to give him anything good to hit. If the pitcher is thinking defensively here, the strategy is to see if you can get a guy like Ramirez to bite at a pitch out of the strike zone. But Ramirez didn't offer at Sosa's first two pitches, so Willie Randolph decided to put him on intentionally. That's how it often happens. It goes down as an intentional walk, but it's really more of a white flag; it's not wanting to let this guy beat you, and giving him a free pass only after you realize he's not about to beat himself. You start out hoping he might be a little impatient, but once he displays patience you give him the base and pitch to the guy with a few more holes in his swing.

That brought up the hard-hitting and free-swinging second baseman, Dan Uggla, with runners on first and third. In Willie Randolph's mind, this was a better matchup for Sosa, with the promise of a more predictable result for the Mets. As a pitcher, you try to forget about the base runners in this type of situation—because, really, it's all about the confrontation between you and the batter. Of course, you don't want to forget completely about Ramirez at first, because you'd like to keep the force in place and keep your defensive options on a ground ball open; yet at the same time you don't want to worry too much about the runners because it might drain your focus from the batter. Uggla, then, should be priority No. 1 at the plate, but Ramirez is right there at No. 1A.

Now, Sosa's ability to hold Ramirez on effectively would be dictated in large part by his bench. The way the game is played today, the manager calls all the throws to first, all the step-offs, all the pitchouts. That doesn't mean a pitcher can't pay some extra attention of his own, but he'll be required to at least follow his manager's lead, which of course will be relayed to him by the catcher. When I pitched, I rarely looked directly into the dugout, because that seemed to me a sign of weakness. The only time I'd pick up that signal myself was if I knew we were about to walk someone. The manager would give the wiggle sign, and I wanted to see it first. But other than that, I'd never look for a sign from the bench. I didn't want it to appear as if I was looking for someone to bail me out of a tough spot.

This is where you want to attack the strike zone as a pitcher. That's another phrase you hear a lot around the game these days, but most fans misinterpret it. They think it means to throw the ball right down the middle for a strike, to make the hitter beat you, but it's really all about being aggressive and shrinking the plate. Give the batter something to hit, but give him a little *less* of something to hit. The breaking pitch you might throw when you're attacking the strike zone is the one that starts out right at the batter and then breaks down the middle; the fastball you throw is not up in the zone but down. Every pitch is dependent on the previous pitch; it's all about the sequence, and keeping the hitter off balance, and moving the ball around the plate in such a way that you maintain your advantage. You throw balls over the plate early so you never have to throw the ball over the plate again in the at-bat. That's the idea.

Against a guy like Uggla, you know as a pitcher that you can get him out if you're outside the strike zone. He's the kind of hitter who generates his power early, so if he's down in the count he's liable to go into his swing a beat too soon. That's why he strikes out so often, because he gets behind and he swings so hard, and here Sosa got him to foul off two pitches off the plate to work the count to 1–2. This set up a scenario where Sosa could take two shots outside the strike zone, but it turned out he needed only one of them. He got Uggla to swing and miss at a fastball down and away to end the inning—and put the Mets in position to tie the game in the top of the fifth on a sacrifice fly.

The way Uggla approached this at-bat reinforced my long-held belief that ballplayers tend to hit and pitch according to their personalities. Players who have very aggressive personalities off the field, like Pete Rose, tend to be very aggressive hitters. And people who are very passive or patient tend to perform that way with a bat in their hands as well.

The game-within-the-game aspects of our national pastime are never transparent in a nothing-special inning, in a nothing-special game to start the season, but there are always a lot of factors at play on the field, in the dugout, and in the bullpen—certainly a lot more than the casual fan might take in at first. Here, there was the drama and excitement of the day after Opening Day. There was the first real opportunity for Mets fans to see if Pedro Martinez could be a factor in the long season ahead. There was the strain and struggle of a veteran pitcher trying to return to form. There was the reaction of Willie Randolph to an unexpected stretch of adversity, and the chance to see if a guy like Jorge Sosa could pitch his team out of a difficult situation and be counted on in the logjam innings that would surely find the Mets in the season ahead.

There was a glimpse at the defensive maneuverings and second-guessings that are sometimes put in place as you look to manage and countermanage an inning and keep a game close. There was baseball, all around.

INNING SUMMARY

MATT TREANOR: groundout to third baseman
  Jorge Sosa replaces Pedro Martinez as pitcher
ALFREDO AMEZAGA: ground-rule double to right center field
REYNEL PINTO: sacrifice bunt to third baseman
  Amezaga advances to third
HANLEY RAMIREZ: intentional walk
DAN UGGLA: strikeout swinging

The Longest Walk

August 7, 1984
New York Mets vs. Chicago Cubs
Wrigley Field, Chicago
Attendance: not reported

Wrigley Field has always been a tremendous proving ground for a pitcher. Chicago is famous for its swirling winds, and these are nowhere more apparent than when they're swirling in the friendly confines of this grand old ballpark. In retrospect, I wasn't ready for my first Wrigley appearance, which came at the tail end of my rookie year. I'd logged over 140 innings at this point in the season, about what I'd been throwing in the minors, so my arm was stretched to its accustomed limit. I was used to making twenty to twenty-two starts in the minors, and far fewer in college, but this game in

Chicago would mark my twenty-third start, so I was inching into new territory.

For a rookie pitcher, there's almost always a fade in effectiveness toward the end of your first full season; your arm needs time to adjust to the extra workload. You see it all the time. It's like training for a half marathon, then deciding to complete a marathon. You're not up to it at first. It takes time to build the arm strength you'll need to last out a full major league season. It's emotionally draining as well, because you're flying all across the country for the first time, visiting all these new cities, meeting new people, having new experiences. There are all kinds of impulses and influences requiring your full attention, all kinds of pressure you've never before experienced, and it can all get a little wearying after a while.

My first April was pretty much a bust, as I have already detailed, but I kicked into gear in May and June. I was 10–3 by the first week of July, including one incredible run where I got the win in seven straight starts. The Mets were off to a strong start, too. We spent most of the first half of the season in first place, and ended our last July homestand with a one-and-a-half-game lead, despite losing three straight at home to these same Cubs. (The ensuing road trip did us in; we went 3–8 on a midwestern swing to St. Louis, Pittsburgh, and Chicago, and returned to Shea on August 9 trailing the Cubs by four and a half games.) I struggled, too—and I would continue to struggle the rest of the way. I ended up going 2–6 after that promising start and adding more than a half run to my earned run average, so I clearly ran out of gas.

My second-half slump included a complete shellacking at Wrigley Field, which came midway through that dispiriting midwestern road trip. It was probably the worst start of my career—and, at that early stage in my development, it was certainly the most disappointing. It was one of the few times I felt out of my element, and the first and only time I felt fear as an athlete. Real, abject fear—and I was powerless against it. I hate to admit it, but here it is: I was scared shitless. There was actually a moment or two when I stepped back and thought, Whoa, Ronnie, you're not ready for this.

What do you do when that happens? Well, you try to talk yourself out of it. You think, Of course I'm ready! Been ready my whole life. But the reality for a pitcher is that you need to get spanked around a time or two. It doesn't usually happen that you can meet all comers straight out of the gate. Even Willie Mays struggled famously through his first few games. He was hitless in his first twelve at-bats, after which he went to his manager, Leo Durocher, and asked to be sent back down to the minors. Durocher responded, "You're my every-day center fielder, kid." Next time up, in his first at-bat at the Polo Grounds, Willie smothered a pitch from future Hall of Famer Warren Spahn and sent it over the left-field roof—but he didn't get another hit in his next thirteen trips, so you never know when you'll finally catch up to your expectations.

Me, I'd thought I was headed for some immortality of my own. When you get to ten wins that early in the season, when you string together seven consecutive wins, you spend a lot of time patting yourself on the back, especially if you're a rookie. You start to think you can do no wrong. You imagine the whole of your career unfolding in the same way. But then when you get taken down a couple notches, you start to think of all the work you still have to do to etch out a real and mean-ingful big league career.

In every off-field respect, however, I was starting to think of myself as a full-fledged big leaguer. When I first came up, I tried to stay out of everyone's way, but now I felt like I truly belonged, and when you feel connected to your teammates there's a spillover effect on your performance. You're looser, I think, more comfortable. You're not always worrying so much about what your teammates think of you, because now they're telling you what they think of you, in no uncertain terms. Major league baseball players don't pussyfoot around. If you're stinking up the joint, your teammates will tell you, and when they happen to be your friends as well as your teammates they'll tell you even sooner—maybe even with a word or two of encouragement or insight to help lift your game to the next level.

A core group of us on that 1984 team tended to stick together. My closest friend on the Mets was probably Ed Lynch, a fellow pitcher. He was funny, smart, and a great storyteller. He'd been around long enough to know which restaurants to go to when we were on the road, where to get a cold beer after the game. Also, the Manhattan contingent became pretty tight: me, Eddie, Danny Heep, Keith Hernandez, and Rusty Staub. Keith and Rusty took us under their wings. We were all single, save for Danny Heep, a valuable reserve on those late-1980s Met teams, but his wife, Jane, was a sweetheart and an all-time good sport.

The routine back then was that the five of us would pile into Rusty's van after every home game and head into Manhattan. We used to call that van the Emerson Fittipaldi Brazilian Rib Machine. At the time, Rusty had a rib joint on Seventy-third and Third, so all day long drivers would run his van all over the city, carting raw meat back and forth to his restaurant. There were no seats in the back—just metal runners on the floor and some shelving. Someone from the restaurant would drop the van off at Shea so Rusty would have a set of wheels to drive back to the city after the game, and we would hitch a ride. Keith got to ride up front with Rusty, while the rest of us sat in the back on milk crates and tried not to notice the stench of pork. (In the heat of summer, those slabs of uncooked ribs could get pretty damn ripe.)

We must have made an incongruous picture, barreling through the streets of New York in the back of Rusty's delivery van—but that's where I came of age as a pitcher. That's where I started to eat, drink, sleep, and think baseball. We'd usually spill out of the van at eleven o'clock at night, and at one or two o'clock in the morning, we'd still be talking about the game. We'd talk about situations. We'd talk about the game we'd just played. If I started a batter off with a hook, Rusty would go over it with me and say, "You never throw a slow curveball to a right-handed hitter, you hear me?" He'd grab my leg as he talked, and then shout it again for emphasis: "You hear me?"

His thinking was that a right-handed batter would have a full, long view of a slow curve. He'd have too much time to adjust, and when Rusty laid it out for me, it made sense. He's right. That ball just hangs there for such a tantalizingly long period of time. It's different for left-handers, but I'd never really thought about it before. It turned out there was a lot I'd never really thought about before. Over the course of that season, I came to realize that when a guy like Rusty Staub tells you how it's done, you listen. I hadn't really known Rusty before this season, but I became one of his guys—and I was the richer for it. I suppose there are guys like that all around the league, but I was lucky to have Rusty as *that guy* on my team. He'd signed his first contract the year I was born, hit his first home run at age seventeen, hit another one after forty, and along the way managed to collect at least five hundred hits for each of four different teams. He was now on his second go-round with the New York Mets, and for this tour he'd recast himself as a wily pinch hitter—one of the best in the game. He'd been around. He had a ton of stories. And we soaked them all in.

After listening to Rusty for that first half season, I had picked up a thing or two—like the lore and legend of a place like Wrigley, which certainly didn't help as I was looking to make my debut there. I'd heard a few too many stories about what those famous Wrigley winds could do to a pitcher's stat line, and as a result the place had started messing with my head long before it could mess with me on the field. This was different than the lesson I took in from Davey Johnson during that drubbing against the Phillies earlier in the season, when he told me to stop worrying about the scoreboard because he wasn't going to take me out of the game no matter how much I floundered. This was me about to let an external factor like the weather or the stadium dimensions determine my approach to a game—treacherous territory if you hope to be effective.

The line among pitchers was that if you woke up in Chicago and the sun was shining it usually meant the wind was blowing out at Wrigley. That's a real alarm to us pitchers. Over time, I wouldn't want to know what the wind was doing at Wrigley until I got out to the stadium. I wouldn't even take batting practice at Wrigley, because I didn't want to see all these scrawny middle infielders jacking them out like nothing at all, so I'd just stay in the clubhouse. Early on, though, I fell hard into the rookie habit of checking the weather, and when I woke up on this August morning before my first-ever Wrigley start, I pulled back the blinds in my hotel room and saw a brilliant, sunny day. My heart sank. I thought, Aw, shit. I'm in for it now. I hadn't even thrown my first pitch, and already I was defeated.

That's the mind-set I took with me to the ballpark—and it's tough to win when you're expecting to lose. I'd already been nervous enough, before I'd factored in these ballpark concerns. It was a big game for the Mets; we needed a win to suspend our recent slide. But all I could think about now was the wind, and how I had to win the game all by myself. My head was filled with the stupid, scared thoughts of a stupid, scared rookie, and that's no way to approach the game. It's a doomed enterprise, really.

It was a big game for the other guys, too, and this played with my head as much as anything else. The Cubs hadn't won anything in the longest while, and here they were building a comfortable lead late in the season, playing good baseball. (They'd end up winning the division that year, before falling to the Padres in the National League Championship Series, three games to two.) The thought of pitching in a big spot, in a game that stood as a must-win for each team, was probably a little more than I could handle at that point in my career— and I think this played into my sense of unease and foreboding as well. I'd always thought of myself as a player who was good under pressure, but here the pressure seemed to have the better of me.

As I continued on in baseball, I came to appreciate Wrigley Field. Walking in that first time was such a nerve-racking experience, but over time I realized that the Cubs had some of the best fans in baseball. It's such an intimate place to watch a game. It's virtually perfect. Everybody talks about the great sight lines from every seat, but when you're on the field it's the *sound lines* you notice. You can hear everyone rooting for their Cubs. That's the great thing about Chicago fans— they root *for* their players, not *against* the other guys. That's unusual in baseball. They don't really boo the other team— although the fans managed to come down pretty hard on me when they thought I was retaliating after their Cubbies took me deep twice in the same inning, as I will explain.

IT WAS ONE OF those days. I couldn't get anything right. I couldn't even order breakfast that morning at the hotel. I wanted one thing and ordered another; to this day I can't figure out why. I was all bent out of shape before I even went out to the bullpen for my warm-up—and here I'll admit it again, for the record: I was afraid. Panicked.

Fear is a powerful emotion. Some guys are able to rise above it. Others are buried by it—and that was me on this day. Swallowed up. Overwhelmed. Unable to put any kind of stamp on the game. My teammates tried to give me a lead, but I kept giving it back. We went up 2–0 in the second on a George Foster two-run homer, but then I threw a leadoff gopher ball to Leon Durham in the bottom of the second, allowed a single, a walk, and a single to the six, seven, and eight hitters, and next thing I knew we were back where we started. I led off the third with a single off Rick Sutcliffe, who had come over to the Cubs in June and proceeded to go on a monster 16–1 tear. This earned him a National League Cy Young Award, which was unusual because he'd already made fifteen starts for the Cleveland Indians in the American League by the time of the trade. I came around on a two-run double off the bat of Keith Hernandez, with Mookie Wilson trailing right behind, to give us another two-run lead.

I settled down after that, but only for stretches. I was getting people out, but I was being hit hard. You know the old baseball maxim that suggests that hitters have it easier the second and third times they face the pitcher in a game? Well, I always thought the opposite also applied. When a guy had some success against me the first time up, I could make a few adjustments the next time around. It cut both ways, and here I was able to keep the Cubs off the scoreboard the second time through the lineup. (Not off the bases, mind you, but off the scoreboard.)

By the fifth inning, though, I was looking at my third time through the order, and the Cubs seemed ready to pounce. If it's true that the edge tilts back to a thinking pitcher on second and subsequent matchups over the course of a game, my edge was dulled by my continued inability to fool these guys. I dug myself a mental hole, convincing myself that the more success these Cubs had against me, the more success they would continue to have. Later on in my career, during the third time through a lineup, I wouldn't necessarily react to the same situation in the same way. I grew more confident in my ability to adapt. For one thing, I wouldn't rely on the book at all. Whatever history I'd had with a batter, whatever book I'd consulted before the game, I tossed it all aside. There might have been a script, a composition going into the game, but at some point it turned into a kind of jazz. I'd improvise. Each matchup became about the last at-bat. It wasn't about how this guy had hit me over the years; it was about what he'd *just* done, and what I could do *right now* to keep him off the bases.

Bob Dernier, the Cubs' speedy center fielder, kick-started the damage in the fifth with a double down the left-field line. Dernier used to stand right on the plate; you had to pitch him in to get him out. Mercifully, he was erased on a fielder's choice to Rafi Santana at short—a base-running blunder you don't see too often at the major league level. Typically, with a runner on second, nobody out, you're not looking to cross to third on a ball hit in front of you—that's Baseball 101. You take your lead and check the shortstop's position; if the ball is hit to your left, or hit weakly, you proceed to third; if it's hit to your right, you better hustle your butt back to that second-base bag.

Here, Dernier misread the play and got caught in a pickle. His gaffe put Ryne Sandberg on first with one down, and I was happy with the exchange. The game hadn't gotten away from me just yet, but already I was scrambling. I was pitching scared. Tentatively. Like I didn't want to make a mistake. Gary Matthews was at the plate, but all I could think about was Leon Durham in the on-deck circle. He'd crushed that home run to start the second, and I didn't want to face him again with a runner on.

Gary Matthews certainly deserved my full attention. We'd always get an earful about Gary from Keith Hernandez. The two of them were close. When Keith was going through his divorce, he used to drive down to Philly and stay with Gary during the off-season, and he would always tell us not to let this guy beat us. Keith thought Gary Matthews was a tremendous clutch hitter, and he was. By now I'd heard it so many times that I think I let it get to me. Here again, I allowed fear to become a factor. I was afraid to give Gary anything good to hit, and while I was busy pitching around him I forgot about Sandberg over at first, and he stole second. It was one mistake on top of another. Sandberg was a solid base runner—not especially fast, but smart and fine and sure. He had a way of picking his spots. A couple pitches later, Matthews was on first with a walk, Sandberg was on second, and I stepped off and tried to think how I'd gotten into such a jam. I was unable to execute, unable to concentrate, unable to do much of anything but climb back up that hill, stare down another batter, and hope for the best.

Durham hit the ball hard and deep to center field. I thought it was going out when it left his bat, but somehow the ballpark held it and Mookie Wilson made the catch, for the second out of the inning. Still, this was more of a worry than a reprieve, and I turned to face Keith Moreland, the Cubs' stocky right fielder. Keith was in the frustrating habit of getting big hits off us—off Doc Gooden in particular. I didn't really have a good book on him, but I knew I had to move the ball around because anything up and predictable would be a disaster. And sure enough, he crushed a high fastball over the fence in left center for a three-run homer. Now the Cubs had the lead, 5–4, and even though there were two outs in the inning, I wasn't liking my chances of registering a third.

It's tough to compete when you're rattled—and I was definitely rattled. I walked the next batter, catcher Jody Davis. I wasn't anywhere close to the plate. Mel Stottlemyre came out to the mound after that, to settle me down. He always said the same thing in these spots. He'd say, "We're still in this game. Let's get a couple outs and hold 'em right here." I listened, but I don't think I really heard him. Anyway, I'd heard the same line before, more times than I cared to remember. It didn't really mean anything that day; it was just something to say, a point of pause. I just waited for him to finish. A part of me didn't want him to leave, because that meant I'd have to face Ron Cey and finish the inning, but another part, a bigger part, didn't want Mel anywhere near me.

The best pitching coaches recognize that it doesn't really matter what you say when you make one of these crisis-point trips to the mound. It's that you're making the trip at all that counts. That's what the trip represents, in the flow of the game, but as long as you're out there you try to help your pitcher find a way to clear his head and move forward. Mel Stottlemyre understood this as well as anyone, and as he finally retreated to our dugout, the one thought that kept bouncing through my head was, Don't let this game get away. Keep it close. We'd been ahead to start the inning, and now we were down, so Mel's words were dead-on. We were only down by a run; all I needed to do was keep the Cubs from scoring and we could take another crack at the lead.

Instead, I left another fastball out over the plate, and Cey deposited it over the wall in left center—almost the same spot that Keith Moreland had taken me a couple batters earlier. Cey's ball was hit a lot harder than Moreland's, but the result was the same. The lid was off the game.

The next batter was Dave Owen. At six foot two, he was a little on the tall side for a light-hitting utility infielder. He was the older brother of Spike Owen, the Red Sox shortstop who would loom as a point of pause in that turning-point second inning in Game 4 of the 1986 World Series. (After that, Spike would briefly be my teammate when I played for the Montreal Expos for a couple of weeks in the summer of 1991.) There was no reason for Dave Owen to be bunting, and yet he turned to bunt as if it had been called for. At first, I couldn't figure this out, so I looked to bust him inside with a fastball high and tight. Actually, if I'm being completely honest, I looked to hit him. Hard. It made me angrier than I'd ever been on a baseball field, seeing this guy turn to bunt. I thought, Not only are these Cubs hitters teeing off on me and embarrassing me, but now this weak-ass hitter wants to bunt and embarrass me even more. I drilled him with the next pitch, that's how mad I was. And I didn't just hit him—I tried to hurt him so badly that he'd feel it for the rest of the game, maybe even knock him out of the lineup.

I'm ashamed of my actions now, all these years later, but at the time I felt completely justified. I felt pretty mighty out there on that mound; these guys were trying to show me up, so I responded in the only way I knew. The Cubs players were immediately ready to chew my head off. I could hear them screaming at me from their dugout, calling me a "chickenshit" and an "asshole." I look back now and think, Ah, the friendly confines of Wrigley Field. Back then, of course, I was plainly unsettled by the taunts coming from the Cubs dugout.

These guys knew I'd thrown at Dave Owen. I mean, I'd just given up two long home runs, with a walk sandwiched in between. Three batters, five runs. In the process, I'd surrendered a two-run lead.

Now, of course, I don't think Owen was looking to show me up by turning to bunt; that was just his game. But at the time I was too green, too scared, too stupid to realize that. He wasn't someone looking to feast on my inadequate stuff, like these other Cubs hitters. He was simply trying to get on base, any way he could, and you don't throw at a guy just because the batters ahead of him in the lineup crushed a couple balls. That's a real no-no in baseball. Dave Owen hadn't done anything to set me off. I could practically hear Rusty Staub, my new pal and mentor, giving it to me after the game: "What the hell were you thinking, Ronnie? You don't plunk some utility infielder just because his teammates hit a couple home runs off you, you hear me?"

RETALIATION HAS ALWAYS BEEN a part of baseball. It was a much bigger part in my day than it is now, but it's so deeply woven into the fabric of the game that it will never go away entirely. I always understood it for what it was: a last-resort opportunity to stand up for your teammates. What most fans don't realize, though, is that both sides recognize it as an inevitable outcome in certain spots. It's expected. And, in its own way, it's accepted. Perfect example: when I was in the minors, pitching for Tidewater, we played a heated series against the Syracuse Chiefs, then the Triple A affiliate of the Toronto Blue Jays. In one of the games before my scheduled start, the Syracuse pitcher drilled our big power hitter, for some reason or other. Baseball convention, then as now, was to return the favor in kind, which meant that at the next appropriate opportunity, our pitcher would have to drill the Chiefs' big power hitter. It's always been an eye-for-an-eye sort of deal, except that you don't go after a guy in a situation that could cost your team the game. The payback might not come until the next game, or the next series, but it will always come. Eventually.

It's understood. In fact, if the chance presents itself when you're on the mound and you don't retaliate in an appropriate manner, your own teammates will treat you like some kind of coward—and that's the situation that came around in that game against Syracuse. The Chiefs' big power hitter happened to be George Bell, who would go on to have some big years for Toronto, and here he finally came to the plate with nobody on. The players in both dugouts knew I'd be throwing at him. George Bell knew I'd be throwing at him. So I threw at him.

Of course, you just don't *throw* at a hitter. There's a whole strategy to it. When I was with the Mets, the pitchers used to have a spring-training drill where we threw at a scarecrow-like figure that was meant to represent the opposing batter. The drill was designed to get us to pitch inside. None of the hitters wanted to stand in against a pitcher working on his inside game, and none of the pitchers were too keen on busting back one of their teammates anyway, so we used this dummy in the batter's box. We'd put a helmet on the thing, and for our last pitch of the sequence we'd try to knock it off. The idea, when you're throwing at a hitter, is to place the ball about an inch or two behind him. The tendency for a batter trying to get out of the way of a pitch is to fall back, so by placing the ball slightly behind him you'd get him to invariably fall *into* it and you'd accomplish your goal. You'd never throw at a batter's head, of course. Ideally, you'd try to keep the ball between his armpit and his rear end. You wanted him to feel it, but you didn't want to mess with his career.

Throwing at another player is not something you do lightly, but you do it anyway. Most hitters I know seem to think of it as an occupational hazard; as long as you don't throw at their head they'll shrug it off. So I never really worried about any retaliation to my retaliation. I should have, though, because it's no fun being on the receiving end of a major league plunking. I was never thrown at intentionally in my career, but I did get hit in the head once. Marty Clary, a pitcher for the Atlanta Braves, did the honors. I came up with runners on base, and the ball got away from Marty on a 3–2 count. I was certain I'd be getting a fastball. Pitcher to pitcher. He had to throw a strike. He probably didn't think I could do much with it, even if it was right over the plate. I knew there was no way he'd throw me a breaking ball, so my plan was to just swing hard and hope to make good contact, but I never got the chance. I can still remember the sick feeling I had as the ball came at my head. It seemed to slow down—not so much that I could get out of the way, but enough that I had time to think about it. I actually had this thought: Oh, my God! That ball is gonna hit me in the fucking head! And it did. I was rattled, but I stayed in the game, and by the time I walked down to first base that pitch to the head had awakened the old ballplayer in me. I told myself if the next batter hit a ground ball and there was a force play at second, I'd put the other team's shortstop or second baseman into center field, so I guess I was none the worse for wear.

In that game against Syracuse, I followed the script and drilled George Bell in the back. He flipped the bat and made like he was going to charge the mound. This was an unusual turn, I thought, given the circumstances—and certainly unexpected. I stepped off and inched toward home, making ready. It looked for a beat or two like there'd be a scuffle, but then George backed away and headed down to first.

In those days, on the Tidewater Tides, pitchers would chart the next game after each start from the stands behind home plate. I never really liked to chart pitches, but I didn't mind it so much on that team, because we were in our street clothes, lounging in the stands, enjoying the game. For some reason, George Bell was also in street clothes that game. He might have been suspended, for (nearly) charging the mound, or maybe he just had the day off; in any case, he was in the seat right next to me. What are the odds of *that*? It was such an awkward scenario, but it played out to the good. We wound up having the nicest, most enjoyable afternoon. He turned out to be a great guy. We talked about how I'd had no choice but to hit him. We talked about how pissed he had been, how much it had hurt. And then we moved on, and for years afterward, whenever we crossed paths in the game, we talked about our first meeting, on the back of a beanball that had us both fuming.

FUMING. THAT'S THE WORD OF CHOICE for sportswriters looking to describe the emotion that invariably follows a brushback or payback pitch. Cubs pitcher Rick Sutcliffe was certainly fuming. He was in the on-deck circle, and he made a beeline for the pitcher's mound, like he was coming after me. He was screaming. I couldn't make out what he was saying, but I figured he wasn't wishing me a nice day. Rick was a big guy. He had this flaming mop of red hair, and an unusually large head, and I took one look at this big fat red head coming at me and thought, Holy shit, I've never been involved in one of *these* before. It felt like both benches were about to empty out and we were all going to get into it, but then Rick turned and made for the batter's box and it appeared a brawl would have to wait.

The worst part was that Dave Owen seemed to be hurt. I'd hit him in the leg, and he couldn't really run, so Cubs manager Jim Frey lifted him for a pinch runner—Larry Bowa, the Cubs' regular shortstop. At this point, the Cubs fans were on me pretty good. No, they don't usually boo the opposing players at Wrigley Field, but when it appears that you've intentionally drilled one of their own, in such a way that he has to leave the game . . . well, then they're inclined to tear you apart.

What a horrid sequence. Five runs already across, Larry Bowa on first, and the Wrigley faithful calling for my head. The only good news in this scenario was that the pitcher was at the plate. That is, it would have been good news if it had been any other pitcher in the National League. But Rick Sutcliffe? This guy could hit! In his Rookie of the Year season for the Dodgers in 1979, he went 21 for 85 with a home run and 17 runs batted in. Here I thought I'd worked my way down to the pitcher's spot and might find some relief, but Sutcliffe drove a first-pitch fastball to left center for a statement single. No, he wouldn't charge the mound and beat the crap out of me. He'd just rope a hard single to left and knock me out of the game instead. He was still yelling at me when he got to first base.

The grace note to this disastrous outing came as I walked back to the Mets dugout after Davey Johnson finally pulled me from the game. The Cub fans were pissed that I'd hit Owen—and rightly so. But then one idiot fan crossed a line: he threw a cup of beer at me. He aimed it perfectly, and if I had been a little less dejected and despairing I might have noted that if I had been able to spot my throws as well as this idiot fan I wouldn't have been in this mess. The fans are right on top of the dugouts at Wrigley, so this guy didn't have to reach all that far; I was in his face, just about, and now I was doused with a cup of warm beer and perfectly humiliated.

I was pissed—at myself, to be sure, but also at this idiot fan. My day hadn't gone well at all, and my first impulse was to retaliate. Rusty would rip me for it later, but I started to double back up the dugout steps and make for my attacker. It was a fool move, born mostly of frustration. Luckily, our hitting instructor, Bill Robinson, known to all of us as "Uncle Bill," was there to pull me back into the dugout and save me from myself. He was our first-base coach and our hitting coach, but he never called himself the hitting coach. He liked to be known as the hitting instructor. It was a pride thing; he thought of himself as a professor of hitting, and this was his way of reinforcing that. We all thought it was pretty funny.

Whatever we called him, Bill was one of the game's good guys, and he had my back that afternoon at Wrigley. He fairly threw me to the dugout bench, then proceeded to take the steps himself. For a beat or two, it looked like he might climb into the stands and go after the guy, but he restrained himself. He just shouted this idiot down, and when the Wrigley security guards came down the aisle to escort the fan from the stadium, Bill backed away.

The great lesson here for me as a young pitcher was that I was part of a team. Despite being embarrassed, and despite the fact that I had embarrassed the Mets, I still had players and coaches who cared enough about me to stand up for me. That was something. Davey Johnson didn't chew me out for stinking up the joint or for needing to be held back from jumping into the stands after I was hit with that beer. That was something, too. We were competing for the top spot in the division, this was true, but he knew we were young. He knew we weren't ready. Anyway, *I* clearly wasn't ready, as this day at Wrigley had demonstrated.

Another something: after Bill Robinson stepped back into the dugout, he flashed me a look that said, *Hang in there, kid. It'll come.* Actually, I don't know if that's what the look really meant, or if that's merely what I took it to mean, but it was good enough for me, and with that I stood and made for the clubhouse. At Wrigley, the walk to the clubhouse stretches on and on. It's just horrible. And on this day in particular, it felt like it would never end. It was hot as hell out there on that field, and here in the bowels of Wrigley, with the air conditioner on full blast, it must have been fifty degrees. When I finally reached the chair in front of my locker, I began to shiver. Maybe I was shaken up by what had just happened. Maybe it was the refrigerated air coming up against my beer-wet skin. Or maybe it was just really, really cold.

I sat and shivered for the longest while. Somewhere, a radio was blaring the play-by-play, so I half-listened to what my teammates were doing. We scratched back with a couple more runs in the seventh, but the Cubs held on to win 8–6, and within a couple weeks we'd dropped so far out of the race it was hard to believe we'd ever been in it. I don't think I left that chair in front of my locker for the balance of the game. Normally, whenever I came out of a game I'd ice my arm for fifteen minutes, do a series of stretches, and then take a shower. I had a whole routine. But on this afternoon in Chicago all I could do was sit and think. And make promises to myself that I hoped I'd have the will and the wherewithal to keep.

I told myself I would never let this happen again. Not getting knocked out of a game—that happens. No, I would never be fearful of a game or a team or a situation. I would never quit on myself. And I would never take a game or a hitter for granted. When you're a major league pitcher, there's a bad patch waiting for you around every corner, but that doesn't mean you don't make the turn. It's how you get past that bad patch that determines your course going forward.

INNING SUMMARY

BOB DERNIER: double to left

RYNE SANDBERG: fielder's choice groundout to shortstop

Dernier out at third

Sandberg steals second

GARY MATTHEWS: walk

LEON DURHAM: flyout to center field

KEITH MORELAND: home run to left center field

Sandberg and Matthews score

JODY DAVIS: walk

RON CEY: home run to left center field

Davis scores

DAVE OWEN: hit by pitch

Larry Bowa pinch-runs for Owen

RICK SUTCLIFFE: line-drive single to left field

Bowa advances to third

Brent Gaff replaces Ron Darling as pitcher

BOB DERNIER: single to center field

Bowa scores

RYNE SANDBERG: flyout to right

Taking Chances

September 11, 1987
St. Louis Cardinals vs. New York Mets
Shea Stadium, New York
Attendance: 51,795

Baseball has a way of repeating itself. That's part of its appeal, I guess: what goes around comes around. If you miss an opportunity one turn, one game, one season, chances are you'll get another crack. That's how it felt to me in a key series against the Cardinals in September 1987. We were just a couple games back in the standings—a scenario that was eerily similar to one we'd faced in 1985 against the (mostly) same bunch of guys. The first time around, we hadn't won anything yet, so it seemed like everything was on the line. Here, in 1987, we were the reigning world champions, so the pressure was on us to repeat, and on the Cardinals to hold off our late-season push.

I'd ended up playing an important role in that 1985 series, although for a while it appeared that my biggest contribution might be as fodder for second-guessing fans and pundits. Davey Johnson made a controversial decision going into the series to start me in the opener instead of Dwight Gooden. To his thinking, it was more of a no-decision than a decision. It was, simply, my turn in the rotation, but there had been an off-day in our schedule, which meant Doc could have pitched on his regular rest to start off the series. Gooden was having a ridiculous year, on his way to his only Cy Young Award, and the beat writers all assumed he'd start the first game. That's conventional baseball wisdom: start your best pitcher to open a big series, if he's available. Gooden was certainly available. It was a three-game set, and we needed all three, so why not go with your strength and make sure you get one in the bag?

Davey Johnson didn't always buy into conventional base-ball wisdom. Or maybe he did, and rejected it anyway because he liked it when folks couldn't figure him out. He liked standing apart from the crowd. He was a bit of a maver-ick, which made it great fun to play for him. You never knew what he might do—and even when you had some idea, you couldn't always understand why. Here his thinking was to give the ball to me for my regular turn, and then if we got the win there'd be this huge momentum shift because we'd have our best pitcher going the next day. In success, it would be a masterstroke; in failure, the second-guessing would probably continue for years.

I was still a young pitcher. I had a full season under my belt, and I was pitching well in my second full year, but I didn't pay attention to the noise and nonsense. I always read the papers, because I wanted to see what people were saying about me and my teammates, but I wasn't fully aware of the back-and-forth going into this series, the way people wanted to tear Davey's head off over his decision not to leapfrog my turn and give the ball to Gooden.

It was only later that I puzzled together the controversy. I couldn't touch Gooden's year, true enough, but I was having a strong season on my own terms. I'd wind up winning sixteen games, which was certainly solid. I'd also go on to lead the league in walks. I always told people Doc was number one in every other pitching category, so if I wanted to lead the league in something it had to be walks. It rankled, but at the same time it really didn't. I might have been wild, but I was competitive, and I found a way to work through my control problems and keep us in ball games; that was my thing.

Wrapped up in my season and myself, I was blissfully unaware of any debate over my turn. *Is this kid a put-up or shut-up kind of pitcher? Can he handle the heat of a big game? What's he made of? Will he justify his manager's faith in him?* All I knew was that it was my turn to pitch and that we needed this game, so I went at it hard.

And it shook out to the good: I matched zeros with John Tudor through nine innings. Tudor was lights-out that year— probably the only other NL pitcher with a legitimate claim on Doc's Cy Young Award. We won it 1–0 in the tenth on a Darryl Strawberry home run. (The ball hit the scoreboard clock— a signature Met moment.) Jesse Orosco got the win in relief, and it was the first time I experienced the full intensity of the professional game. I'd never seen my teammates so emotional, so *invested*. Ray Knight, our third baseman, actually had tears in his eyes in the clubhouse after the game. He was pumping his fists for sheer joy, that's how much the game meant to him, and it meant much the same to every guy in that room. It didn't matter how much money we all made. It didn't matter that we were having the time of our young lives, living in New York City, playing the game we loved. And it certainly didn't matter that we were meant to be hardened professionals. No, these games were important. Winning was important. This was how we were measured—and this game would be a huge yardstick for me. Guys came up to me afterward, congratulating me, treating me differently. In their eyes, I went from a kid pitcher still finding his way to a full-fledged team member, just on the back of that one start. It was a real, welcome-to-the-club moment for me personally, and I remember taking some small offense at that. (Not a lot, but some.) I mean, I'd won twelve games the previous season. I was on my way to winning sixteen. I'd thought I was already *in* the club, but this game put me on a whole other level with my teammates.

I got to the ballpark early the next day, the same way I always did. I got my running in before batting practice, the same way I always did. But then just before BP, as I was making my way out to the outfield to shag flies and continue my day-after workout, I found a batch of about forty reporters hovering in my path. There was the usual pregame scrum around the manager, and when the press was done with him they moved on to me, right there on the field. Jay Horowitz, the Mets' press secretary, saw the reporters headed my way and tried to get to me first, to give me a heads-up. He said, "Hey, Ronnie. Got a minute? We're gonna meet with the press here."

I said, "Huh?"—or something equally eloquent. As a pitcher, I was used to talking to the press the day before I pitched, and then again right after my game. That was it. Nobody wanted to hear from me between starts.

Jay said, "We've set up a little press conference. There are too many reporters here to just do interviews."

Normally, a dozen or so beat guys covered the team, but I

guess with the division championship in our sights that number had grown.

I said, "A press conference? For what?"

He said, "These guys just want to talk to you. You pitched a helluva game last night, Ronnie."

So I sat down in front of all these reporters. I still remember the first question: "Ron, how do you feel, now that you're recognized by all of your teammates as a big-game pitcher?"

I'd always thought of myself as a big-game pitcher, but I guess my teammates hadn't seen that from me yet, and it took hearing it from these beat reporters to put it in context. They're the ones who filled in the blanks about all that pregame controversy. They're the ones who hailed Davey as a genius, for holding back Doc Gooden for that extra day of rest. They're the ones who helped me take my new measure.

NOW, IN 1987, WE WERE TRAILING these same Cardinals by a game and a half. There was a fairly intense rivalry between our two teams in those days. Most of that had to do with the fact that we were two of the stronger teams in our division, but it also ran to personnel. Keith Hernandez had been traded to the Mets from the Cardinals in 1983, and Keith always felt that it was a vindictive move by Whitey Herzog and the Cardinals, because Whitey knew how much Keith hated New York. Keith, who'd had some off-field problems in St. Louis, believed Whitey was trying to bury him on the Stems, as Keith used to call the Mets. (They were a backward team, he said, so they rated a backward name.) He didn't want to be in New York, but as soon as he got here he helped legitimize us as a team, and he fell in love with New York as a city and with New Yorkers in general, and I think that fueled the rivalry, at least from our perspective.

It ran to our styles, too. We were the pitching-and-power team. The Cardinals were the defense-and-running team. There was a real contrast. They manufactured their runs. We were aggressive on the bases, but at bottom we were station-to-station hitters, and we counted on our starting pitchers to keep the games within reach. The Cardinals' lineup reflected the team's style of play. Vince Coleman was probably the best base runner in the game. Willie McGee was as fine a hitter as I ever faced, and another demon on the bases. Tommy Herr was a clutch-hitting second baseman who'd somehow managed to drive in 110 runs a couple seasons earlier—with only eight home runs. Ozzie Smith had always been a spectacular glove man at short, but late in his career he had blossomed into a patient, purposeful hitter as well. Terry Pendleton was an up-and-comer at third who would eventually lead the league in hitting. No question, these guys could play. It was always a real test, going up against that group. You had to deal with their hitters *and* with their running game. There weren't a whole lot of teams who could hurt you that way, but these Cardinals could—and a few ways more besides. (And when they could throw a guy like John Tudor at you every fifth day, you *really* had to keep sharp.)

Personally, I liked matching up against the Cardinals. Their running game suited me—I had a good pickoff move and varied my deliveries to the plate. In those days, pitchers were required to manage their own running game—that is, we decided when to throw over to first, when to pitch out, how long to hold the ball between pitches. We developed a real feel for it. Today, all of this stuff is called from the bench. The manager relays the signs to the catcher. There are signs for a throw-over, for holding the ball an extra couple beats so the runner on first feels like he's sinking into quicksand, for a quick move to first, for an easy move to first, for a step-off, and so on. Pitchers today can always throw over on their own, of course, but most don't even bother because waiting for the signal has been programmed into their games.

In my time, it was all sense and feel. You could sense that the runner was inching farther off the bag, stretching his lead. You could feel it somehow, or see it with the eyes in the back of your head. There was a real rhythm to it. Baseball people talk all the time about how certain runners, like the Mets' José Reyes, can take a pitcher out of his game—and this is true, if you're talking about an inexperienced pitcher. A pitcher with a good feel for the running game, however, can fit even a gifted base stealer into his overall game plan. Still, a fast runner can almost always upset a pitcher's tempo. A general rule of thumb: the faster the runner, the slower the game; and, it follows, the slower the game, the greater the margin for error or miscalculation.

We used to say a guy was particularly "runnerish" if he was dancing off the bag at first. It was a twist on the more familiar baseball expression for a batter who was antsy in the box, and possibly overanxious; we'd say he was "hitterish." It meant he was ready to go, and "runnerish" applied similarly on the bases. You just knew when a guy was going; it was in the way he stretched his lead, the way he leaned, the way he flapped his fingers in the air above the infield dirt. (Think Rickey Henderson!) You could take it all in from your perch on the mound and just *know.* Young pitchers today don't have the same feel for the running game because it's been taken away from them, but I always felt like I had an advantage when there were runners on. It didn't matter how fast they were: *I* had the ball. *I* set the pace. In fact, I was so confident of my ability to pitch with runners on that I used to look ahead to an assignment against a running team like the Cardinals and think they'd be playing into my strength.

This was my mind-set going into this 1987 showdown with St. Louis, a game that would offer up a season-ending, career-changing moment in an otherwise innocuous sixth inning—one that stands as a cautionary reminder of how the game can turn on a single play. The sixth inning is an under-appreciated marker for a starter. I've always thought of it as a real hump inning. After all, it's when you take your team deep into ball games that you start to make a real contribution, and when you can get past the sixth and into the seventh you've done your job. You've turned the lineup over a couple times by this point, you're facing hitters for the third and fourth times, and if you're still getting outs you're on your game. Trouble is, sometimes you're on your game and it can still get away from you on an unlikely (and unlucky) bounce of the ball.

Too, the sixth inning has become the minimum threshold for a "quality start"—the standard by which today's pitchers are measured. Six innings or more, three earned runs or less. Not exactly the high standard to which we held ourselves back when I was playing, but the bar of expectations has been lowered over the years. Here again, the game has changed—and I think today's big-money, long-term contracts are to blame. Clubs have so much money tied up in their top-tier pitchers that they don't think they can afford to let them pitch beyond a certain pitch count, so it's the club-imposed cap on a starting pitcher's workload that lowers the bar. Do the math: if you're limiting a pitcher to eighty, ninety, one hundred pitches, it follows that he won't make it much past the sixth inning, and so the sixth inning has become a kind of bare-minimum marker.

As a result, you hear pitchers say things like, "I did my job." Or, "I kept my team in the game." Or, "I gave us a chance to win." You never heard that stuff back when I was pitching, and I hear it now and bristle. It's a half-empty kind of approach, don't you think? At some point, a starting pitcher has to take it upon himself to do a little more than put his team in a position to compete. He can't simply content himself with the thought that he's part of the reason his team wins the game. He has to be able to stick out his chest and say, "*I* am the reason we're going to win."

John Tudor was once again on the mound for the Cardinals for this 1987 showdown (see what I mean about the game repeating itself?), but here we touched him up early—in front of one of those rocking, boisterous Shea crowds that always seemed to turn out for big games. Darryl Strawberry hit a three-run home run in the bottom of the first to set us up, but then I gave one of those runs back in the top of the second with a couple of walks and a couple of groundouts to the right side of the infield.

Mookie Wilson hit a solo shot in the fourth, to stretch our lead to 4–1, and at one point, around the fifth inning, I looked up and noticed that the Cardinals had yet to get a hit off me. Typically, that's not something a pitcher pays attention to until the sixth or seventh, but here it registered. I'd allowed a bunch of base runners, and that early run, but no hits, and once it registered I couldn't shake it from my thinking. I don't think I approached the game any differently after that, because right then a no-hitter was far less meaningful to me personally than the game itself. (I know that sounds like a line, but in this case it's legit, although if it had been the seventh or eighth I probably would have been a little more "no-hitterish.") All I really cared about was putting my team in a good position to cut the Cardinals' lead in the NL East to a half game.

Lance Johnson came on to pinch-hit for Tudor to lead off the sixth. Lance would later play for the Mets and in 1996 notch one of the best single-season offensive outputs in team history (.333 batting average, 227 hits, 117 runs scored, 50 stolen bases, and 21 triples), but back then he was just another speedy young outfielder cut from the same cloth as Vince Coleman. He lined the ball to Keith Hernandez for the first out, bringing up Coleman at the top of the order. This guy always gave me fits. He'd waited out a walk to start the game, but then I got him swinging in the third, and here in the sixth he turned to drag a bunt for a base hit.

You hardly ever see a batter look to break up a no-hitter in the late innings with a bunt. Some baseball people think it's a bad play, although I'm not one of them. My thinking is, if you can find a way to get on base, that's great—especially in a big spot in a big game. We had only a three-run lead. Coleman had some tough hitters behind him. Absolutely, it was a solid play. Plus, you always had to expect a bunt from that Cardinals lineup. They had four or five guys who could lay one down for a hit, so you had to keep ready—although in this case, keeping ready might have been my undoing.

Coleman dragged a textbook bunt to my left. He couldn't have placed it better if he'd written out a script. I got a good jump on it, but in the back of my mind I was thinking, Shit, this guy is just too damn fast. I didn't think I'd have a shot, but I dove for it, both hands forward, and I somehow managed to collect the ball with my glove hand and flip it to Keith Hernandez at first with my right in something resembling the same motion. In reality, I had no shot at Coleman, who fairly flew down the line, but in my head it felt like one of those beautiful plays you used to see on *This Week in Baseball*. When I finally had a chance to watch it on tape sometime later it was a little less graceful than I'd imagined it; it was quick enough, and athletic enough, but also a little clunky.

I couldn't really get anything on the throw, and Coleman legged it out by a step, but that was the least of my worries. I landed awkwardly on my pitching thumb, and right away I could tell something was wrong. I didn't feel anything pop. I didn't hear anything. But I'd jammed it in such a way that I knew it would give me trouble. An athlete can always tell when it's more than just a bruise or a sprain. When you know your body, you know when you're hurt, and here I came up thinking that if I hadn't gotten such a good jump off the mound, if I hadn't been thinking bunt and drifting toward first, if I hadn't taken an unnecessary chance, I would have never had a shot at the ball and therefore never gotten hurt.

Alas, there's no kicking yourself over good instincts and a solid effort. There's no brooding over an injury that may or may not have any long-term impact on your game, your season, your career. There's no rush to poor judgment, for failing to weigh the possible risks of an overly aggressive play against unlikely rewards. And there's certainly no blaming a bad bounce for misfortune.

In this particular situation, there was no room in my agenda for injury, so I pushed it aside. Adrenaline is a wonderful thing, and I climbed back on that hill and shook off the pain. I didn't really care about the busted-up no-hitter, and just then I didn't care very much about my jammed thumb; Coleman was my front-and-center worry. I always threw over with a guy like that on first, and now, with this apparent injury to my hand, I wanted to take a soft toss or two, a couple of trial runs. I didn't want to ask for time and stop the game to make some practice throws, because I didn't want the Cardinals to know I was ailing. (Just as important: I didn't want Davey Johnson and his coaches to know, either.) But a soft toss to first, disguised as a pickoff attempt, would do just fine—so that's what I did. And it's a good thing, too. The ball didn't feel right. My hand was starting to swell. I had some trouble gripping the ball. Nevertheless, my plan was to power through. It never even occurred to me to call for the trainer, because of course there was nothing the trainer could do except advise Davey to take me out of the game.

Meanwhile, Vince Coleman had his own idea about how the game should go. He'd come to the plate thinking his team needed base runners, and now his thought was to get down to second. It was automatic with him. When I threw to the plate, Gary Carter didn't really have a chance; my thumb was practically hanging at my wrist, and I can't imagine I put a whole lot on that pitch.

Now Coleman was two up on me. He'd broken my no-hitter with a bunt and had gotten a great jump and stolen second on my first pitch. I knew he'd be thinking about stealing third. He used to love to do that, to steal his way around the horn, and Ozzie Smith, hitting behind Coleman, had become a very patient batter at the plate, giving Vince plenty of chances to run.

This might have worried another pitcher, but it didn't worry me; I always thought it was easier to pick guys off second than it was to pick them off first. Runners on first are always alert. On second, they sometimes fall asleep, and I used to have an eye-contact play set up with shortstops Kevin Elster and Rafael Santana that tended to work pretty well. We nailed a lot of guys with this play. It was our variation of the daylight play used by every team, all the way down to the high school level. Normally, your shortstop lines up in the pitcher's sight line directly behind the runner as he's taking his lead off second. With the daylight play, the pitcher turns and makes his move to second the moment the shortstop breaks toward second and the pitcher sees a sliver of light between the base runner and the shortstop behind him. But I thought to go the daylight play one better, and figured out a way to trigger it a split second sooner.

Here's how it worked: the shortstop would stand behind the runner, but just before he'd make his break he'd drop his glove to his left. As soon as I could see that leather come out from behind the runner, I'd make my break. It bought me an extra fraction of a second, and that fraction was everything. Elster and Santana and I had worked out this eye-contact thing, to let each other know the play was on. It was just a long stare. I'd get the throw back from the catcher, and then I'd turn and look at my infielders. Here, when I caught Rafi's eye, I held it for another beat or two; it was just a shade longer than normal eye contact, but that was our sign to put the play on. I didn't want to give Coleman a couple pitches to pick his spot. I wanted to go at him right away. (Plus, to be honest, I didn't like the way my right hand was swelling up, so I didn't trust myself with the ball for too much longer.)

The great thing about our glove-daylight play was that it was foolproof. As with any play to second, the fallback was that you didn't have to throw if there was a miscommunication between the pitcher and the shortstop. If your shortstop wasn't there, he wasn't there. You're allowed to spin and fake a throw to second; it's just a step-off. But I rarely turned and didn't make the throw. When we put the play on, it was on. We had our timing down. We knew we'd have a good shot at the runner.

Mercifully, that's just what happened here. Coleman was his runnerish self, and we caught him leaning the wrong way. (How's that for sense and feel?) The Shea crowd went nuts, because Met fans never really liked that guy. Even when he came to New York a couple of years later, the fans never fully warmed to Vince—maybe because his best baseball was behind him by that point, or because he once tossed a lit fire-cracker into a crowd of fans.

That gave me two outs. One hard-hit ball right to Keith,

one perfectly placed bunt between the mound and first, one stolen base, and one well-timed pickoff move at second. Not the most dominant two-thirds of an inning, but it would have to do—that is, until I let Ozzie Smith get away from me at the plate. I'd spent so much time "managing" Vince Coleman at second that I'd taken Ozzie for granted, and I ended up walking him.

This brought Tommy Herr to the plate—a tough assignment at this stage in his career, but especially tough here, with my damaged thumb. Tommy wasn't exactly a power threat, but he was a dangerous hitter, and his hits had an uncanny way of leading to runs. I stepped off the mound and thought, How the hell am I gonna get this guy out? My hand was messed up pretty good. I didn't have any pain just yet, but there was considerable swelling, and because of the swelling there wasn't a whole lot of hop on my fastball. (And you could forget about any movement.) I couldn't grip the ball for trying. In fact, even to call what I had a fastball would have been to give real fastballs a bad name, so I tried to change things up and get Tommy to chase a pitch off the plate. He did just that—grounding to Keith at first to end the inning.

I had to cover the bag on that grounder to first, and I hustled back toward the dugout with the ball still in my glove, hoping our trainer Steve Garland might forget about my hand. Instead, of course, he came right over to me. I knew something was horribly wrong, but I was one of those dumb jocks who wanted to play through every pain. Guys in my day were pretty stupid about this type of stuff. (Guys before me were even worse!) We prided ourselves on our ability to play hurt, to put the team ahead of our aches and pains. Already that season, I'd taken eleven cortisone shots, just to keep pitching. I don't set this out to whine or bitch or moan—that's what we all did back then. I was starting to have some trouble with my elbow that year—bone chips, primarily. I was in constant pain, but we'd lost Sid Fernandez to a knee injury and David Cone to a broken thumb, so our ranks were already thin. Earlier in the year, we'd lost Dwight Gooden right out of spring training when he'd failed a drug test and been sent to rehab, and Rick Aguilera missed almost three months. We were hobbled and depleted, and it fell to me to hang in there for the team. Here I thought it would take a lot more than a jammed thumb to get me out of a 4–1 game in the sixth.

My thumb was swollen to the size of a golf ball. Steve Garland tried to move it, and I guess I winced. Then he got up and headed to the other end of the bench. As he left, he said, "That's it."

"What do you mean, 'That's it'?" I called after him. "I got this game."

Somehow, I convinced Davey to send me back out to start the seventh. (The lesson? Never underestimate a major league baseball player's power of persuasion—or delusion.) Clearly, I didn't belong on that mound. I couldn't tie my own shoes, much less throw a baseball. But there I was, on that mound. I was exposed soon enough: I walked Dan Driessen to start the inning, and that was it for me. For the game. For the season, it turned out. That was it for the Mets, too, although we didn't realize it just yet. At that moment, I didn't know the extent of the damage to my pitching hand, just that if we could hold on to win, we would be only a half game out of first. I came out for Randy Myers and went into the clubhouse to ice my hand. Everyone who knew what they were looking at said the thumb was broken, but there was still hope that an X-ray might turn up negative. I certainly wasn't thinking that I would miss my next start—not yet, anyway.

In those days, most teams didn't have X-ray equipment in the clubhouse, so plans were quickly put in place for me to drive myself to the hospital. Nowadays, with star players commanding eight-figure salaries, no team is likely to trust its investment to an ER technician without its own medical personnel in place to oversee the examination, but there were no such contingencies back then.

I hung around the clubhouse long enough for Randy to get out of the small, no-out jam I'd left in the seventh, and long enough to see Roger McDowell get through the Cardinals lineup in the bottom of the eighth as well. We were still up 4–1 after I was showered and changed and ready to head out. I didn't want to wait for the game to end, because these emergency room visits could drag on, so I moved along, thinking the game was well in hand.

I used to park my car out beyond the scoreboard in right, beneath a small overhang near the famous home-run apple in the Shea Stadium outfield. I drove a 1966 Mercedes 220— silver, English-drive—and I liked that spot near the apple because it was like a carport. The overhang offered some protection in case of rain.

By the time I got through the tunnel to our bullpen, the Cardinals had closed the gap to 4–2, with a run off Roger McDowell in the top of the ninth. There were two outs and a runner on first, so I wasn't worried. The guys in the bullpen didn't appear worried, either. As I passed, I wished them luck the rest of the way, and they shouted back some words of encouragement.

I was certain that the injury to my thumb wasn't anything serious. I'd never missed a start in my career, and I wasn't planning on missing one now—not in the thick of a pennant race, not over something as insignificant as a jammed thumb. (Frankly, the bigger worry was how I'd manage the stick shift on my car, with the steering wheel on the right and my bum hand on the wheel.) I assumed I'd be ready to go in five days.

I was conditioned to believe that four days of rest could cure anything. I also assumed that Roger would hang on to get the last out of the game, and that I'd earn my thirteenth win of the season. I had three or four scheduled starts left, so I caught myself thinking I could get to fifteen wins—a good year. Not a great year, but a good, solid year.

It was a beautiful night as I slipped through the gate to the parking area beyond the fence, and the Shea crowd was making noise, willing Roger to put the Cardinals away. Fifty thousand people can really make themselves heard when things are going their way, so I started to project the scenario for the rest of the night and the rest of the season in best-case terms. Just then, as I approached the overhang that protected my car, the crowd went suddenly quiet.

I knew that meant there'd been a long drive by an opposing hitter, so I held my breath for a moment and listened for a clue to what might happen next. But the silence held. For the longest time, it held. It was a killing hush, and it was finally broken by a sickening hissing sound. It was like a missile, whistling past, and when my eyes caught up to it I could see a baseball short-hopping into the door of my Mercedes. It was the strangest thing. It took me a beat or two to process it. Terry Pendleton had belted a two-run home run to the right of the home-run apple—he'd managed to tie the game, erase the lead I'd left behind, and dent my car all with one swing. It was almost surreal—so much so that I could never bring myself to fix that dent. I drove around with it for the next ten years, until I finally sold the car. It was a constant reminder of a distressing Shea Stadium moment that was tied inextricably to that jammed thumb on Vince Coleman's drag bunt in the sixth.

We ended up losing the game, on back-to-back-to-back singles from Coleman, Smith, and Herr in the tenth, dropping us two and a half games back. I ended up with a condition called "gatekeeper's thumb," which is apparently very common, although I'd never heard of it. There was no break, as the Mets trainer and coaches had originally thought, but I'd pulled all the ligaments in and around my thumb so severely that I needed surgery. A hand surgeon put a metal rod in my thumb, which I still have to this day. Then he put me in a cast, which plastered over any false hope I might have had about pitching anytime soon. The only thing that kept me off the disabled list for the first time in my career was the fact that it was September and we had an expanded roster, so Davey didn't need to make any kind of move.

WHEN PEOPLE ASK ME about my most memorable moment at Shea, I invariably drift to this game against the Cardinals. It was just one game, but it cost us a shot at first place. At least, that's how it had me thinking. Realistically, we would have had a tough time down the stretch, with Sid Fernandez and David Cone out for the season, but with me out of the mix as well, Davey was down to only two-fifths of his starting rotation. He used a patchwork of starters that year—twelve in all, I think: guys like John Mitchell, Jeff Innis, Don Schulze, John Candelaria, Tom Edens, and Terry Leach. (Terry actually had a big season for us, going 11–1.) We even used a pitcher named Bob Gibson—a journeyman who of course couldn't touch his namesake.

I'd had a no-hitter going in the sixth, and that dive to my left for Vince Coleman's bunt put an end to that. It put an end to my season and an effective end to the Mets' postseason chances. And it set up one of the most backbreaking losses in anyone's memory. It also changed the course of my career. It cost me my curveball, because once I got that cast off I couldn't straighten my thumb anymore, and I could never manage that classic overhand hook again. Even after over a year of intensive rehab, the motion was lost to me, and I had to develop a different kind of breaking ball. I was able to pitch effectively, but I was a different pitcher. I couldn't rely on my old breaking ball, so I developed my split-finger, which turned out to be an effective pitch for me over the next phase of my career.

I'm a big believer in things like karma and mojo and good fortune, so you'll never catch me wishing to replay a game because I pitched poorly. If you stunk up the joint, you stunk up the joint—end of story. No sense bothering the baseball gods because you messed up. But if there's one moment in my career I'd take back, it would have to be this one, because in retrospect my overhustle coming off the mound and trying to make a play out of Vince Coleman's picture-perfect bunt was probably ill-advised. My chances of making the play? Negligible. My chances of hurting myself and possibly derailing my career? Also negligible—but why take even a negligible chance when there's only a negligible chance of return? It was a cruel, bittersweet reminder that it doesn't pay to go all out when there's no real hope of a return on your investment.

Going in, I'd felt like this was my game—the same way I'd felt in that 1985 late-season start against Tudor, and in Game 4 of the 1986 World Series. There are certain checkpoints in games after which you just know you'll be the one to shake hands after the last out, but sometimes you pass those checkpoints and you still run into a roadblock or two.

Few things in this life hinge on one moment, but every now and then a ball game can turn on a dime. This game could have gone a different way. It could have been a solid eight-inning effort, or maybe even a complete game—a competitive outing against a great opponent to put us in position to make our run. That's how I had it written in my head. But instead, with everything that had happened to our pitching staff that year, with all of our starters going down, and with me now being the last piece to fall, it was almost like we were destined to sit this one out—and now I would have to reinvent myself as a pitcher.

INNING SUMMARY

LANCE JOHNSON: lineout to first base
VINCE COLEMAN: bunt single to pitcher
    Coleman steals second
    Coleman picked off second
OZZIE SMITH: walk
TOM HERR: groundout, first baseman to
             pitcher covering

Righty-Lefty-Righty

June 16, 2008
New York Mets vs. Los Angeles Angels of Anaheim
Angel Stadium of Anaheim, Anaheim
Attendance: 39,229

From time to time, you run into an inning that has as much to do with the off-field distractions that surround the game as anything that unfolds between the lines on the field—and these distractions can play with a pitcher's thinking and take him out of his game before he even gets into it. Front-office intrigues, organizational strategies, and shifts in the prevailing winds of baseball theory invariably come into play, along with the usual ebb and flow of a long campaign, and as the New York Mets neared the midpoint of the 2008 season these factors bubbled forth in a meaningful, instructive way.

The 2008 Mets were struggling—two games under .500 nearly seventy games into a season that was meant to be theirs. Their underperformance had to do with injuries, assorted failures in execution, and a dark cloud that seemed to hover about the club. It wasn't for lack of effort, and yet nothing seemed to go consistently right for this group. As a result, Mets manager Willie Randolph was under the gun. I suppose this was inevitable. His Mets were coming off a giant fade the season before, a September to forget for a team that had been in first place for most of the 2007 season and had been expected to win the division going away. Instead, they hadn't made it into the postseason at all. Now, a little more than two months into the 2008 season, there were rumblings in and around Shea Stadium that the manager's job was in jeopardy. The talk among the beat writers covering the team was that Willie's days were numbered.

I should mention here that I'd been through some version of this as a player. There was a long stretch in there when Davey Johnson was on the firing line, ultimately to be replaced by Bud Harrelson, but in that case the scrutiny wasn't necessarily over our underperformance as a team. It had more to do with Davey's repeated clashes with the front office, over one issue or another, so there was no real spillover effect into the locker room. In 2008, though, with Willie Randolph's job in jeopardy, the players were feeling it too—especially the younger players, who had no frame of reference for this type of baseball drama. Also, for a young pitcher like Mike Pelfrey, who was struggling, it's hard to approach a significant turn in an interleague contest against a top team with all of this other stuff going on outside the lines.

Willie heard the talk, of course. He saw the same dark cloud the rest of us could see. But to his great credit he tried to maintain an upbeat tone. The day before—Father's Day, no less—the Mets had split a doubleheader at Shea against the Texas Rangers, winning the nightcap, and still the talk continued as the team prepared for a six-game road trip clear across the country. It was reported that Willie Randolph even approached the Mets' general manager, Omar Minaya, after the second game and said, "Omar, don't make me fly out to the West Coast if you're planning to make a change."

Reportedly, Minaya told his manager his job was secure for the next while—and it was, I guess. Later, Omar Minaya would tell reporters that he made the decision to remove Willie Randolph as manager sometime that Sunday night, while the team was on the plane to California, but that he wanted to sleep on it one final night before making the move. That's standard procedure for Omar Minaya, for every significant roster move—and a move like the one being considered here was surely significant. He'll even sleep on a trade before pulling the trigger. He apparently woke up Monday morning convinced of his decision: he would have to fire Willie Randolph in order to jump-start his team and salvage the season. Sometimes you have no choice but to fire your manager—not because he can't manage the team, but because his situation has become such a distraction.

Meanwhile, there was a game to be played that Monday night in Anaheim. Naturally it wouldn't do to dismiss Randolph over the phone, so Minaya made plans to meet the team in California and tell his manager personally that he was letting him go.

And so, there was *that*.

There was also this: second-year pitcher Mike Pelfrey was continuing his difficult adjustment to the bigs. The organization had high hopes for Pelfrey, but the young man had done little to justify those hopes by this near midpoint in the 2008 season. He remained a top prospect, but there was talk of sending him to the minors or possibly bouncing him from the rotation until he could find a way to pitch more effectively.

Why does a young pitcher sometimes struggle early in his career? He can't seem to throw strikes. He doesn't trust that he's good enough to pitch at this level. He's got brain overload, from processing all the information he gets from his catcher, from his manager and pitching coach, from the computer printouts that every club receives going into each series. I struggled with all of these issues when I first came up, and the biggest pitfall for me was that I gave the opposing hitters too much credit. You watch these great players on television, in the All-Star Game, in the postseason, and now they're staring you down with a bat in their hands. As a pitcher you try to beat your chest and convince yourself you're their equal—and maybe you are, but it takes a while.

MONDAY'S GAME AGAINST THE ANGELS loomed as a real test for this young pitcher, and it didn't get off to a great start. The Mets scored two runs in the top of the first, but Pelfrey gave one of those runs right back in the bottom of the inning—never a good sign from a struggling young pitcher. In those spots, you want your starting pitcher to power through the opposing lineup and establish a tone for the innings to follow, but so far it appeared that Mike Pelfrey could do no such thing.

Pelfrey's outing was a test for Willie Randolph as well, because the manager was backed into the unenviable position of having to win ball games every night while at the same time trying to lay a positive foundation for a young pitcher's career. Those two assignments are sometimes at cross-purposes.

These Mets must have sensed a special kind of urgency to this particular game, because they added a run in the second, and another in the third. Pelfrey seemed to settle in for a stretch, retiring the Angels in order in the second and third, but then he allowed them to slink back into the game with two runs in the fourth, on four singles—another red flag to a manager on the same short leash as his starting pitcher.

Here again, Pelfrey appeared to regain his toehold after briefly losing his footing. He didn't allow a hit in the fifth or sixth innings, and in the top of the seventh the Mets exploded for another four runs, knocking Angels starter Jered Weaver out of the game and giving Mike Pelfrey an 8–3 lead going into the bottom of the seventh—in all, a welcome turn for Pelfrey and Randolph and the New York Mets.

The baseball cliché to describe a pitcher's approach to this scenario is *Put a zero on the board.* After your team scores a bunch of runs for you, the idea is to hold the other guys so you don't give back the ground you've just gained. It becomes a real hammer inning for your team. You don't want the other guys to sniff any chance for a comeback, so as a pitcher you want to be exponentially more aggressive than you might have been to that point in the game. It doesn't mean you have to throw only strikes, but you certainly don't want to walk anybody. A lot of times, when you pile on the runs in one inning and your pitcher retires the side in the next frame, you get back up to the plate and pile on a few more. That's just how it goes. Your hitting shoes are on, the laces tied tight. It's like taking care of a great gift—that's what it means to put a zero on the board. Your teammates have just given you a nice cushion, and the last thing you want to do is let the air out of it. You don't want to be caught laboring, not even a little, because then you let the other guys sniff an opportunity later on in the game.

You can be sure these were the types of thoughts running through Mike Pelfrey's head as he stepped back on the mound to start the bottom of the seventh. He'd thrown a lot of pitches by this point in the game, and the score had been 4–3 when he left the hill after the sixth inning. Now he had a five-run lead, and it fell to him to take good care of it. Too, it fell to Willie Randolph to take good care of Mike Pelfrey, which he felt called upon to do after the very first batter. Howie Kendrick, the Angels' fine young second baseman, managed to squeak a grounder just beyond the reach of his opposite number, Luis Castillo. Pelfrey actually made a good pitch—a changeup away—but Kendrick got his bat on it and found a hole. It could have just as easily been the first out of the inning, but now Kendrick stood on first with a leadoff single.

To a veteran pitcher, a hit like that is nothing, a mini-hiccup. It shouldn't take away from whatever mojo might have come your team's way in the last half inning. But to a laboring and possibly uncertain pitcher, with a manager operating as if his every move is being analyzed and dissected, it's a potential trouble spot, so Willie Randolph made a quick trip to the mound. Willie always did a great job of visiting the mound in big moments to settle his pitchers—and the reason he succeeded so well was because he so rarely did it. To a pitcher, it's always a big deal when you see your manager coming out there to talk to you. You could tell from Pelfrey's body language that he was mad at himself, but there was nothing he could have done differently. He didn't give Kendrick anything good to hit; the guy just pushed the ball past Castillo's glove—no big deal. It was probably a sound move by Willie Randolph, to come out to the mound like that and give Pelfrey a chance to catch his breath, given all these other circumstances, but I couldn't help wondering if Randolph would have gone out there if his own job wasn't so clearly on the line.

However it came to pass, and whether or not it was justified, it didn't seem to me, upstairs in the broadcast booth, that Randolph's trip to the mound had the desired effect. Actually, from anywhere in that ballpark it appeared to miss its mark, because Mike Pelfrey certainly didn't help himself or his teammates with the next batter: right fielder Gary Matthews Jr. If you're Pelfrey and you see a fleet-footed contact hitter like Gary Matthews Jr. stepping to the plate, you should be thinking ground ball. At this point in his career, Mike Pelfrey was primarily a one-pitch pitcher—he had that great hard sinker that had everyone in the organization so excited about his future. You can't expect to double up a guy like Matthews, and Pelfrey was not the kind of pitcher who could expect to strike him out, so the pitcher's best outcome here was to keep the ball on the ground. His main objective, with that sudden gift of a five-run lead late in the game, was just to get an out. Collect enough of them, and you'll help your team to a win.

One of my college coaches used to describe a pitcher's job as filling a basket with outs. I'd never really pitched as a starter before I got to Yale, and I had some trouble with the role at first, until this coach came up to me one day and said, "Just keep it simple, Ron. Think of it like there's a basket behind you and it's up to you to fill that basket with outs. If you're having a good game, that basket will be full. If you're not, you'll be a little light."

That made sense to me as a young pitcher. It broke things down in such a way that I started to think of the game in smaller increments, one out at a time, and it occurred to me that Mike Pelfrey would do well to grasp the same analogy. He seemed to want to do a little too much with each pitch, meaning he was trying to make each pitch a perfect, on-the-corner sinker, instead of just enough, meaning he should just try to get the batter to hit the ball on the ground and hopefully into one of his fielders' gloves. Here, Pelfrey got off to a good start against Matthews, quickly running the count to 1–2, but then he let the batter hang in there for the longest time.

Mets catcher Brian Schneider called for a fastball down and in, but to a left-handed hitter that's the danger zone. You're better off coming in belt-high or higher against a lefty. Generally, there's one exception to this rule, and I learned it from Mel Stottlemyre: when the batter happens to be a natural right-hander. In this case, the right arm is dominant, which means the bottom hand on the bat is stronger as it comes through the zone, in a powerful backhand motion, so when you assemble a book on a left-handed hitter you need to know how he throws as well. Normally, the stronger hand is on top and can only guide the bat through the hitting zone; when your bottom hand is your lead hand, you're better able to drive a ball that's up in the zone, so this is where the pitcher will do well to keep that ball down and in.

The Achilles' heel for a right-handed sinker-ball pitcher has always been an inside pitch to a left-handed batter, because that ball tends to drift naturally over the strike zone. The sinking action of the ball will take it from the inside corner back over the middle of the plate, so one of the things Mike Pelfrey was working on at this stage in his career was the ability to come inside to left-handed hitters with something else—either a cutter or a straight fastball.

At 1–2, Pelfrey should have thrown a fastball up and in, for effect. (And, possibly, to set the batter up for the next pitch, away.) Instead, Pelfrey threw it down and in, and Matthews was able to foul it off. At that point, I would have come back up and in, like I might have done in the first place, but Pelfrey kept pushing his pitches toward the outside corner—away, away, away. The pitch selection came from the dugout, but Schneider knew what he was doing. In my day, the catcher made the calls on pitch selection, and you never knew what you might get behind the plate. Obviously, some catchers around the league were known to be a whole lot smarter than other catchers. Of course, the flip side of that also held true: some catchers didn't have the insight or the intellect to track all the tendencies and nuances a major league catcher has to consider. Maybe he had a great bat, or a good glove, or a solid arm—but no head for the game.

Fortunately, this was not an issue for the young Mike Pelfrey, because Brian Schneider was a sharp defensive catcher, well-equipped to execute the game plan put in place by the Mets' bench. And Pelfrey, too, had a good feel for the ebb and flow of the game.

Still, the at-bat continued. Each time Pelfrey came to the plate, Matthews managed to foul off the pitch, until he finally pushed the count to 3–2 and whatever advantage Pelfrey might have had in the matchup was long gone. Now, at 3–2, Matthews continued to foul off pitches, and the remarkable piece here was that Howie Kendrick was running on each pitch. I thought, There's not a manager in baseball other than Mike Scioscia who would put that runner in motion, down five runs with nobody out—but that's how Mike played the game. Hard. All out. All the time.

Mike Scioscia had always been one of the slowest players in the league, but at the same time he'd been one of the best base runners. That's not a contradiction, and for a pitcher it's a helpful distinction. A lot of times, slow runners make the best base runners because they've had to compensate. They've had to study the game and learn how to get a good jump. As a pitcher, you have to recognize that guy who might appear as something less than a threat on the base paths, because he can hurt you if you take him for granted. These 2008 Mets needed to know that about Scioscia as well, because his tendencies as a player may spill over into how he manages a team—the out-fielders most of all. You can't assume that one of Scioscia's base runners won't be going first to third on a hard-hit single—he might have gotten an outstanding secondary lead, or he might cut the bag at second like a diamond cutter and be headed toward third before you know what hit you.

In addition to worrying over Kendrick at first, Willie Randolph and his pitching coach, Rick Peterson, were becoming more and more concerned about Pelfrey's pitch count, as Gary Matthews Jr. pushed him deeper into the 3–2 count. It was a real battle—and all credit goes to Matthews for stretching things out in just this way. As it unfolded, you could feel the advantage in the at-bat shifting from Pelfrey to Matthews, to where finally it seemed a foregone conclusion that this would be one of the last batters Pelfrey would face, no matter what happened here. After seven, eight, nine pitches, a turn like that can really change the dynamics of an inning, even though nothing of moment has really happened. After twelve pitches, Schneider called for a fastball in, but Pelfrey couldn't get the ball over the plate and Matthews earned a meaningful walk. It would have been better for Pelfrey and the Mets if the guy had gotten a single on the first pitch, because now Pelfrey had thrown eighteen pitches in the inning without recording a single out, and there were runners on first and second.

That gift the Mets had given Mike Pelfrey in their half of the seventh? It was about to be sent back.

At this point, Carlos Delgado walked over to the mound from first base to talk to his pitcher. Normally, this is a good, veteran move—but here again, not a whole lot gets said during one of these visits. It's just a point of pause, designed to tell a young pitcher that he's not in this thing alone. The message underneath, of course, was that Willie Randolph wasn't going to allow Pelfrey to dig himself a deeper hole. In the back of his mind, even a young pitcher like Pelfrey had to know that he would be pulled from the game if he slid into further trouble.

It gets that way sometimes, for a pitcher. You half-expect your manager to come out with a hook, and then you're surprised when he stays in the dugout and leaves you in the game. It's a non-event—nothing has happened to change your role—but a lot of pitchers start to lose their rhythm and their confidence when they realize they might be pulled from the game at any moment. It messes with their head. All of a sudden, they're too fine with their pitches or they try to do too much with each pitch, and the trouble they were hoping to avoid now knows where to look for them.

Next up: catcher Jeff Mathis, and here Pelfrey should have been thinking about strike one. That's all. Just get that first pitch over for a strike—and don't really worry about the runners. Most managers, down five runs, wouldn't think of running their team out of a potentially big inning, not even Mike Scioscia, but at the same time it wouldn't have been a terrible play for Mike Pelfrey to glance over to second and look Kendrick back a time or two before turning his attention to Mathis. It's a relatively simple thing for a pitcher to pay cursory attention to that lead runner on second. You can do it in a few different ways. You can vary your looks, so that you turn your head toward second once or twice before the first pitch, two or three times before the next pitch, and so on. You can deploy that effective swing move with your front leg, where instead of moving toward the plate you rotate to second. Or you can simply step off. Any one of those moves will put enough doubt in the base runner's mind to keep him close.

With runners on first and second and nobody out, Willie Randolph made the key decision to play his infield back, at double-play depth. With a five-run lead, there was no good reason to hold the runner at first—a good move, I thought. The only move, really.

Pelfrey jumped out ahead of Mathis with a called first strike, but then he followed that with a ball in the dirt that Brian Schneider managed to keep in front of him. With this, Schneider made a quick trip to the mound, and I looked on and thought, Enough with the visits to the mound. Just let the kid pitch. First it was Willie Randolph, then Carlos Delgado, and now Brian Schneider. These repeat visits don't always leave a pitcher on point—they might leave him on tilt instead. With all of these people coming out to talk to him, he's got to think he's doing something wrong—a young pitcher, especially.

My thought here was that Schneider's trip was one of those paranoid visits that have mostly to do with the fear that the runner on second is stealing signs. This was probably true, because the Mets' signs tended to be fairly simple. I'm able to figure them out every time, from up in the booth, so Schneider was right to be concerned, but I wouldn't have made this third trip. At some point, all those interruptions start to mess with a pitcher's tempo. Whatever rhythm he had going falls away. Sometimes, it's better just to keep moving forward and try to start putting a couple outs in that basket.

Jeff Mathis wouldn't be one of those outs. He worked the count full, then laced a hard grounder between third and short—a solid hit, against a pitcher who was now on his heels. That 3–2 pitch from Pelfrey should have been his put-this-guy-away pitch, a sinker down and in, but he tried to be too fine with it and caught a little too much of the plate. Instead, it was his take-me-out-of-this-game pitch. True, he accomplished one of his objectives—to get Mathis to hit the ball on the ground and hopefully into a double play—but he allowed him to hit it hard, scoring Kendrick and moving Matthews down to second.

At this point, Willie Randolph had seen enough. His pitcher was laboring. Pelfrey had shown a marked inability to put these Angels hitters away. He was working more slowly, more meticulously than he had earlier in the game—even earlier in the inning. His pitch count was becoming more and more of a concern—and now, with the score 8–4, runners on first and second, and nobody out, a comfortable lead was looking a whole lot less comfortable.

Armchair managers watching a game at home—or up in the broadcast booth—might catch themselves wondering why a manager leaves a pitcher in a ball game for a couple batters too long. But you never really know what a manager is thinking, and our second-guessing usually comes with the benefit of hindsight. At each juncture here in this seventh inning, Willie might have pulled Pelfrey, but obviously he thought he had something left. That, or maybe his bullpen wasn't ready, or maybe a laboring Pelfrey was still his best option.

Certainly, there's no denying that it's harder than ever before for a big league manager to know when to pull a pitcher. There's such a great emphasis placed on pitch counts and innings that managers no longer understand when to trust a pitcher to let him know he's truly gassed. Whenever I hear a manager or a pitching coach talk about the importance of capping a pitcher's workload, I wonder what the careers of some of the all-time great pitchers would have been like in today's ultraconservative environment. I think, Bob Gibson on a pitch count? Are you kidding me?

I used to strike a kind of bargain with my managers. I'd say, "Look, there are going to be certain games when I'm on, where you won't have to worry about me. There are going to be other games when I clearly don't have it, where you won't have to worry about me. It's just those games in the middle we have to worry about." My thinking was that we were investing in each other, and when I'd hit one of those trouble spots I should be able to say, "Okay, I'm in a bit of a jam, but I think I can get this next batter out and maybe hang on and earn a win." Conversely, my manager should have been able to say, "Okay, Ronnie. I'm giving you some rope here. Just make sure you don't hang me with it."

In any case, the Mets' comfortable lead was looking a whole lot less comfortable. The left-handed sidearmer Pedro Feliciano got the call in the bullpen. It was a no-brainer move. Chone Figgins, batting next, in the leadoff spot, was a speedy switch hitter, who'd already hit from the left side of the plate three times in the game. It made sense to turn him around, on the thinking that it might take an at-bat or two for him to find his groove from the right side. That's the essence of situational pitching, which I've always thought of like a dance; you try to get the other guy out of his groove while you attempt to find yours.

Feliciano is not a classic sidearmer, in the mold of the old-time submarine-type pitchers who would really reach down and scrape their knuckles over the dirt as they came to the plate. He's one of those guys who have made an adjustment somewhere along the way, in order to compete at the major league level. He'd been a traditional over-the-top pitcher, with a big hook, but at some point he realized his stuff wasn't good enough to cut it in the bigs, so he dropped down and refashioned himself as a sidearm left-hander with a sinker, a changeup, and a slider—the slider being his out pitch against left-handed batters. Nowadays, most contending teams have a guy like Feliciano in their bullpen, a specialist who is often called on to get just one out against a tough lefty in a tough spot.

Here Willie Randolph needed Feliciano to do a little bit more besides. He needed him to turn Figgins around to the right side, then stick around for another couple batters. That's a dangerous assignment. You want to be careful as a manager when you try to extend a relief pitcher who has developed into a late-inning specialist. A guy like Feliciano is used to pitching to one batter, maybe two, three, tops. It was almost always a lefty-lefty matchup when he was in the game. Sure, there was a time in his career when he could go longer, when he could face batters on either side of the plate with equal confidence, but that hadn't been his comfort zone for a while.

Here, the number two hitter, shortstop Maicer Izturis, was also a switch hitter (he's since refashioned *himself* as a straight right-handed hitter), and he would be followed by Garret Anderson, a dangerous left-handed hitter, so Willie Randolph was hamstrung by the flexibility of Mike Scioscia's lineup. Sure enough, the move didn't exactly work out according to plan. Figgins managed to bounce a ball up the middle on the third pitch of his at-bat, just out of the reach of a diving José Reyes, allowing Matthews to score and the Angels to inch ever closer on the scoreboard.

Looking at the replay, it appeared as if José was a little too concerned with fielding the ball in such a way that he might be able to turn and start a double play, but the better move here might have been just to knock the ball down and keep it on the lip of the outfield grass, to prevent that lead runner from scoring. Also, the Mets should have taken the elements into consideration; you've got to know the field. That hard-baked infield in Anaheim is notoriously quick, so you have to be prepared for the ball to skitter through with a little more pace on it than it might at home at Shea. It wasn't a bad pitch by Feliciano, and Figgins didn't get a whole lot of bat on the ball, but he managed to put it just out of reach and keep the rally going.

As a manager, you couldn't look on at that at-bat and think Feliciano didn't have his good stuff. He was just unlucky, is all, and Randolph had no choice but to leave him in to face Izturis and hope for the best. Feliciano got the hitter to put the ball in play—this time, a slow roller to second baseman Luis Castillo. The ball wasn't hit hard enough for the Mets to execute a double play, but Castillo was able to flip the ball to Reyes, covering second, in time to get the force on Figgins. (Figgins also made a good hard slide, to prevent Reyes from getting off the throw to first, but it didn't appear that José would have had time to nab the runner at first even with a strong throw.)

Now the Mets were looking at runners on first and third, with just one out, as Garret Anderson dug in. This was the guy Feliciano had really been brought on to face. Those first two switch hitters could have gone either way, but Anderson, with his 2,000-plus hits and his MVP-caliber seasons, had loomed all along as the important out in the inning. Before the inning had even started, Feliciano had probably been sitting out in the bullpen, working his way through the Angels lineup in his head, thinking he might be called on to face Anderson, and now the moment was upon him. Vladimir Guerrero, one of the most feared hitters in the game, stood in the on-deck circle, and Feliciano knew it was essential that he go after Anderson, to minimize any further damage. It was a pick-your-poison moment—but Anderson came around first in the order, so he was the first order of business.

Feliciano got Anderson to foul off the first pitch, and then he unfurled a perfect slider, down and away. Anderson lunged at it, but he couldn't come close. He actually looked bad on his swing, and I thought Feliciano might come back with the very same pitch. That was the move—and it appeared that's the pitch Brian Schneider wanted. Anderson has a great ability to go the other way with a pitch, but you don't want to take a chance busting him inside and putting him in a position where he can turn on a pitch and pull it. The better move, the safety move, was to keep the ball on the outside of the plate, away from Anderson's strength. When you get to 0–2 against a good hitter, that slider has to be even farther off the plate, because all the batter can do at that point is protect the plate. He's forced to shorten his stroke, which means he's a different hitter than he was at the top of the at-bat. Feliciano failed to execute, however. He didn't get the ball far enough away, and Anderson was able to stroke a crisp line-drive single into center field, scoring Mathis from third.

Just like that, the Angels were back in the game—primarily because of the contagious inability of the Met pitchers to execute—and here Willie Randolph was forced to summon hard-throwing right-hander Aaron Heilman from the bullpen to face Guerrero. It was the kind of righty-lefty-righty maneuvering we see so often in today's game, which of course stands in marked contrast to how the game was played in my day. Back then, there were usually only two relievers on most staffs who could pitch worth a damn. The rest of the guys were filler, and if they came in at all it usually meant you were looking at a game that had already been decided, one way or another.

Nowadays, though, with starting pitchers being shut down after a hundred or so pitches, the game has changed. Now major league managers regularly reach for their middle relievers to pitch them out of tough spots—a formula that's doomed to fail more often than not. Why? Simple math, really. If you're using a five-man rotation, it follows that those five guys are probably your five best pitchers. In any case, they're the guys who (at least in theory) have the stuff to work their way through an opposing lineup three times and get batters out consistently. It follows, too, that your closer and possibly your two setup guys are your next-best options. Maybe they have exceptional stuff, but it's the kind of exceptional stuff that can't get hitters out two times in a row; or maybe they just have the kind of bounce-back arm that allows them to pitch on consecutive days. That still leaves three or four guys at the bottom of your bullpen who are now being called on to get meaningful outs, in meaningful situations—not just every once in a while, but day after day after day.

With this game in Anaheim, it's possible to suggest that Willie Randolph was dipping into the well a few too many times—putting too fine a point on an inning that shouldn't have gotten away from his starter in the first place. And, once it did, it shouldn't have gotten away from the guy the manager called in to put out the first fire. But because of the way the game is played today, pitchers like Mike Pelfrey aren't expected to go deep in most ball games, and as a result they don't expect it of themselves—and, as an even further result, they tend to pitch down to the low expectations managers and coaches and front-office personnel have lately set for them. Pitchers like Pedro Feliciano are rarely called upon to face more than one or two batters or to pitch away from their strengths, so they, too, may falter when they're asked to do more.

It's difficult to fault Willie Randolph for any one move he made in this seventh-inning showdown. He was just going by the book, and here his final move happened to pay off: Heilman got Guerrero to swing through the first pitch, a slider away. Then he came back with another slider—normally his third-best pitch, but against a guy like Guerrero probably his best shot. Most of the time, the stuff of a dominant pitcher will trump the abilities of a dominant hitter, but that equation didn't really apply in this case. Guerrero was such a strong hitter that his abilities forced a pitcher like Heilman to react to *his* strengths as a batter, rather than the other way around.

Now, at 0–2, Heilman faced a small dilemma. Should he come back at Guerrero with his third straight slider? Or should he change it up and hope to catch Guerrero off guard? If it had been me on that mound, with the same arsenal of pitches, I would have come back with a fastball, head-high, just to change the look of the at-bat and keep the batter guessing. Maybe Guerrero would swing at it, maybe he wouldn't; but either way, it would set up the next pitch. I never liked to go at a guy three times in a row with the same pitch, in the same spot. It scared me. A slider, especially, is a difficult pitch to reach for three times running. You're more apt to make a mistake with a breaking ball—and that nearly happened here.

Schneider called for that third straight slider away. That's the catcher's role, and it's not an easy one when you're dealing with relief pitchers. You have to make a quick judgment call on each guy who comes in during the game. You'll know what he throws, you'll know his best pitch, but then on top of that you'll have to decide right away if his best pitch is with him or against him this night. The slider is usually Heilman's third-best pitch, but tonight it appeared to be his best pitch, so that's what Schneider called. Heilman meant to deliver it and failed to execute. He put it right over the plate, but he caught a break. Guerrero swung through it for the second out of the inning.

That brought Torii Hunter to the plate. Hunter, who'd signed as a free agent, had been the Angels' big off-season acquisition, and he was a tremendous ballplayer. He lived in big spots—and this was surely a big spot. One swing, and the game could turn back in his team's direction. So what did Heilman throw? Another slider—his fourth in a row! Hunter swung right through it. Clearly, Brian Schneider was playing his pitcher's hot hand, but he couldn't keep reaching for that same pitch indefinitely. Hunter knew it. Heilman knew it. Every thinking fan in that stadium knew it. Plus, three of those four sliders had been out of the strike zone, so all Hunter had to do to force Heilman to change things up was exercise a little patience at the plate. And that's just what he did—he let the next two pitches go, a fastball in and another slider away, and the count ran to 2–1.

Up in the booth, I could see a tight shot of Willie Randolph on the monitor. Willie was standing on the top step of the dugout wearing the look of a major league manager with a game, a season, a career on the line. Heilman had just gotten a huge out, but now he'd pitched himself into a hitter's count, and Willie Randolph clearly didn't like it that the advantage had tilted away from his pitcher yet again. The slider had been working for Heilman, but the Mets couldn't count on a disciplined hitter like Hunter to swing at a slider off the plate—not with a 2–1 count.

Heilman threw over to first before the next pitch. That call came from the bench, and it was a good one. The Mets had to keep Anderson honest, because he represented the tying run—but more than that, the move forced Hunter to think a little longer about the next pitch. Then Heilman came back with his first changeup of the night, which Hunter fouled off for strike two. Now Willie Randolph could allow himself to think the advantage had tilted back in Heilman's favor. There was no way Hunter could sit on another pitch. Heilman had thrown two sliders away, a fastball in, a changeup down. Hunter had to be in hit mode; he had to be up there thinking, *See the ball, and put it in play.* If the count had run to 3–1, it would have been a different story. He could have waited on his pitch and, if he got something he liked, teed off on it.

Another call from the bench: Brian Schneider put down three fingers to indicate a fake pickoff to third, so Heilman dutifully stepped toward David Wright and pumped a throw. I had to think Randolph had him do that to get a read on Mike Scioscia—an aggressive manager who might be inclined to put on some type of running play in this situation, now that Hunter was on the defensive. Remember, Scioscia had already tipped his hand on how aggressive he would be that inning when he ran Kendrick on all those 3–2 counts, so you really do have to think along with the other manager—as a pitcher, as well.

The next pitch was off the plate, to run the count full—and now it was probably a push as to who had the advantage, the hitter or the pitcher. Heilman came back with another changeup, down and in, and Hunter swung through it for the third out of the inning—so on this night, at least, the righty-lefty-righty choreography paid off for Willie Randolph and the Mets. There was some collateral damage—the Angels pushed across three runs and brought the winning run to the plate in the form of two big-time hitters—but in the end Mike Pelfrey, Pedro Feliciano, and Aaron Heilman helped their team dodge a pretty serious bullet.

It wouldn't be enough to save Willie Randolph's job, but it was enough to keep the Mets in the game.

I don't think any inning like this would have played out in quite the same way back when I was pitching, but the game has changed. Relief pitchers are asked to do less, but at the same time, what they're being asked to do matters more. This particular seventh inning, which took place in the swirl of all kinds of controversy and uncertainty, stands as a case in point and a full-on reminder that results on the field don't always match our expectations in the dugout—or the front office.

INNING SUMMARY

HOWIE KENDRICK: ground-ball single to right field

GARY MATTHEWS JR.: walk
Kendrick advances to second

JEFF MATHIS: ground-ball single to left field
Kendrick scores; Matthews advances to second
Pedro Feliciano replaces Mike Pelfrey as pitcher

CHONE FIGGINS: ground-ball single to center field
Matthews scores; Mathis advances to second

MAICER IZTURIS: ground ball to second baseman
Figgins retired at second on force-out; Mathis advances to third; Izturis reaches first safely

GARRET ANDERSON: line-drive single to center field
Mathis scores; Izturis advances to third
Aaron Heilman replaces Pedro Feliciano as pitcher

VLADIMIR GUERRERO: strikeout swinging

TORII HUNTER: strikeout swinging

On a Roll

July 12, 1992
Oakland Athletics vs. Toronto Blue Jays
SkyDome, Toronto
Attendance: 50,392

A two-hit shutout is a beautiful thing. It's doubly so when you manage to throw a pair of them back-to-back—or just about. And when those matching gems turn up at a kind of career crossroads that has left you thinking you might be done as a top-of-the-rotation pitcher, well, then it's off the charts.

Baseball is a quirky game. It's shot through with symmetry and chance and weird blips that tend to come in clusters. You can go your entire career without reaching one goal or another, and then out of nowhere you might achieve a flurry of extraordinary feats and catch yourself thinking, *What the hell was that?*

For example, despite my accomplishments as a hitter in college, I hit only two home runs in my major league career. The relevant piece here is that the home runs came in consecutive starts: a solo shot on June 24, 1989, against the Phillies' Floyd Youmans and a three-run job off the Reds' Norm Charlton on June 30, 1989. Not exactly Tony Cloninger (the Atlanta Braves pitcher who in 1966 miraculously smoked two grand slams against the San Francisco Giants *in the same game*—just a couple weeks after going deep twice in a game against the lowly Mets), but close.

What are the odds against a pitcher taking a no-hitter into the late innings on his way to a complete-game, two-hit shutout in consecutive starts against the same team? Pretty damn long, I'd say. And what if those no-hitters were broken up by the same batter, leading off one of those late innings? Pretty damn longer, right? And—get this!—what if those games were bunched together in such a way that there was only one other start in between? Well, now we've drifted into the outer reaches of far-fetchedness, but that's what happened in the middle of the 1992 season, when I started to turn around a rocky first half for the Oakland A's on the back of a neat trifecta of complete-game outings. The dueling two-hit shutouts came against the Toronto Blue Jays, who would go on to win the World Series that year, after besting us A's in the American League Championship Series. The opposing hitter who foiled both no-hit bids was Candy Maldonado, who put together a solid enough career over fifteen seasons but always seemed to hit me like an all-time great. The game sandwiched in between was a 1–0 complete-game loss to the New York Yankees. The three outings, taken together, helped to drive my earned run average from 4.78 to 3.82, and to set right the pendulum of my career after a swing in the wrong direction.

That first outing against Toronto reinforces the sheer serendipity of our pastime and stands as a reminder of the momentum shifts that can sometimes stamp a game, a season, the back of a baseball card. We've all heard hitters give postgame interviews about how they're seeing the ball particularly well, or maybe they'll say they're feeling particularly "locked in" at the plate, but pitchers can also fall into that zone where they feel like they can do no wrong on the mound. You don't hear that very often in reference to a relief pitcher, primarily because they're not in the game long enough to go on one of these rolls, but it happens for starting pitchers all the time. Every now and then, a guy gets locked in and goes on a tear, and that momentum roll can stretch from a couple of starts to an entire season. They'll tick off ten, twelve, fourteen wins in a row.

I was certainly locked in for this batch of starts—and it was a good thing, too, because I hadn't really pitched all that well for nearly two complete seasons. The 1990 season—my last full year with the Mets—had essentially been a bust, from start to finish. I just couldn't get it going, and my ineffectiveness bled into a lost 1991 campaign, where I wound up pitching in long relief for the Mets before being shipped to the Expos in a change-of-scenery deal for their closer, Tim Burke. I stayed in Montreal for only a couple weeks, logging another few lousy starts before heading on to the A's for a pair of minor leaguers, and once I got to Oakland I didn't do much to distinguish myself for the balance of the year, winning only three games in a dozen tries.

One of the reasons the A's traded for me, I learned later, was that Tony La Russa consulted with his friend and colleague Jim Leyland, the manager of the Pittsburgh Pirates.

Tony wanted to hear from someone who'd seen me pitch a few times from the opposing dugout, and Jim Leyland said unequivocally that I still had something to offer a big league pitching staff. He said the Mets—or, now, the Expos—would never trade me to a competitive team within the division; otherwise, he'd grab me in a heartbeat.

My performance when I got to Oakland didn't exactly justify Leyland's endorsement, at least not on a micro level. You could watch me pitch an inning or a game and there might be nothing to distinguish me from any other pitcher looking to hang on in the bigs. My value to a ball club at that stage in my career was really my durability as much as anything else. I was a workhorse. I'd take the ball thirty-four times a season, every fifth day, so you had to consider my contributions over a somewhat longer stretch—in a macro way, if you will. I'd keep us in ball games, so we'd have a better than even chance to win, more times than not. That's something—enough, it turned out, to get me an extension with the A's after that dismal 1991 season. Tony and his pitching coach, Dave Duncan, must have appreciated my macro contributions, because they seemed to want to keep me around—at least for one more year.

Dave Duncan took me aside during my first spring training with the A's and gave me his take. He said, "Remember that pitcher you were with the Mets?"

I said, "Yeah."

I thought Dave was going to tell me what we needed to work on in order to return to form, but he went another way. He said, "Well, say good-bye to him."

I wasn't expecting that, and he kept at it. He said, "Say good-bye to the pitcher you used to be. Reconcile yourself to the fact that you're no longer able to do what you used to do when you first came up, so you need to think about all those great games you pitched for the Mets, all those great seasons you had, and set them aside. Say good-bye to that pitcher, because he's no longer here."

It was a brilliant approach, really. Dave had been a catcher during his big league career, so he knew his stuff. (We actually had a little history between us, although Dave certainly didn't remember it. As a kid, I had gone with my Little League group to a game at Fenway, and, of course, I spent most of my time chasing around the stadium trying to collect autographs. After the game, we ran to the Red Sox players' lot, but were turned away, so me and my buddies doubled back to catch the visiting team, which just happened to be the Oakland A's, as they left the stadium. Those 1970s-era A's teams were pretty colorful, with their long hair and distinctive mustaches and bright uniforms. They were good guys, too, and the very first autograph I snagged was Dave Duncan's. I never forgot that, and here he was, helping me get my game back after a career speed bump.) Dave knew what it took to get his pitchers going. He knew when a guy had lost some hop on his fastball or some movement on his breaking ball. He knew what I was capable of doing and what I needed to do in order to be effective and win games. He said, "I know about your personality, Ron. Your makeup is why you're here. You're competitive. We like that you're competitive. It doesn't matter what your stuff is, as long as you're competitive. I can work with that. You can work with that. You've still got a major league arm. But you can't go at it like you used to and think you're going to get people out."

This was harsh, but it was a message I needed to hear if I wanted to continue on as a ballplayer, so I took it in. It had nothing to do with the shift in organizational thinking that would soon keep pitchers to lower pitch counts in order to preserve their arms and their careers, even though a lot of baseball people consider Dave Duncan and Tony La Russa to be at ground zero in the game's move toward situational pitching. They were the very first to keep a tight rein on their pitchers, and to stick so religiously to the concept of the one-inning relief pitcher that came into prominence during this period. One year in there, the A's had a pitcher named Storm Davis who managed to post a 19–7 record, while pitching only 169 innings. That's not a whole lot of work for a starter who somehow managed to figure in 26 decisions—less than five and a half innings per start, including a handful of no-decisions. But that was the beginning of the game's emphasis on the quality start, a stat line that in my day would have gotten you nowhere in the estimation of your teammates. Back then, we looked at numbers like seven innings, two runs or less as a baseline measure of effectiveness, and compared to today's standard of six innings and three runs or less, there's all the difference in the world. It was pitching to a 2.57 earned run average instead of a 4.50 earned run average.

But this wasn't about pitch counts, I don't think. This was about me no longer having the velocity or the stuff to continue on as the type of pitcher I had been earlier in my career. I'd have to pull it back if I wanted to keep pitching effectively. One of the biggest shifts Dave had me make in my approach was to separate myself from the notion that I could overpower hitters for an entire game. That had been my attitude all along, and here Dave was telling me it would no longer do. I might make it through nine innings from time to time, he allowed, but that couldn't be my goal. He said, "We don't want you to get twenty-seven outs a game. We don't want you to get twenty-four outs a game. But we're gonna get you to where you can get us eighteen or twenty-one outs and put us in a position to win."

That meant leaving something in the tank for the next outing, and the one after that. It meant pitching around some batters. It meant reaching for my changeup when the pitcher I used to be would have reached for the fastball. It meant tweaking my pickoff move, which had always been one of my strengths, so runners wouldn't have such a predictable time of it trying to figure me out going forward. And it meant relying on my teammates to make the plays behind me, and on our bullpen to finish what I started.

I admired Dave Duncan's approach, and underneath that admiration I had to hand it to Tony La Russa as well. Managers can communicate with their pitchers in any number of ways. They've got a whole bag of tricks. They can talk to you directly, as Tony would do with great effectiveness later on in my Oakland career. They can reach out to you through their pitching coach, as Tony was apparently doing here. They can communicate with you through the press, which I suppose can be effective in some cases, if a little gutless. Or they can use a veteran catcher to get an important point across.

I'd been on the receiving end of each approach, with varying results. One of the more anxious moments in my Met career came early on when Davey Johnson deployed two of these strategies to get through to me after a miserable outing in Philadelphia at the front end of the 1985 season, and his double-barreled method paid off. I'd given up five earned runs in five innings in that start against the Phillies, on the way to a 10–6 loss. After the game, Davey told one of the beat reporters that I'd put out an unprofessional effort, and that watching me pitch that game had been one of the most difficult things he'd ever had to do as a major league manager. For two years now, he'd been trying to get me to mix up my pitches and throw strikes. It wasn't about holding a key pitch in reserve so much as varying my timing, my speed, my movement. For two years now, I'd resisted Davey's entreaties to keep hitters off balance in this way, and now he was sick and tired of watching me throw a hundred or so pitches and fail to make it to the sixth inning.

Davey Johnson was a thoughtful guy. He spent time on this stuff. He must have decided that this coaching-through-the-press tactic might have an impact. It did, and it didn't. I was pissed that Davey thought it was okay to chew me out in public like that, but he did have a point. I was walking too many hitters, no question. I was pitching myself into tough spots, no question. I was always, always, always behind in the count, no question. And there's no question that I was relying way too much on my fastball to get me out of jams, when I should have been finding ways to stay out of those jams in the first place.

I had a couple days to process Davey's comments before my next start at home against the Pirates, and in that time I went from being mad to being open to his point of view. Not all the way open, mind you—but open a crack at least. Joe Orsulak was the Pittsburgh leadoff hitter that day, and I started him off with a fastball down the middle for a strike. It felt good. I had good control, good velocity, good movement. On the next pitch, Gary Carter called for a curveball, but I shook him off. He called for the curve again, and I shook him off again. It was a real standoff. My thinking was, Joe Orsulak isn't a power hitter. He isn't about to hit one out. It felt like I had my fastball working, so why not go after him with it? But Carter was firm. He put down two fingers and called for the curve a third time—clearly on Davey's orders.

Gary's style was to hold his glove hand in front of his face when he was ready to receive the pitch, and he always held it just below his eyes so he could maintain eye contact with his pitcher. This time, however, he held his glove in front of his entire face. He wasn't budging on this. He didn't want to see me shake him off a third time. He was telling me that I was throwing a curve or we were not going.

Davey's strategy here was to take me out of myself and out of my game, whether I liked it or not. But my thinking was, I had such persistent control problems that the best game plan was to be super-aggressive in the early innings, to go with my fastball as long as it was working, then add my other pitches into the mix as I started to feel comfortable. Only I wasn't talented enough to simply go after these hitters. I had to show them something more. To be successful in the bigs, Davey believed, you needed to mix up your pitches right away, starting with the first batter of the game. And he was right. You need to develop a rhythm and a confidence, and to keep the hitters guessing. Otherwise, if you keep going at them with the same pitch, they'll catch up to it before long. So that's what I did that day. Reluctantly. Gary Carter and Davey Johnson won the stalemate and forced me into it. I came back with a curveball to Joe Orsulak, and after that I settled in and let Gary and Davey call the game. At the other end I looked up and I had pitched a complete-game shutout for my first win of the young season, with eleven strikeouts thrown in for good measure.

I was a new pitcher—all on the back of this little head game Davey had played out with me in the media, with Gary Carter backing him up behind the plate.

All of these approaches can work. The one that's most appropriate depends on the manager, the pitching coach, and the pitcher and their personalities. It has to make sense, and in 1992 the A's took the position that I was a mature professional athlete and should be able to hear a direct assessment of my strengths and weaknesses.

Dave Duncan's ideas about how I should think of myself as a pitcher put me in a whole different mind-set, I'll say that—and it took some getting used to. Indeed, it took the first half of the season. I was a middling 7–7 going into this start against Toronto, and a record like that can sometimes make you feel like you're not even there. You're not making a meaningful contribution. You're at .500, dead even, treading water. But then everything started to click as we looked ahead to the All-Star break. As a team, things were going well. We were trailing by a game or two in the standings, but we were playing good, smart, winning baseball.

Off the field, I was really enjoying my new surroundings. I mention this because frame of mind is a big part of a pitcher's makeup and game plan. It was for me, anyway; I needed to feel relaxed, and welcomed, and very much a part of things. Happily, there was no problem on that front with this Oakland team. We were a close-knit group. We played a lot of day games, for some reason, and usually, after a day game at home, we'd gather in somebody's backyard for a barbecue. With the Mets, usually just a few players would go out to a restaurant or a bar after a game, but here in Oakland it was a family affair. The players would take turns hosting, and we'd sit around the yard, sipping beers, eating burgers and steaks, talking baseball, watching our kids horse around. It was great. We all lived in Alameda County, within a couple miles of the stadium, so getting around was easy. Some weeks, we'd have a day game on Thursday, and another on Saturday and Sunday, so we'd bounce from house to house. For the most part, the older, more veteran players did the hosting. They were the ones who were set up to handle a large group, and they were the ones who could afford the steaks and the beer. Everybody was welcome. Out of twenty-five guys on the major league roster, maybe twenty would come, and they'd bring their wives and their kids. We'd shoot hoops, or play Wiffle ball, or toss around a football. It was just a nice time— and it rubbed off on some of the kids. Chris and Shelley Duncan were always around, soaking up the life of the major league ballplayer, as were Carney Lansford's kids, who also went on to play professionally.

That Oakland A's team was a talented group. We had Lansford, who won a batting title; Harold Baines, who'd go on to collect nearly three thousand hits; Willie Wilson, who'd been such a sparkplug for those strong Kansas City teams in the early 1980s; Dennis Eckersley, the dominant closer in the game; and Rick Honeycutt, our eighth-inning setup guy, back before the role had a name. Rickey Henderson and Mark McGwire were on that team, too, and José Canseco started the season with us but was traded midway through the year to Texas.

These guys cared about one another, which was great, but they cared about winning most of all, which was even better. I'd never been around a group of players who prepared so diligently for a ball game. They were real professionals—and they treated one another with enormous respect. Carney Lansford was such a respected presence in that clubhouse that no one would touch the postgame spread until he gave the nod; after a tough loss, he'd sit in front of his locker, and no player would eat until he moved to the table. He could sit there for a half hour, and guys would be dying to grab a bite of a sandwich or take a swig of beer, but no one would move. If Carney hit the shower directly after the game, we all had to wait for him to come back out to eat. It was an unspoken thing, but no one went against it. I'd never seen anything like that before, and I loved it.

These Toronto Blue Jays were a tough bunch, too. Dave Winfield, Robby Alomar, Joe Carter, Devon White, a young Jeff Kent, and an even younger John Olerud—there was an all-star in pretty much every spot in the batting order, and they could throw in guys like Jack Morris and Jimmy Key and Juan Guzman and shut you down. It felt like you didn't have a shot against these guys, but this was baseball and you always had a chance.

For whatever reason, I was on my game in that first matchup against Toronto, heading into the All-Star break. I had my good curveball working. My fastball was crisp. It felt like I could put the ball wherever I wanted, and I could get these guys to chase when I wanted them to chase. The one exception, early on: I walked Devon White to start the game. Devo fouled off four pitches before earning his pass. This might have rattled the old Ron Darling, but I kept hearing Dave Duncan's eulogy for the pitcher I used to be and decided to redouble my focus on Devo now that he was on base. The old Ron Darling might have walked him and forgotten about him, but the new Ron Darling wanted to erase him from the picture before focusing on the next batter, Roberto Alomar. It wasn't just about erasing him, of course. It was about managing an entire inning—defensively, as well as from the mound. It was about being a good caretaker of your team's fortunes, and putting yourself in a position to hand the game off to one of your bullpen guys with a lead. Sure enough, that's just what I did. I made that base runner a priority. I threw over to first straightaway. Then I fired a fastball past Alomar for a called strike. Then I threw a ball out of the strike zone, to see if the runner was going. He wasn't, so I threw over to first again, to keep him close. I varied my timing with each throw. When the count went to 2–1, a classic runner's count, I spun into my full-tilt pickoff move and caught Devo leaning. After that, I got Alomar to fly to right on the very next pitch, and Joe Carter on a strikeout swinging. I walked another batter in the second, but I settled down after that and retired the next sixteen batters, bringing me all the way to Candy Maldonado in the five hole to start the eighth. I'd thrown only about eighty-five pitches at this point in the game, which meant my arm was strong and good to go and I could forget for the time being about being a twenty-one-out pitcher. The game was stacking up as mine to finish, with the no-hitter just six outs away.

Now, I've always been fascinated by the thoughts that run through a pitcher's head when he's facing down immortality— and by the thoughts that don't. I found myself in this situation a handful of times in my career, and my thoughts tended to run along the same lines as they did in any other game. Giving my team a chance to win was paramount. Going deep into the game was also up there, along with finishing what I started and finishing strong. I can't stress this enough: I never gave a percolating no-hitter much thought. I was always aware of it, in a back-of-my-mind sort of way, and certainly I was more and more aware as a no-hit bid reached into the late innings, but it was never my focus.

There are just too many factors out of your control as a pitcher for you to count on throwing blanks for a full nine innings. It always struck me as the kind of thing you couldn't really shoot for. If it fell your way, that would be great. If it didn't, that'd be okay, too. It made more sense to focus on getting through each inning. Oh, I might dwell on a near no-hitter after the game, and run through all these *What if?* scenarios in my head, but while I was in the middle of the thing it was always just another ball game, just another hitter who was hoping to stand in my way and give me some trouble.

That was my view here. I'd taken a no-hitter into the eighth inning only one other time in my big league career, so this was new territory for me, but I tried to set that aside and go about my business. The guys on the bench weren't really saying anything about it, either. It was like the elephant in the room—we all knew it was there, but we dared not acknowledge its presence.

The score worked against me in a way. We'd gotten out to a big lead early, which always helps when you're shutting down your opponent, but I'm not so sure it helps when you're chasing a no-hitter. It removes a certain layer of pressure for a pitcher. You don't have to be so *fine* about things. A no-hitter, however, is built on pressure and precision. You can't exactly coast your way through a lineup; this is true even when you don't have a no-hitter going. As a pitcher, you always want the lead; you might even want a comfortable lead; but you don't want to be too comfortable because then you can get yourself into trouble. You want a cushion, but not too big a cushion. A score of 4–0 seems about right—enough of a lead to absorb a mistake or a misstep, but not so much of one that you take your foot off the gas.

Here we were up 8–0, so it's not like the outcome of the game was really in doubt. The only uncertainty was whether I could finish off this no-hitter, and as Candy Maldonado strode to the plate to lead off the eighth I allowed myself to think, Sure, Ronnie, what the hell, why not?

Candy Maldonado had a different thought. I left a 1–1 pitch out over the plate, and he drove a hard liner up the middle and into center field. It was a clean hit, which I guess is the way you want to lose a no-hitter. Here again, the old Ronnie might have been thrown, but the new-and-improved Ronnie bore down. I got Derek Bell to pop out in foul territory along the third-base line on the very next pitch, and then Tom Quinlan, who'd come on for Jeff Kent at third, grounded weakly back to me, and I trotted over to first and stepped on the bag for the second out while Maldonado advanced to second. Then the Toronto catcher, Pat Borders, worked me to a 3–1 count before flying out to center field to end the inning.

I wasn't exactly dejected as I stepped back into the visitors' dugout after the inning. *Disheartened* is probably a better description. *Disappointed,* maybe. But I also used that hit to recharge and refocus. Yeah, I'd lost the no-hitter, but I still had the shutout going, and we had the game in hand, so I turned my attention to finishing out the string.

LESS THAN TWO WEEKS LATER, we met up with these same Toronto Blue Jays, this time in Oakland. Once again, Devon White led off the game with a walk. Once again, I shook it off. I threw to first a bunch of times, but he stayed put. He moved to second on a groundout, but he was stranded there. With one out in the second, I found another small patch of trouble: I hit a guy, and walked the batter behind him, but I pulled it together to retire the next two batters to get out of the inning. After that, the Blue Jays went down one, two, three in the third, fourth, and fifth. I walked Roberto Alomar on four pitches with one out in the sixth, and he promptly stole second, but Joe Carter went down swinging and Dave Winfield lofted a 1–0 fastball to left for the third out of the inning.

By the seventh inning, we'd cobbled together a 3–0 lead, and the scoreboard once again showed that the Blue Jays had not gotten a hit. Candy Maldonado stepped to the plate to lead off the seventh—and he hit the ball to the deepest part of the infield, behind second base, allowing him to leg out Toronto's first hit of the game. It went down as an infield hit, but there was nothing cheap about it. Here again, I caught myself thinking that you want to see your no-hit bids broken up by something solid, but however it happens, a broken no-hitter is just that: broken.

Just like that, my second no-hit bid in two weeks was spoiled—by the same damn guy. Two first-pitch fastballs, and each one came back to bite me. But I couldn't fault myself for those pitches. Whenever I faced a guy who hit me pretty well, like Maldonado, I always liked to make sure I got the first pitch over for a strike, just to give myself a chance in the at-bat. It didn't do to hunt and peck with batters like that. The only way to get them out consistently was to pitch with some kind of advantage in the count—and the only way to do *that* was to get out in front. Even if it meant putting a fastball right down the middle of the plate at a time in the game when another pitcher might have looked to paint a couple corners.

My catcher that day was Jamie Quirk, who's now a bench coach for the Rockies. We were on such a high in that game, the two of us. Each pitch had a purpose. Each pitch hit its target. If Jamie called it up and in, I gave it to him up and in, and before it even reached Jamie's glove I knew he would call the next pitch down and away, and I knew I would give it to him. We were really in sync. In fact, we were so in sync that we made up a brand-new pitch during the game. It's the only time in my career I ever did *that,* but there it was. We just pulled it out of the air. Things were going so well that at one point Jamie put down two fingers and wiggled them. The two was our signal for a curveball. The wiggle was for a changeup. He wiggled the two, and I knew exactly what he meant: *take a little off the curveball.* I'd never gotten that sign from him before, we'd never talked about it before, but there was nothing to discuss. It just happened. And it worked. Everything worked that day. It gets that way sometimes, out there on that mound. It doesn't happen very often, but when it does it's a little bit magical.

After the game, Jamie came out to congratulate me, and to this day the exchange stands as the nicest compliment I ever received as a pitcher. Terry Steinbach was our main catcher; Jamie Quirk caught only once or twice a week, tops. But when it was Jamie's day to catch he'd be the first one at the ballpark, eight o'clock in the morning, excited and ready to go; that was just his personality. After that near no-hitter, he came out to the mound with this bubbling, infectious enthusiasm, and he reached for my hand and shook it and said, "R.J., you can fucking pitch."

I should mention here that when the no-hitter was finally broken, I didn't fully make the connection that it had been Maldonado on the spoiling end of the game in Toronto. I suppose I knew on some level, but I had put it out of my head during the course of this carbon-copy game in Oakland. It was only later, when the dust had cleared on this follow-up two-hit shutout, that the pieces fit themselves back together and I started to think how freaky and strange it was, the way these two games unfurled along the same lines.

That's baseball, I guess, and as I set out to chronicle the happy coincidence of these two games, I had meant to focus on just that. But there was more than mere serendipity at work here. There was a change in focus that every pitcher has to make at some point in his career. There was a survival-of-the-fittest adaptation, on the back of Dave Duncan's directive to shift my mind-set and remake myself into the finesse pitcher I might become. There's some chance mixed in here, too, for good measure, but chance doesn't just happen. You've got to work at it.

INNING SUMMARY

CANDY MALDONADO: line-drive single to
center field
DEREK BELL: foul pop-up to third baseman
TOM QUINLAN: groundout to pitcher (unassisted)
Maldonado advances to second
PAT BORDERS: flyout to center field

Clincher

September 22, 1988
Philadelphia Phillies vs. New York Mets
Shea Stadium, New York
Attendance: 45,274

There's no overstating the talent and expectations attached to the New York Mets teams of the late 1980s. We'd set the bar pretty damn high with our 108-win season on the way to the 1986 World Series championship. We had been fairly dominant that season, arguably the best team in recent baseball history, which meant that most folks thought we were a lock to contend for the division every year. That's a kind of double-edged prospect. In and around New York, there was all kinds of talk about how the Mets of the late 1980s could be like the great Cincinnati Reds and Oakland A's dynasties of the 1970s. The only trouble with the chatter was that it got ahead of our accomplishments.

Unfortunately, we didn't get it done in 1987, as I have mentioned, because of various off-field distractions and on-field disappointments and injuries, but we returned to form in 1988, on our way to another 100-win season. All was once again right with our world, at least for the time being. The World Series seemed ours for the taking. It had been a tight race for much of the summer, but by mid-September the Pittsburgh Pirates were the only NL East team in our rearview mirror—and they were well off the pace. Remember those great Pirates teams from that period? Bonds, Bonilla, Van Slyke; Doug Drabek and John Smiley in the rotation. They were solid, top to bottom, but we were deeper, stronger, *better.* Plus, we'd been down this road before, so we had that going for us, too. We were eleven games up in the standings with just twelve games to play when my turn in the rotation came around—against Philadelphia at Shea. The way it fell on the calendar, the Mets could potentially clinch the division if I pitched well enough to help us get the win. Even though first place seemed comfortably in hand, it's always a big deal to lock things up, and here it was a serendipitous big deal that I'd be handed the key to turn the lock.

I remember being jealous in 1986 when Dwight Gooden got to pitch the clincher against the Cubs at home. It was every young ballplayer's fantasy. If you're a golfer, you grew up dreaming about that last long putt to win the U.S. Open. If you're a basketball player, it was sinking a buzzer-beater to give your team the lead and the championship as time ran out. For a pitcher, it meant being on the mound for the final out of a clinching game. It didn't matter if it was a division championship, a league championship, or a World Series title—only that you would have the chance to jump into the arms of your teammates and go a little bit crazy. That was the ultimate fantasy, and I watched Doc go through those motions, finishing off a complete-game victory against the Cubs, as the Shea Stadium faithful spilled out onto the field and proceeded to tear the place up. Doc had to run through a gauntlet of fans, just like Chris Chambliss when he hit that game winner against the Royals, and I hung back and thought, Gee, wouldn't it be great to be in that scrum? Just once?

On paper, the 1986 division clincher was even less dramatic than this 1988 game would turn out to be. That first time around, we were up by nineteen games, so by August the division was never really in doubt. The clincher came in mid-September, and if it hadn't come that night it would have found us soon enough. Still, it's a wonderful, gratifying, wish-fulfilling thing to know with finality that you have outpaced and outperformed your peers, and to look ahead to a league championship and (hopefully!) a World Series title, so we celebrated the hell out of the thing.

This was my shot to be in the mix as we closed out the 1988 season, just as Doc had been two years earlier. I'd been watching the scoreboard for days, hoping things might shake out in just this way, but it was a secret hope. It wasn't exactly the kind of thing you could share with your teammates. Even among us pitchers, it wasn't discussed. About the only thing you could say publicly in this regard was that you were hoping the Mets could tie things up in front of the home crowd. You could even make a statement like that on the road and get away with it, for the way it suggests selflessness and wanting to give something back to the fans. It's not like I was rooting for the Mets to lose and thereby put me in a position to pitch the deciding game, or for the Pirates to keep winning, but I wouldn't have minded too much if we had to keep putting off our celebration until I could *fully* participate.

Of course, it wouldn't be enough to simply pitch well and give way to our bullpen in the eighth or ninth inning. It would have to be a complete-game victory if I wanted to run around on the field like a lunatic after recording the last out, and complete games were hard to come by. I would notch seven complete games that year—the high-water mark for my career—but a lot can happen over a stretch of nine innings. You can pitch great, but your team might not get it going offensively. You can pitch into some hard luck. Your pitch count can run away from you to where there might not be a whole lot left in the cannon by the late innings. You can pitch into a jam and find yourself facing a tough batter who's had some success against you over the years. You can be lifted for a pinch hitter to help push across a run in a close game.

There weren't a whole lot of complete games being pitched in that era, at least not compared to the 1960s and 1970s. I remember looking at Mel Stottlemyre's career stats one day in the locker room and marveling at the fact that he had pitched 152 complete games in his eleven-year career, including a career best of 24 in 1969. From 2000 through the 2008 season, no pitcher has led the league in complete games with a double-digit total. So while a complete game in 1988 wasn't exactly the tall order it would be today, it was close— and it was certainly a bigger deal than it would have been when I came of age as a baseball fan.

To my thinking, on this night, it was a complete game or bust. If I didn't finish the game and we still managed to win, I supposed I would pop a bottle of champagne and celebrate with my teammates, but it wouldn't be the same. I wanted what Dwight had had. I wanted that moment where Jesse Orosco throws his glove in the air, and that image shows up on the back pages of the New York tabloids. Those guys had had it, and now it was my turn.

I'd pitched in a momentous deciding game before—Game 7 of the 1986 World Series—but I hadn't recognized it as such at the time. It doesn't get much more momentous than that, and yet for some reason that game didn't register on my schedule in any kind of personal way. It was a big game for us as a team. It was a must-win—the quintessential win-or-go-home scenario—but it would have been unrealistic to think I could go nine innings against the Red Sox in Game 7. It was my third start of the Series—my third start in ten days. My approach to that game was to go as hard as I could for as long as I could, and hope that the effort would be enough to put us in a position to win. In the end, I didn't go as hard or as long as I would have liked, but we got it done.

This time around, I did the math and consulted the standings as soon as all the scores were in from the games of September 21, and I knew I'd have my shot the next day. I looked ahead to the opposing lineup, the same way I always did as a start approached. These Phillies were the weak link in the NL East that season, thirty-three games back in the standings, but our recent experience with Philadelphia was that they took it to us when the games mattered most. In 1986, before Doc's clincher, we went to Veterans Stadium with a chance to lock up the division. We had to take two out of three, but we ended up getting swept, so we'd seen what the Phillies could do when a Mets team was poised to clinch.

Up and down the Philadelphia lineup, there were players who could hurt you. (At least, they could hurt *me*, as they had shown in the past.) At the same time, they could be vulnerable at the plate; the baseball maxim is that good pitching can always keep a lid on good hitting, and it applied here. Don't misunderstand me: these Phillies had some talent—guys like Phil Bradley, in the leadoff spot; Ron Jones, a terrific athlete who would have probably gone on to a stellar career if he hadn't run into an outfield wall and messed up his knee; Ricky Jordan, a tall, free-swinging first baseman; Von Hayes, who always gave me fits. It's just that along with their raw talent, there was also a dose of impatience. A perfect example was my old nemesis Juan Samuel, who during his first couple years in the bigs had emerged as the next Rogers Hornsby. (It didn't exactly play out that way for him, but he had a good long run as one of the preeminent players in the game—and, alongside Ryne Sandberg, the most explosive second baseman in the league.) Juan was the kind of hitter who could carry his club for a week or two, but he was streaky, and here I hoped to catch him in one of his rough spots.

Lance Parrish was the Phillies catcher. We used to call him the Human Muscle, because he was just that—all muscle. One of the first ballplayers to really work out, he was a formidable presence in those days, with those big guns sticking out of his short-sleeve jersey. No other ballplayer was cut quite the same way, and while he wasn't hitting for average that year, he was still a fearsome presence in the middle of that lineup.

The crafty left-hander Don Carman was the scheduled starter, but to tell the truth I never paid that much attention to my opposite number on the hill, because it never felt to me like I was directly opposing the other team's pitcher. All that stuff you read and hear, about head-to-head matchups between pitchers, I don't think it really exists—at least not in the heads of any pitchers in my acquaintance. I was going up against the other team's lineup. My teammates were going up against the other team's pitcher. That's all. The two of us just happened to be working the same game.

Here, though, I gave Carman's assignment some thought, because the game loomed in such a significant way. I kept coming back to the fact that Carman always managed to pitch

Keith Hernandez tough. Keith gave Carman trouble, but then Carman gave it right back. He always used to throw at Keith's head, right under his chin, in such a way that Keith's helmet would invariably go one way off his head and his bat would fall out of his hands in the other direction. Almost every game, it seemed, Carman would come in high and tight to Keith, who had a habit of leaning in over the plate, and Carman must have hated that Keith always managed to get big hits off him.

That's the battle I knew we'd see between Keith Hernandez and Don Carman. I should have been thinking about the rest of the Phillies lineup. How Juan Samuel hit me pretty hard. Von Hayes, too. There were a couple guys in there who'd had some success against me, but overall they were a team that could be pitched to. If you had your stuff, you could keep these hitters off the bases. That sounds like an obvious assessment, but it's not always the case. A lot of times, you can bring all your tools to the game and the other guys can keep battling until they wear you down. The good teams are like that, up and down the order. They break you down after a while. They hang in there and make you work for it, hard.

These Phillies weren't like that. Nothing against them as individual players, but as a team they could be beat—which I guess explained their 60–91 record going into this game. As individuals, though, they could be tough. Even their bench was tough. Greg Gross was one of the premier pinch hitters in the league at that time, and I thought back to one of the last times I'd faced him. It was June 28, 1987, at Veterans Stadium. This was the one other time I'd taken a no-hitter into the eighth inning; Greg Gross pinch-hit for Kent Tekulve to lead off and promptly stroked a triple to deep center. That put an end to that. The next guy up was Juan Samuel, and he singled to left, bringing home Gross and sending me to the showers. The Mets had been up 4–0 going into the eighth, and we ended up losing the game, so these Phillies could break your heart if you gave them the chance.

The plan, then, was not to give them that chance.

This was easier said than done, because the Phillies had me wired for disappointment. Once, that wiring left me a little red-faced out there on that mound; this one requires a bit of a setup. I was at the point in my career where I'd gone from not looking at the guy as he rounded the bases after hitting a home run off me to not even following the flight of the ball as it left the ballpark. I gave up a lot of home runs in my career, and after a while you can tell from the crack of the bat; I'd just gotten sick of looking. I'd gotten sick of giving the hitter the satisfaction of seeing my head jerk around toward the outfield fence, to watch the ball go over the wall. (Not exactly the most mature response to getting beat, perhaps, but I still had a lot to learn.) Instead, I would listen to the sound the ball made as it hit the bat, and for good measure I'd watch the body language of the other guys on the field and in the dugout. At home, if it got really quiet that usually meant it was a home run, and on the road, if it got really noisy that usually meant I'd given one up. And so over time I fell into the bad habit of walking off the mound and raising my glove to face the catcher or the home plate umpire, ready to receive the new ball to be put in play.

And that's just what happened here—sort of. With two outs, the Human Muscle rocketed a ball to deep center field. I couldn't watch, but I could see Gary Carter brushing the dirt around home plate, getting ready for the next batter, looking down. Catchers, too, have their own routines, especially when it comes to winning the head games we tend to play with our opponents. He was like me. He didn't want to give the other guys any additional satisfaction, any extra edge, so he went about his business, tidying the batter's box for the next hitter, putting out the all-important message that the home run was no big deal. I caught Kid's eye for the briefest moment, but he quickly looked down, and I thought, Aw, Parrish got all of it.

So what did I do? I raised my glove, pocket ready, and waited for someone to throw me a new ball. I hung there for a long few beats, until finally Kid smiled and ran off the field and into our dugout.

He got me pretty good. As it happened, our center fielder, Mookie Wilson, had been camped out under the ball and had made the catch for the third out of the inning. Carter was a great student of the game; he was also a great needler. He knew my strengths and my weaknesses and my lazy habits. He knew I wouldn't follow the crack of a hard-hit ball like that. I'd had no idea Kid had realized what I was doing, but he had, and he nailed me for it and left me hanging, and as I threw my glove onto the dugout bench I turned to him and said, "You fuckin' asshole. I can't believe it. You got me."

IN 1988, WE HAD THE DIVISION WON, going away, but you never know, right? And it's not like any of us were so damn used to winning that it was old. Winning never gets old. Plus, we wanted to do it on our terms. It wouldn't do to lose a ball game and then have the Pirates lose a game so we'd just kind of back into the pennant.

The Phillies scratched out a run in the fourth to open the scoring, and I was mostly to blame, hitting Phil Bradley to start the inning and then walking right fielder Ron Jones on six pitches. A Ricky Jordan grounder to second moved the runners up, so the Phillies had men on second and third with one out when Von Hayes arrived. His first time up, I'd gotten him to ground out to first base, but here he scorched a ball to left that Kevin McReynolds managed to grab for the second out. Bradley tagged and scored, and we were down 1–0.

We came back to tie the game in the bottom of the fifth. Shortstop Kevin Elster led off the inning with a double to left. I stepped to the plate with a chance to move Kevin over to third, but I couldn't get the job done and ended up grounding out to Chris James at third. (When you take special pride in the well-roundedness of your game, these are the missed opportunities that eat at you over the years.) Then Mookie Wilson legged out an infield single between first and second, moving Elster to third the way I should have done; Gregg Jefferies, our rookie third baseman, brought Elster in to score with a ground ball to second base.

We scored another run in the sixth, on a wild pitch, and as I stepped out to the mound to start the seventh inning I realized there was no margin for error in this game. Judging by the standings and the calendar, it should have been a laugher, but these Phillies just wouldn't go away. Don Carman was pitching a tremendous game. I looked on and thought, Why does he care? What does this game matter to him? And for all I know, he was looking across the diamond at me, wondering the same damn thing.

But it *did* matter to me. And it mattered to my teammates. To a man, we didn't want to let an opportunity to clinch get away from us. We didn't want to send a signal to the Dodgers, or whoever we would end up meeting in the playoffs, that we let the last-place Phillies stiff-arm us out of a celebration. It was a statement game, as much as anything, so we battled. Plus, those Mets teams of the late 1980s had a real love affair with the fans, and we wanted to wrap things up at Shea—for them as much as for us.

Carman wasn't giving anything away, but we eked out another run in the bottom of the seventh. (That's the sign of a championship team, we all thought: to small-ball our way to a run in three straight innings against a pitcher who was on his game.) Mookie pounded a single through the hole between short and third. Jefferies flied out to right. Keith grounded to second, sending Mookie to second base. Phillies manager Lee Elia came out to talk to his pitcher at this point—either to settle him down or to take his temperature.

I'd been on the receiving end of these types of visits a bunch of times, and it's never pleasant. It's usually routine, but it's not the good kind of routine. You watch the manager walk out to the mound, and all you can think is, Hey, if I'd done my job, I could have saved him the trip. The conversations aren't much, but it's the visit that matters, and here I could imagine what transpired. Lee Elia, one of the game's good guys, probably asked Carman if he had anything left. Carman probably said he wanted to take it to Strawberry and finish out the inning. It was a lefty-lefty matchup, so the outcome of the visit was already tilted in Carman's favor. As long as he expressed confidence in his ability to get this last out, Elia would leave him in the game. If he wavered or waffled in any way, he was gone.

Strawberry was probably the most dangerous power hitter in the game at that point. He'd hurt the Phillies all year long. Carman might have said he wanted to pitch to him, but judging from his approach he didn't want to pitch to him, not really. First he missed with a fastball, low and away. I thought it was interesting that he threw a fastball, because conventional baseball wisdom said that if you were trying to pitch around a guy you started him off with a breaking ball. I never liked that approach—you could always hang a breaking ball—so I tended to go against conventional wisdom on this one. Carman did, too, apparently. He missed with another fastball on his second pitch, and I thought for sure he'd come back with a breaking ball. When you're behind 2–0 to a dangerous hitter with a runner in scoring position, you should always be thinking breaking ball, out of the strike zone. You've pitched yourself to where you're now thinking you don't *really* want to face him. You have a base open. Maybe he'll get himself out.

Lee Elia must have been furious. His pitcher had just told him he wanted to go after our cleanup hitter, but he couldn't get it done. He'd missed badly with two pitches, and now he was looking at a 3–0 count; Elia gave the signal to walk the batter. Four fingers down—the Wiggle Four. No pitcher ever likes to see that sign, especially when he knows he's coming out of the game. I mean, who wants to put a runner on and then leave his fate to the next guy in line?

Carman completed the intentional pass, and the Phillies manager was out of the dugout and halfway back to the mound before Darryl was halfway down the first base line. Let me tell you, Lee Elia didn't look happy. And Don Carman wasn't exactly happy to see him again so soon after his last trip. Carman had known Elia would be coming, but he wasn't thrilled about it. As tough as it is for a pitcher to wait on the mound for the manager to come out to talk to you, it's even tougher when he comes right back out to pull you from the game, because you know he's thinking he should have made the move on the first trip.

Meanwhile, I was sitting on the bench thinking, Man, this is taking a long time. Two trips to the mound, back-to-back. A lot of time between pitches. When it's late in a close game that's fallen into one of these long innings at the plate, a pitcher in the dugout whose team is taking its turn at bat can find that his thoughts run away from him. On the one hand, you want those long innings, because you need the insurance runs they usually provide, but on the other hand, if you're sitting for too long, you might lose your timing. You probably had a nice rhythm going. It's a real catch-22 situation. In this game, however, it's not like we were piling on any runs. In fact, we'd yet to push across another run that inning, so all we were doing was giving my arm a chance to cool down and my rhythm a chance to fall away.

There are a couple things you can do as a starting pitcher to help counter the negative effects of a long inning at the plate for your team. I used to try to stay on my feet as much as possible. I'd walk up and down the dugout, pacing, or I'd slip into the clubhouse for a cup of coffee. I didn't like it when I sat for too long. The main thing I used to do, after a long half inning at the plate, was take a more purposeful approach to my warm-up when I got back out there. Normally, my warm-up before each inning was basically just going through the motions, but after a long inning I'd bear down. I'd concentrate on how I planned to face the next hitter. If it was Lance Parrish, say, I'd finish off my warm-up with four targeted pitches: fastball away, curveball, fastball in, and split-finger. This way, I'd throw all my pitches in succession, and hopefully I'd place them where I wanted to. It didn't always happen that way, but that was my intention.

Kent Tekulve came on in relief of Carman, setting up one of the most dazzling plays I got to see in a Met uniform. Kevin McReynolds hit a soft ground ball to third that he managed to beat out for an infield hit, but the dazzling piece was that Mookie Wilson came around from second to score. You don't see that very often. It wasn't a hit-and-run, and Mookie certainly wasn't trying to steal third. He just went on contact, and when Phillies third baseman Chris James made the throw across the diamond Mookie kept going. He didn't hesitate. I can't be sure he didn't get any kind of sign, but I don't think he did. It was just good, hard, smart baseball, and it caught

Phillies first baseman Ricky Jordan napping, because he certainly didn't expect the runner from second to head home on an infield hit. But he didn't know Mookie, I guess. He didn't know that this guy played with such exuberance you could never be sure what he might do. That's why Mookie was always one of my favorite teammates. He was such a beautiful player. He made the game exciting, and I can't recall a more thrilling, more typical Mookie moment than this mad sprint to home to give us a little bit of a cushion going into the final two innings of a close game.

That seventh-inning insurance run was key, because when I went back out there for the top of the eighth I knew I couldn't be beat. I felt loose, strong. I was working quickly now, with a little more confidence behind each pitch. I knew full well that baseball is a game that feasts on mistakes, but now I had a cushion, so that even if I made a mistake we'd be covered. I might hang a breaking ball, but I wasn't about to hang two. Once we got that 3–1 lead, it felt like 8–1 to me. Greg Gross came out to pinch-hit for Tekulve to lead off the eighth, and I tried to push his previous eighth-inning pinch hit against me from my head. This time, I tried to nibble. I knew Gross liked the ball away, so I planned to come in on him.

Tom Seaver's mantra was Get the first out of the inning. You always hear how important it is to throw the first pitch for a strike, but Tom didn't care about the first pitch. He would waste a first pitch if he felt he had to. He cared about the first batter. Set him down, and you're on your way. That was his thing, and he drummed it into me that one August we pitched in the same rotation, and that's what I caught myself thinking here: *Just get this first out, Ronnie. Keep the ball inside. Work quickly. Help your teammates stay sharp in the field.* Happily, I did just that. I busted Gross inside and all he could manage was a grounder down to Keith Hernandez at first.

Keith collected the ball and stepped on the bag, and then he ran it back over to me with a rallying-cry roar. He screamed, "Five more, Ronnie! Five more!" That's the type of player he was. There was no such thing as a meaningless game to Keith. There was no such thing as routine. He played with a kid's enthusiasm, always firing himself up. His teammates, too. It didn't matter that this was a bad Phillies team. It didn't matter that we had a big lead in the standings, or that first place was a virtual lock. He played hard, all the time, and he expected everyone around him to play hard, too. So he screamed. Loud. "Five more, Ronnie! Five more!" Counting out the outs. Like everything was on the line.

Not everyone responded to Keith's brand of enthusiasm, but I found him to be a great motivator. I liked it whenever he singled me out and tried to lift my game, but some of my Met teammates found it a little unsettling. Once, Doc Gooden came out on the short end of a 1–0 game after balking in the lone run from third when Keith called to him from first while Doc was getting ready to pitch. Keith was only trying to motivate Doc, but Doc thought he had some important piece of advice, so he stepped off in the wrong way, thinking he'd ask Keith to repeat himself.

At last, my clinching moment was close enough to taste, and looking back I think I let it get ahead of me a little bit because I promptly gave up a line-drive single to right center, to Phil Bradley. That brought Mel Stottlemyre out to the mound. This was a bit of a surprise. It shouldn't have been a surprise, but it was just the same. I knew it was late in a close game. I knew my manager, Davey Johnson, wasn't going to give me a huge margin for error. I knew we had one of the best closers in baseball in Randy Myers, to shut things down if I got into trouble. But I still felt like I could close out this game on my own. I hated it that Mel was coming out to talk to me, but I might have expected it. Still, I turned away from him as he approached, and as I did I saw Randy Myers throwing out in the bullpen. It was the first time that night a relief pitcher had been summoned to get ready, and that's always a powerful signal to a starting pitcher that he's on a short leash. I knew as much, of course, but I didn't like to be reminded of it in such an obvious way. It's a public vote of no confidence, just like a trip to the mound from your manager or pitching coach.

Mel told me later that this was one of the longest walks he ever made as a pitching coach. Davey Johnson told him to come out to talk to me, but Mel had no idea what he should say. It was a tough spot. If it had been a World Series game, there was no question they'd take me out if I gave up another hit. If we were in the middle of a pennant race, they'd be watching me closely. But I'd been fairly cruising through this Phillies lineup, my pitch count was low, and I was still throwing hard. There were a ton of games left on the schedule. There was really nothing on the line here. If we didn't wrap up the division on this night, we'd wrap it up the next.

"How you feeling, Ronnie?" Mel said, when he finally reached.

"Feeling great, Mel," I said. "Let me finish this up."

Revisiting that moment, I see that there was no reason for me to be so confident—the tying run was at the plate!—but when you're a young athlete and things are going well, you tend to overestimate your control over certain game situations. And here I thought I was in complete control.

For some reason, Mel seemed to think so, too. He was just out there to take my pulse, that's all. That, and he wanted to give Myers some time to get warm, if it turned out we needed to go to him after all. So Mel kicked at the dirt a little bit, and then I kicked at the dirt a little bit, and together we looked at the ground for a while, and after a couple beats of neither one of us really saying anything he made to leave. He said, "All right, Ronnie. Let's do it."

Ron Jones came up next, and he hit the first pitch on the ground past Keith's glove hand, moving Bradley to third. I didn't even have a chance to settle into the at-bat. Just like that, I had runners on the corners with only one out, and I'd let some of the air out of that two-run cushion. Still, I wasn't *really* worried, but then I looked up and saw Mel and Davey talking in the dugout. I could only imagine what they were talking about. I knew Mel was always on the side of his pitchers. He knew I was still strong. He knew how much I wanted to stay out there and finish the job. Davey probably wanted to give me the hook and bring in Myers, to avoid the second-guessing that would surely find him if I faltered, but Mel must have won the argument because I stayed out there to face Jordan.

To be honest, I wasn't all that worried about Ricky Jordan. I wasn't all that worried about that runner on third, either. Maybe I should have been, but I wasn't. I was too cocky to worry, too full of myself. Plus, I always felt like, for me, Ricky Jordan was an out. To be fair, he was a dangerous hitter, and he could always run into one, but I tended to get the better of him in our matchups—and that was my plan here.

Meanwhile, the crowd was going completely crazy. It was insane. I hadn't really noticed the crowd until just now. The New York fans were tremendous in those days, and they really pulled for us. For this game, the Mets front office had requested a greater police presence than they'd had at Shea in the past—folks had spilled onto the field when we clinched in 1986 and they didn't want the fans to dig up the grass—so there were dozens of mounted New York City cops gathering in the outfield. I first spotted them out in the bullpen, when I snuck that peek at Randy Myers warming up: about eight or nine horses hugging the bullpen fence, waiting to be let out of the gate. It was an odd sight. (Horses in the bullpen? Come on!)

Jordan swung at the first pitch. He hit the ball hard—he actually had a better swing than Ron Jones, who'd pushed that last pitch through for a single—but he happened to hit it to Kevin Elster, our smooth-fielding shortstop. I loved when Kevin played behind me, because he made all those tough plays, and he made them look easy. Here he glided to his left and scooped the ball to Timmy Teufel covering second, and Timmy pivoted and threw down to Keith to complete the double play. One pitch, two outs. That means I got a little lucky, I guess, but that's the great thing about baseball. Bad luck can get you into sudden trouble. Good luck can get you out of it. And sometimes it balances out.

I came back out to start the ninth to the biggest swirl of crowd noise I could remember. Bigger than during the World Series, it seemed—although I can't believe that this was the case. And yet, when I was in its middle, the moment loomed pretty damn large. Folks were caught up in it—me especially. Everyone was standing, stomping, cheering. The guys in the dugout were on the top step. It was all I could do to shut out the din and focus on the next three hitters.

One of the first thoughts I had, as I completed my warm-ups, was that I didn't want to be the guy to disappoint all these people. My teammates. The fans. The Mets front office. My family. It wasn't like me to make room for such a negative thought at such a critical moment, but there it was, and before I could shake it Von Hayes stepped up to the plate. As I went into my motion he turned as if to bunt. He was just looking to take the pitch, to rattle me. There was no way he'd be bunting here, I knew. The Phillies needed base runners, this was true, but you're not about to send up your cleanup hitter to bunt his way on to start the ninth. Plus, the convention in baseball at the time was to take a pitch to start the inning if you were down a run or two, to maybe work a walk and get something going. You don't see that as much these days. Guys come up swinging. That's the great push-me/pull-you of these late-inning matchups. The pitcher is fighting to get ahead in the count, while the batter is fighting to get up in the count. I felt certain Von Hayes would be taking in this spot, and knowing that gave me a little bit of an edge, so I threw him a pitch right down the middle for a strike. I worked him to a 1–2 count, then struck him out with a split-finger fastball.

Juan Samuel was next, and I pushed him to a 1–2 count as well. I looked at the game tape recently and noticed that I stepped off the mound here. I took a deep breath. I spit. I hadn't remembered that. It meant I was a little nervous, because I rarely spit when I pitched. I used to chew a little bit of tobacco between starts, but never when I was pitching, so it strikes me now as a show of nerves. It was something to do, is all. Then I climbed back on the mound and got the sign from Gary Carter. Kid wanted me to throw a split-finger, down. I thought that was a good call. I put the pitch just where I wanted it, and Samuel chopped it right back to the box for the second out of the inning.

Here I stepped off the mound again—this time to take in the scene. For the first time in my career, I allowed my focus to drift at a critical point in the game. I took myself out of the moment. It's a rookie mistake, only I was no rookie. I should have known better, but I couldn't help myself. I quickly scanned the crowd, looking for my parents. I wanted to see the smiles I knew I'd find on their faces, and sure enough, after peering into the section where I knew they'd be sitting, I found just that. Man, they were beaming. They were surrounded by members of the extended Mets family. Wives, kids, parents . . . everyone was pumped, ecstatic. The faces of the crowd were painted with sheer joy.

And then I lost myself in all those smiles.

It took just two or three seconds for me to take all of this in, but in those few beats I had time to think that this was what actors must feel like at the end of a great Broadway show, when they step out from behind the curtain to take a bow and get a chance to look out on all the people in the audience. I don't know why that thought popped into my head, but it did. Of course, most actors wait until the end of their performance to survey the crowd. Not me. I still had some performance left, and no less a menacing presence at the plate than Lance Parrish to keep me from taking my bow.

Finally, I climbed back onto the mound and tried to get my head back into the game, but when I reached into my glove for the ball I couldn't feel the seams. It was the strangest, most terrifying thing, almost like an episode of *The Twilight Zone.* The ball felt like a cue ball in my hands, and I have to think now that I brought that feeling on myself by stepping out of the game for a moment. Nothing like this had ever happened to me before—not in the bigs, not in the minors, not in college, not even in Little League. I could have kicked myself. Throughout my career, I'd taken great pride in being a dependable teammate. I might get beat from time to time, but I never beat myself. I'd take the ball every fifth day, and I'd give myself over totally to each start, and I'd do everything in my power to give my team a chance to win. Here, I'd let that dependability slip, because I'd lost my focus.

I'd let the moment get the better of me, and now I couldn't even feel the damn ball.

I felt like such a dolt.

When I stepped off the mound and studied the crowd, I moved out of that competitive box I climbed into at the start of each game. I flung off that cape that all pitchers put on before they take the hill. I took this great, grand moment for granted, and looked to soak it in before it was mine. It was selfish, really. Amateurish. And I regretted it right away. Parrish had gotten a hit off me in his last time up, so there was that thought rattling around in my head, alongside all these other terrifying thoughts that had to do with not being able to get a grip on the ball. All in all, I was a mess.

For these last couple batters, I'd been throwing the ball as hard as I ever had in my career. A radar gun would have clocked me at 92, 93 miles an hour—hot stuff, for me. But speed is nothing without control, and I got behind Parrish 2–0 with two balls so far out of the strike zone I'm amazed they even found their way into Carter's glove.

Whatever mojo a pitcher has when he's out there on the mound, it had up and left me in a foolish hurry. I look back on that moment and realize that you can't ever let that concentration slip away. You cannot treat it lightly or take it for granted, because you only have a tenuous hold on it in the first place.

Carter knew right away that something was wrong, and he came out to talk to me, to settle me down. He said, "You all right?"

I nodded.

He said, "How you feeling?"

I said, "I'll get it, Kid. I'll get it."

I couldn't exactly tell him my mojo was gone, could I?

Parrish helped me out on the next pitch. He swung at a

ball out of the strike zone, and after that I clicked back in. I got the feeling back in my hand, I got my concentration back, and I ended up getting Parrish on a split-finger in the dirt to end the game and give us the division. But in the adrenaline rush that found me after that final out there was also this weirdly unsettling knot in my stomach, because I knew how dangerously close I had come to giving it all away.

In every other respect, it was the moment I'd imagined. The mounted policemen rode onto the field with their horses. The fans stayed where they were, and did their wild jumping up and down in the stands. And my teammates gathered in that inevitable scrum.

One of the photographers covering the team snapped a photo just before our celebration on the field, and it stands as my single favorite picture of my time in a Met uniform. It's a shot of Gary Carter and me shaking hands in front of the mound. Kid was the first one to reach me, and he came at me with his right hand extended. I remember thinking it was such a professional, businesslike approach. Every other time I'd seen a pennant-clinching game, there were hugs and high fives and backslaps all around. Guys were jumping all over one another. But here Kid just walked purposefully to me with a congratulatory handshake, his eyes wide with excitement.

Of course, we quickly turned that handshake into an embrace, and we all started jumping around right after that picture was taken, but in that one freeze-frame moment was everything I knew and loved about those Mets teams of the 1980s. There was our thoroughgoing professionalism. There was a sense that we were expected to win, and to carry ourselves as winners. And there was a sense of pure joy about to burst forth.

When we were done with our jumping around on the field, we retreated to the clubhouse for more of the same, only here I noticed how tired I was. I hadn't felt tired during the game, not at all, but the feeling came over me right after that final out. I was spent, tapped, done. Relieved, too. Maybe it had to do with how anxious I had been, during those tense few moments on the mound, when I thought I'd let things slip away. Or maybe I was just drained.

Whatever it was, I wandered into the small room behind the trainer's room, where I used to take my pregame naps. No one used that room after games unless there had been an injury. I closed the door behind me. I still wore my full uniform. I'd dropped my hat and glove by my locker, but I had my spikes on, and my jersey, and I moved directly toward the quiet of that small room. All around me, my teammates were going crazy, spraying and chugging champagne, jumping and laughing and hugging one another. That was certainly appropriate, but I wasn't ready to whoop it up just yet. I wanted to sit and think things through. Back in 1986, I'd been all over this celebration. Each time out—the division clincher, the NL pennant, and the Series win—I'd had my arms around my buddies, and I'd made noise with the best of them. This time, though, I sought peace and quiet, and once I found it I shut the door behind me and sat myself down, hard. Then I let out what had to be the biggest sigh in the history of big sighs. You could probably hear it on the other side of the door, that's the kind of relief I felt at that moment.

I sat there by myself for fifteen, twenty minutes. I knew I had obligations on the other side of that door. I had interviews to grant, teammates to thank, congratulations to receive. That was all part of the game, but I figured that stuff could wait. At just that moment, all I wanted was to let the whole of my baseball life wash over me. I tried to think about my parents and the first times we'd stood in the backyard, playing catch. I thought about my dad coaching my Little League teams.

Strangely, I caught myself thinking about a championship game I'd played alongside my brother Eddie. I was pitching. There were two outs. A ground ball came my brother's way and he muffed it, and two runs came around to score. It cost us the game. My poor brother was devastated. I felt terrible for Eddie, and as we walked from the field to the car I took his hand. We walked around the parking lot and headed home on foot. I must have been about ten years old; he must have been about nine. We had to cross this little highway, and it probably wasn't the smartest, safest move, but we kept walking. He cried as we walked, and I tried to comfort him. I told him it was no big deal, that it was just a game.

That's where I drifted, in those first few moments following the final out of this pennant-clinching game. Back to Little League. Back to this gentle point of connection with my little brother. Back to college. Back to my first spring training. Back to my first big league uniform and the wet brown spray of Rod Hodges's tobacco juice that dotted my starched white pant leg for my entire first game. Back to everything basic about me and baseball. Back to everyone who had ever had a hand in my career, even if only to offer a push in the right direction.

After these fifteen, twenty minutes of quiet reflection, I stood and made my way back out to the clubhouse, where the celebration was still raging. (It takes more than twenty minutes to drink all that champagne!) The rumpus had started without me, of course, but I slipped right into it. For some reason, though, I found myself holding back a little. I didn't spray any champagne over my teammates' heads, the way I had in 1986. I didn't jump up and down like a lunatic. I thought, That stuff is for the younger kids. This was their time to strut, their time to go nuts. I was twenty-eight years old, and full enough of myself to think I was some wizened old veteran, but I was a full-fledged professional baseball player by this point. I couldn't afford to let my concentration slip—not after the way it had nearly gotten away from me on the mound before I'd faced that final batter. I still had a job to do—and, in the end, I couldn't quite accomplish it.

The resonant message of this clinching inning? As sweet as this moment was, it turned sour on me soon enough, and I suppose that's the great lesson of the game. We couldn't fight our way past the Dodgers in the National League Championship Series, and I was no help at all. I had the ball for a deciding Game 7, at Dodger Stadium, but I couldn't get out of the second inning. Hell, I couldn't even get an *out* in the second inning. I left with the Mets down 6–0, and that's how it ended. So when I reach back to that 1988 season I rarely catch myself thinking of that clinching game against Philadelphia. I think instead about the series that got away from us as a result of my bad outing. I think about what might have been.

What had been a moment to behold might have been a championship in the making—but, in true baseball fashion, it evaporated in no time at all.

INNING SUMMARY

VON HAYES: strikeout, swinging
JUAN SAMUEL: groundout to pitcher
LANCE PARRISH: strikeout, swinging

The Old College Try

May 21, 1981
St. John's Redmen vs. Yale Bulldogs
Yale Field, West Haven, Connecticut
Attendance: about 2,500

I had the good fortune to pitch in one of the more memorable games in college baseball history—an extra-inning affair in the first round of the 1981 NCAA Northeast Regional tournament—and I offer it here as a textbook example of the beautiful cruelty of our national pastime. The bittersweet takeaway of this game, for me, is that sometimes you can perform gloriously and still come out on the short side of the score.

Let me set the scene: the winner of the regional tournament would receive a spot in the national championships, to be held later that summer in Omaha, Nebraska. This was a big deal, and as luck would have it, Yale had been selected as the site of the tournament. It's always helpful to have the home-field advantage in postseason play, but here it was especially so. Yale Field is a storied baseball-only stadium, with horseshoe-shaped stands partially circling an open outfield that features a thirty-five-foot green metal scoreboard in dead center. The grandstand is rimmed by a string of open arches that lend the place a classic, old-time feel. It's been around for nearly a hundred years. I used to love playing there. Every time I took the field in that ancient stadium, I was reminded of the legends who'd roamed that grass in a more innocent time: Babe Ruth, Lou Gehrig, Ted Williams, Yogi Berra—they'd all turned up for exhibition and barnstorming-type games over the years. Former president George H. W. Bush spent a lot of time there during his Yale days, when he played first base for the Bulldogs. So did another former president, William Howard Taft, who taught legal history at Yale Law School between his time in the White House and on the United States Supreme Court. I'd heard that Taft was such a determined baseball fan that school officials had to remove an iron armrest between two wooden-slat seats so he could fit his large frame comfortably in his favorite spot behind home plate; sure enough, Taft's double-wide perch was still there during my playing days.

Despite this home-field advantage, we came out on the short side of the score that afternoon against the St. John's Redmen (back before they were known by the more politically correct name Red Storm), but the disappointing result did nothing to diminish our shared sense of moment and history. True, it was a discouraging reminder that you can play your heart out in a meaningful game and still come up empty, but the game has taken on such historic proportions over the years that, to a man, we all counted ourselves richer for having been there.

One of the main reasons the game has lived on in baseball annals is because it was given the star treatment by Roger Angell, the legendary baseball writer for *The New Yorker,* who was in the stands that afternoon. The matchup loomed on the calendars of a great many New York–area baseball fans that season for the way it pitted two of the most highly touted collegiate pitchers in the region against each other: Frank Viola of St. John's and me. It also stood out as a stark reminder of a forgotten time in baseball, as the professional game struggled with the prospect of the work stoppage that would stain our national pastime and leave millions of baseball fans with no place to put their enthusiasms for a good chunk of the 1981 season. Roger Angell took note of the game on the schedule and thought he might get an article out of it; as it turned out, he got a whole lot more.

Roger arranged it so that he watched the game alongside Smoky Joe Wood, the great Red Sox hurler who once notched thirty-four wins in a single season. (For good measure, he also won three games in the World Series that year, carrying Boston to the 1912 world championship.) Joe Wood had gone on to manage the Yale baseball team and had been a fixture at Yale Field for decades, although now that he was in his nineties he didn't attend very many games. Happily, he came to this one.

Certainly, if our game had been a dud, no one but the players would have given it a second thought. But it was no dud. Frank Viola and I ended up matching zeros for the longest while, and as the contest unfolded it became apparent to everyone in that grand old stadium that something special was happening on the field. Even more special was the fact that I'd managed to hold the St. John's batters hitless through the first nine innings. Like most pitchers who manage to go deep into a ball game without giving up a hit, I was helped along by some stellar defensive play behind me. Some glove work was mine, too—and looking back I take as much pride in my fielding that day as I do in my pitching. In the fifth inning, for example, I lunged to my left to grab a hot grounder through the box off the bat of the St. John's short-stop, Brian Miller, and got enough on the throw to first to beat him by a half step.

In the sixth inning, I got the first out and then proceeded to walk the next two hitters. As I've noted, in a scoreless game, you don't think about things like a no-hitter; you think about keeping that runner on second from coming around to score. Luckily, I had a strong pickoff move even back in college. Our shortstop, Bobby Brooke, was a tremendous all-around athlete who went on to a successful career in the National Hockey League, and he and I had a version of that play I'd later use with the Mets, where I spun toward second just before the shortstop broke for the bag. Here we caught the St. John's runner leaning the wrong way, and Bobby made a spectacular effort to reach for the ball and place the tag. Then I came back and struck out the Redmen's hard-hitting first baseman, Karl Komyathy, to end the inning with the no-hitter still intact—and, more important, with the score still knotted at 0–0.

There was another fine play in the top of the seventh, with a runner on second and one out. The St. John's batter hit a rising rope, but our second baseman and captain, Gerry Harrington, leaped to grab it and somehow managed to flip the ball back to Bobby Brooke to double-off the runner.

Meanwhile, Frank Viola was doing his part to keep our guys from scoring—and to ensure that our two names would be inextricably linked for the balance of our careers. (Such were the epic proportions the game took on over the years, so much so that when Frank and I ultimately became teammates for a stretch late in my Met career, the local sportswriters dredged up accounts of this Northeast Regional game as if it had just happened the day before.) It seemed like we had our chances every inning, but the rhythm of the game was against us. A line drive here . . . caught. A ground ball up the middle . . . snagged. A shot down the first-base line . . . just foul. A base-running gaffe to take us out of another threat. It just wasn't our day. Not to detract from Frank Viola's work; he shut us down when it mattered. We got a bunch of hits off of him, but the score was what counted, and we couldn't push a run across the plate. He was tough; just one lousy run, and I might have had a no-hit shutout to cap off my collegiate career—but if that's how it had ended, I don't think folks would still be talking about that game.

Let me pull back for a bit and put the game in context. A shot at an NCAA championship was a giant opportunity for us, but it didn't get in the way of our classes and exams. This was Yale, after all. During the season, academics were obviously a priority. Here, in the postseason, classes were already over for most of the guys on the team, but a lot of us still had exams and a few of the guys were taking the LSATs or the MCATs or putting together other postgraduate plans, so very few players turned up on the field for the two or three practices leading up to this tournament. At one session, there were only four or five of us, and we laughed about it. At any other college program in the country, we imagined, guys would be taking extra batting practice, extra infield, extra everything, but here at Yale it was just a game. In the Ivies, they take that whole mind-body connection pretty seriously; sports are merely an adjunct to an overall education. Winning was important, but it certainly wasn't everything.

In the end, I think, this relaxed environment served us well. It kept us loose—and it kept baseball in perspective. A lot of us didn't even think of ourselves as baseball players, at least not in any kind of first-and-foremost sort of way. We had a collection of great athletes on that team, but our best players excelled in other sports. I've already mentioned Bobby Brooke, in the NHL. Rich Diana, our center fielder and one of my closest friends (then and still), came to Yale to play football and ended up playing briefly for the Miami Dolphins. (He's now an orthopedic surgeon, by the way.) Joe Dufek, our left fielder, played quarterback for the Buffalo Bills. Other team-mates continued to excel in the classroom: in addition to the four starters who would go on to play professional sports, our starting nine featured three future law school graduates, another physician, and one art school graduate—and so, for a lot of us, baseball wasn't really a priority.

Don't misunderstand me: we were a competitive bunch, and we played to win. But here in the postseason we'd be going up against guys who were counting on a career in the game. It's tough to match up against teams like that. We had a couple of pure baseball players, to be sure, including Joe Impagliazzo, who ended up pitching in the Montreal Expos organization, and a hard-hitting freshman catcher named Tony Paterno, who briefly played minor league ball, and yet somehow we put it all together that year and ratcheted our game to a whole other level.

Personally, I don't think I could have played such an important role, pitching us into the postseason and shutting down this strong St. John's club through the first nine innings, if I hadn't gone to the Cape Cod Baseball League the previous summer. The experience was a real confidence builder for me—and the first chance I'd had to test myself against some of the best amateur ballplayers in the country. I'd finally decided to give up football and focus on baseball, but I still thought of myself as an all-around athlete. I told myself I was only pitching to help out my team; I was happiest as a ballplayer when I had a bat in my hands. At Yale, when I wasn't pitching, I played in the outfield—and, since they used a designated hitter in the college game, when I was pitching I was also the DH.

But I'd happened to post some big numbers on the mound that sophomore season, going 11–2 with a 1.31 earned run average, and I'd started to hear that I was a legitimate pro prospect. The good news–bad news split here was that any shot I did have at a major league career would come as a pitcher. It was a take-it-or-leave-it deal. I'd never even thought of playing professional ball until that season, and now here I was, getting a lot of press and attention—and yet beneath all of that clamor was an undercurrent of doubt. Some of those doubts were my own, I'll admit. Yeah, I was an All-Ivy pitcher, but that didn't necessarily mean anything. The thinking was that I could never match up against kids from Florida State, or Clemson, or any of the big-time baseball programs around the country.

That's where my short stint with the Cotuit Kettleers of the Cape Cod league came in, and the important takeaway for me as a young ballplayer was that I could compete against guys who were supposed to be the best young ballplayers in the country—with my bat *and* my arm, as it turned out. As a result, I went into my junior year at Yale with a whole new mind-set, and as the season played out I started to think about declaring myself eligible for the draft and finishing my last year of school at a later date—and I did, eventually. There was talk that season that I might even be a first-round prospect, so that was bouncing around in the back of my head as I put together another strong season for Yale.

By the time this regional matchup against St. John's came around, I was used to pitching with scouts in attendance. (In his *New Yorker* account, Roger Angell guessed there were as many as fifty on hand for this game.) I was also used to pitching against big-time talent. The Redmen had some heavy hitters, but I wasn't intimidated by their lineup. We didn't really have a scouting report on these guys, but I knew the leadoff batter was hitting over .400 and the number two hitter was close to .500. After that, I was on my own.

I had some butterflies as the game got under way, but I always had butterflies. Even in the majors, I was always a little uneasy as game time approached, until I started throwing and feeling comfortable. I didn't feel any pressure, though—not the way these St. John's kids were probably feeling pressure. They were expected to dispatch us Yalies without too much trouble; I guess they weren't counting on me to throw the game of my life.

There wasn't much of a crowd, beyond the scouts and the friends and families of the players—and, of course, Bart Giamatti, Yale's president, a passionate baseball fan who would go on to serve a too-short stint as commissioner of Major League Baseball. It was a big crowd for us, though. The attendance estimate at the opening of this chapter also comes courtesy of Roger Angell, who figured in his article that the stadium was about half full, but I didn't think there were more than a thousand or so scattered around the grandstand. Our fellow Yale students? They didn't usually come out to our games, not the way they did for the football and basketball teams; besides, the semester was all but over and most folks had already gone home for the summer. My parents were there, though—they never missed a game—along with two of my younger brothers, Brian and Charlie. The families all sat together, just like they did for every home game. The only difference here was that it might turn out to be one of the last games of our season, so maybe we would all go out for pizza afterward, as a group.

Naturally, I wanted to pitch us to a win and move on in the tournament, but mostly I wanted to pitch well. In the back of my mind, I was already thinking this might be the last college game of my career, and more than anything else I wanted to keep my string of complete games intact. I'd started twenty-seven games for Yale—and I'd finished all of them. I wanted to make it twenty-eight for twenty-eight, which I thought would be a pretty cool record. I didn't know how I would do that against this touted St. John's lineup, but I liked my chances.

Also, I knew there'd be a payday coming my way once I declared myself eligible for the amateur draft—and I wanted to make sure I pitched well enough to earn a signing bonus rich enough to pay off my college loans. A baseball career was no sure thing, but a relatively modest signing bonus was certainly within reach, so these were my two personal goals going into this St. John's game: to finish what I started and to impress enough of the scouts in attendance so that I might set off on the next chapter in my life without any debt.

I got off to a strong start, retiring the side in the top of the first, then setting the heart of the Redmen lineup down in order in the second—the last two on strikeouts. I came off the mound after that second inning thinking I was invincible, untouchable, and in all my years of pitching I don't think I ever felt so *on* my game as I did in the early going that afternoon. Man, it was a heady feeling. I was fluid, strong, focused. That cape I mentioned earlier, the one all pitchers put on before a game? Mine was flapping majestically behind me like a thing of beauty.

Frank Viola must have had a heady, majestic feeling of his

own, because he hung in there all afternoon. We scratched out our hits against him, here and there, but we couldn't seem to package them together in any kind of orchestrated way. He pitched in and out of trouble like it was nothing at all.

As the no-hitter reached into the late innings, I seemed to pick up a head of steam. I got through the eighth without incident, and then I retired the side in the ninth. I doubt that I stopped to think about the no-hitter after notching that third out, because it wasn't a no-hitter in my mind. If we'd had any kind of comfortable lead—any lead at all, really—I suppose I would have been. I'd have been out there pumping my fist, thinking, Let's get this no-hitter done and in the books! But there was still a game to win—and, keeping in mind my goal to complete what I started, a game to finish. I remember thinking I'd just have to get the next guy, and the next, and the next. I was like an assassin out there, gunning down all these hitters. That's the image that popped into my head as we reached extra innings. I wasn't focused on a no-hitter. I wasn't tallying my strikeouts. I was in a zone. I was thinking, Okay, who's next? One, two, three. Let's go. Let's get this over with.

I got the Redmen in order in the top of the tenth, too. I'd thrown a ton of pitches by this point. They didn't usually keep pitch counts in those days, at least not at Yale, but someone— one of the scouts, I think—told me afterward that I ended up throwing 176 pitches that afternoon. Along the way, I collected 16 strikeouts, which was certainly one of the reasons I had such a high pitch count. I must have been well over 120 pitches by the tenth, and yet I was still going strong,

I made another fine defensive play in the eleventh, to keep the no-hitter going and extend the string of zeros. Rather than describe it myself and risk sounding like a blowhard, I'll let Roger Angell do the honors. "With two out in the top of the eleventh," Roger wrote toward the end of his long article, which he called "The Web of the Game," "a St. John's batter nudged a soft little roller up the first-base line—such an easy, waiting, schoolboy sort of chance that the Yale first baseman, Brien O'Connor, allowed the ball to carom off his mitt: a miserable little butchery, except that the second baseman, seeing his pitcher sprinting for the bag, now snatched up the ball and flipped it toward him almost despairingly. Darling took the toss while diving full-length at the bag and, rolling in the dirt, beat the runner by a hair."

A storybook ending appeared to write itself in the bottom of the eleventh as we loaded the bases with two outs, after a hit and a couple walks. Viola was tiring, it seemed—that, or maybe the home plate umpire was growing tired of the extra-long affair, because pitches on the corner that had been going Frank's way during the regulation innings were now going ours. In any case, you didn't hear any complaints from our side, and there was an unspoken sentiment running up and down our bench that our next batter, right fielder Dan Costello, would wait out a third straight walk against Frank Viola to force home the winning run and finally put an end to the contest. As a fellow pitcher, I would have hated to see the game end on such a fizzling note—but I would have taken it. Oh, we all would have taken it. But Costello wasn't quite as patient at the plate as I might have expected; he swung at Viola's very first pitch and grounded meekly to Brian Miller at short to end the rally.

Viola was done after that—and, alas, so were we.

Steve Scafa, St. John's left-handed-hitting second baseman, led off the top of the twelfth for the Redmen. A scrappy guy, he always seemed to get his bat on the ball. My first thought as he dug in was, Okay, Ronnie, you're not striking this guy out, so just make him put it in play. Tony Paterno and I thought we'd start him out with a fastball away. I meant to keep it down, but it hung up there a little, and Scafa reached out and went with the pitch and stroked a picture-perfect line drive that floated over Bobby Brooke's head at short and landed softly on the grass in front of our left fielder. Just like that, the no-hitter was over, and I stepped off the mound to take a deep breath and refocus. When I looked up, there was Scafa at first, tipping his batting helmet. It's like the moment had been put on pause. There was my catcher, standing straight up behind home plate, looking right at me. He wasn't down in his crouch. I thought, What the hell is going on here? I knew Scafa had just broken up the no-hitter, but I was trying to win the game. I was thinking, *Come on! Let's go! Next batter!*

Then a voice came over the public address system, announcing that my eleven innings of no-hit ball was a record for an NCAA tournament game, and everyone in that wonderful old stadium stood to applaud. I wasn't expecting that. I wasn't expecting the guys in the St. John's dugout to stand and tip their caps. I wasn't expecting my own teammates to stand and do the same. (Some of the St. John's players even threw their red caps on the field—the ultimate nod!) I wasn't expecting a long standing ovation from the crowd. To be sure, this was bigger than I'd thought—way bigger. I knew I was having a great game. I knew I hadn't allowed a hit. But you can't allow yourself to go there as a pitcher. You just have to set about it, and pitch, and keep to your game plan.

It took a couple beats for the commotion to settle, and as soon as it did I rushed myself back to that pitching rubber. In retrospect, I probably should have grabbed another few moments to collect my thoughts and return my full attention to the game, but I was so concerned with moving things forward that I didn't give myself time to get back into it. I just stepped back on that hill and made to throw, and I didn't really pay all that much attention to Steve Scafa at first base.

Big mistake. Like I said, we didn't have any real scouting reports back then, so I didn't know Scafa had stolen thirty-five bases that season, but I should have known just by looking at him that he'd be going. He was built like a guy who could run—and it was clearly a running situation. I don't remember all these years later if I threw over to first to keep Scafa close, but if I did, it was only once or twice, and without any real attempt to pick him off—just a soft toss or two to let him know I was there.

One of the knocks on my pitching motion before I got to the bigs was that I was slow to the plate. A keen set of baseball eyes would have surely noticed this at some point in the first eleven innings—and, it appeared, Scafa or one of his coaches had done just that. Scafa was off on the very first pitch. Tony Paterno had some trouble coming up with the ball behind the plate, but Scafa had the base stolen anyway. That one was on me, not my catcher. I should have done a better job of holding the runner on—heck, I could have at least made another soft toss—but I'd allowed myself to get distracted by all that noise and nonsense. It had taken me out of my game, and now I was paying for it.

And then I paid for it again. This time, I barely even looked Scafa back to second, and he took off for third. He went on a 1–1 count, as I recall, which meant he checked me out for a couple pitches before picking his spot—which in turn meant I ignored him for those same couple pitches, allowing him to think he'd have the base free and clear.

It's amazing to me now, looking back, how quickly a game can get away from you. One moment, you're throwing eleven innings of no-hit ball; the next, you've got a guy on third with nobody out in a scoreless game. I may have been an All-Ivy pitcher, and I may have been (mostly) unhittable that day at Yale Field, but I had no idea how to manage an inning. Competitively, I could power my way through a lineup and do a good enough job with pitch selection and placement to win ball games. But intellectually I didn't really have a clue. How do you keep a team from executing its running game? How do you minimize the damage after you allow a base runner? How do you put your catcher in the best position to make a throw if the runner attempts to steal? All the subtleties and nuances that would become almost instinctive as I developed were beyond me just then.

I should have paid more attention to Scafa on first base and made double sure he didn't get a good jump. My attention had been on the St. John's hitters all day long, and I didn't shift over to worrying about the guy on base until it was too late. I could have tried a few more throws over to first, varying my timing with each toss. I could have made a quick throw, then held the ball for an extra few beats, and then taken a slide-step, and a step-off, and on and on. Instead, all I managed was one or two lazy throws—if that.

As a right-hander, I should have found it even easier to hold Scafa on at second than at first, but I ignored him there, too. He checked me out for those two pitches, but I didn't look him back or change my delivery or do any damn thing to tilt the game in my favor, where it had been all along. There was a right-hander at the plate, Karl Komyathy, which made it easier for Scafa to steal third because the hitter was in the catcher's way, but I don't even think I took this into account. I just went after the hitter. I thought my stuff would see me through. And for the time being it did: I managed to get Komyathy swinging.

Next up was St. John's catcher, Don Giordano, who hit a grounder to Bobby Brooke at short. In a perfect world, this would have put the Redmen rally on pause, but Scafa danced off the bag at second in such a way that he rattled my normally sure-handed pal, and Giordano reached safely on the error. Now there were two on and one out, but before I could figure out how to pitch to the next batter, Scafa stole third. Once again, I'd forgotten about the base runner, and I finally paid for it.

I thought St. John's might put on a squeeze with that meaningful run on third—and sure enough, that's just what they did. On a 1–0 count to the next batter, Paul Maruffi, Scafa broke down the line as I went into my motion. He left a little early, which gave me a bit of an edge because I could see him in my peripheral vision, and I could see the batter turn as if to bunt, so I did what I'd always been told to do in that situation: I fired the ball directly at the batter's head. I wasn't out to hit him, but I couldn't let him lean in and get a bunt down either, so I had to brush him back, and as he leaned away from the pitch he pulled in his hands. The ball still found Maruffi's bat, though, and he fouled it off.

Scafa returned to the bag, and I didn't think they'd put the squeeze back on for the very next pitch, so I fired a fastball over the outside corner to run the count to 1–2. Now, with two strikes on the batter, I knew Maruffi wouldn't be bunting, and I was still throwing hard, so I blew another fastball by him for strike three.

That made it runners on first and third, with two out, and here the St. John's manager lifted Giordano for a pinch runner, a speedy infielder named Tom Covino. This got me thinking. It got my manager, Joe Benanto, thinking, too. I know because he came out to talk to me at that point. Joe was one of those straight-talking, no-bullshit managers. He yelled. He cussed. He expected his guys to play hard and to know the situation. I'm sure he'd noticed that I'd mismanaged this inning, but mercifully he didn't say anything. Actually, he let me do the talking. Tony Paterno and all the infielders had joined us on the mound, and Joe Benanto looked at me and said. "What are you thinking?"

Not as in "What the *hell* are you thinking?" Just "What are you thinking?" He wanted my take on the situation.

I said, "First and third, a pinch runner on first, they're gonna put something on."

He nodded. "Damn straight," he said. "And here's what we do. Catcher comes up and fires a strike, right back to Ronnie's head. Makes like he's throwing to second, but it just goes to the pitcher. Let the runner take second. If the guy breaks off third, we're out of the inning."

It was a Little League–type play, but you'd be surprised how often those fundamentals can pay off. It didn't here, though. The pinch runner broke for second on the very first pitch to Redmen shortstop Brian Miller, and Tony Paterno burst from his crouch and gunned the ball back to the mound. The only problem with Tony's throw was that it was a little high. My follow-through left me falling off the rubber in such a way that I couldn't reach the ball as it sailed past—although at first it appeared we'd be okay because our second baseman, Jeremy Spear (who had come on to replace Gerry Harrington earlier in the game), simply stepped in and picked it off in that no-man's-land behind the mound, just short of the second-base bag. Naturally, the pinch runner wasn't interested in continuing on to second, and he pulled up short; his real objective was to get caught in a rundown and thereby give Scafa an opportunity to scamper home.

Spear looked Scafa back to third, which was the proper play, then turned his full atttention to the pinch runner hung up between first and second, which was not. Jeremy needed to make the guy on third his priority; that run was more important than a *chance* at an out. Instead, he ran toward the pinch runner, forcing him back toward first—although at this juncture he still had Scafa frozen at third. Finally, Jeremy threw the ball to O'Connor at first, as Scafa broke for home. O'Connor quickly turned and fired a pea to Tony Paterno behind the plate, but the ball arrived a shade too late, and Scafa slid in under the tag to give St. John's a 1–0 lead.

I ended up striking out Brian Miller to end the inning, but the damage had been done. A right-handed relief pitcher named Eric Stampfl came on and struck out our side on ten pitches. I was his second victim. We just couldn't get our bats going against this guy. (Ironically, he'd be drafted by the Mets a couple years later.) We were deflated, defeated, done—and as we gathered our gear in the home dugout we looked across the field at the whoops and huzzahs of the St. John's players and wondered what had gone wrong.

For the longest while, the loss didn't seem real. For going on four hours, I'd done pretty much what I'd wanted to on that mound. I couldn't just shut that off, now that we had finally breathed our last. It was the first time as an athlete that I felt as if I could will it so. Whatever I wanted this game to be, I could make it happen—that had been my mind-set out there. Certain athletes, like Tiger Woods or Michael Jordan, always seem to will it so. You watch them perform and know they are in complete control. Wayne Gretzky was the same way on the ice. Joe Montana, in his prime. Pelé, I suppose, when he was building his legend. You can see it in their eyes. You can see it in their manner. You can see it in the way their opponents seem to shrink from them. That's how I felt out there on Yale Field that afternoon, through the first eleven innings: like I could will it so. That is, until I couldn't—because, of course, the St. John's guys were also out there, willing it so for themselves.

This right here was one of the great epiphanies for me as a competitive athlete, only it took a while for it to resonate. I was helped along in this the following year, by one of my first managers in professional baseball—a former major leaguer named Tommy Burgess, who worked with me in AA ball when I was in the Texas Rangers organization. Tommy came up to me after a rough outing, put his arm around me, and said, "You know, those guys are trying, too."

It was a really sweet thing for him to say, I thought at the time. Still do. A lot of managers would have chewed me out. A lot more would have left me alone to figure things out for myself. But Tommy just broke it down and made it simple. I never forgot that. Everyone on that baseball diamond is trying to get to the same place, I realized. And from time to time everyone believes that he can will it so. That was Steve Scafa, over in the other dugout. Here's a guy who broke up my no-hitter with a clean single to left field—he tipped his cap and then promptly stole second, third, *and* home to carry the day for his team. And here I'd thought *I* had it going on that day.

I remember looking in the stands for my parents, after our last guy went down on strikes. I wanted to catch my dad's eye, to know that I had done okay. I was disappointed, but it was a double-elimination tournament, so we weren't out of it just yet—and I would take my pick-me-ups where I could find them. We had another game the next day, against Central Michigan. (We came up short in that one, too, by a score of 7–2, and I returned to pitch an inning in relief.) To tell the truth, most of that postgame stuff is a blur. In the college game, there's usually some show of sportsmanship between the two teams, like a handshake line, but I don't have any recollection of that following this game. John Franco, who would go on to a great career as a reliever for the Mets and the Reds, was on that St. John's staff, and he and I had been teammates the previous summer in the Cape Cod league, so I'm sure I said hello to him after the game—but I have no specific memory of it.

I'm sure I shook hands with Frank Viola, too, but I don't recall exchanging words with Frank until a couple years later, when my Tidewater Tides went to Toledo to play his Mud Hens in a Triple A contest. He sent over a note that said, "I'm cooking steaks tonight—why don't you come over?" I went, and we didn't say a word about the game. We talked about our careers, our families, where we grew up. We were joined like brothers because of this one game, but we didn't talk about it. We just talked.

For all I know I congratulated Steve Scafa on the field as well. We were also connected. I don't remember ever speaking to him after the game, and I'm certain we've never spoken over the years, but from time to time I'll hear from a mutual acquaintance and we'll pass along our regards, because of our special bond. That's what Roger Angell wrote about in his *New Yorker* account, the timeless links we share with players past and present. Somehow Roger found a point of connection between this 1–0 game and another memorable 1–0 showdown between Walter Johnson and Smoky Joe Wood, and he used the serendipitous fact that Wood was in attendance to make the point that games like this twelve-inning heartbreaker tend to live on in our shared baseball memories because of those connections.

And yet all I remember from that day's postgame excitement was that I was craning my neck, looking for my folks, wondering if we'd be joining my teammate Rich Diana and his parents at our favorite pizza place in town, just like we did after every other home game. But before I could reach my family, I was swallowed up by a sea of people. Reporters, mostly. There were local camera crews, too. Apparently, during the course of the game, word had gone around on the newswires that something special was happening in the NCAA playoff game at Yale Field, and folks had come out.

People were spilling out of the stands and onto the field. Kids were coming up to me and asking me to sign autographs. It was the first time I'd ever signed my name to anything but a check or a term paper. One little kid just seemed to want to touch my arm.

I thought, This is crazy.

I thought, What the hell is going on here?

I thought, Enough already, let's get something to eat.

But the noise and commotion didn't die down anytime soon. I'd just pitched the greatest game of my life and come up short, but it was all right. Even at twenty years old, I could appreciate the bittersweetness of the moment, and the beautiful cruelty of the game I might be playing for the next while. I had the whole of my baseball life in front of me, and yet I had no idea if the game just ended would be as good as it was going to get for me or if it would be the start of something even bigger and better. For the time being, anyway, it was all right indeed.

INNING SUMMARY

STEVE SCAFA: single to left
   Scafa steals second
KARL KOMYATHY: strikeout swinging
DON GIORDANO: grounder to shortstop; reaches
               on error
   Scafa steals third
PAUL MARUFFI: strikeout
      Tom Covino pinch runs for Giordano
      Covino steals second
      Scafa steals home, completing double-steal
BRIAN MILLER: strikeout

Done

There comes a time in every athlete's career when there's nothing left. For me, it came on my thirty-fifth birthday—although, to be completely honest, the moment arrived long before. That's just the day it announced itself.

I was at the butt end of a miserable 1995 season, with an earned run average over 6.00 and a won-loss record of just 4–7. I was hanging on to my spot in the Oakland A's starting rotation by the thinnest of threads. If I had to guess, I'd say the reasons A's manager Tony La Russa kept throwing me out there were because the front office told him to do so and because he was a good guy. Best I could tell, there was no *baseball* reason for me to keep pitching—it's not like I was helping my team.

Tony and I got along well, but that didn't warrant my having a spot in the rotation. I had a big contract, and I was apparently healthy, and there was likely some pressure to justify the expense of keeping me around on the team. Also, it probably didn't hurt that I'd been around the block a few times, and someone must have thought it might be helpful to have another veteran arm on the staff—even if it hung from the shoulder of a guy who could no longer get major league hitters out with anything resembling consistency.

As bad as I was that year, some of the other Oakland starters were worse, so I wasn't really worried about my job. I should have been, but I wasn't. I'd fooled myself into thinking I was a key part of the team, and that if there were cuts to be made they would come from the bottom. It's like that old line about being fast enough to outrun a bear in the woods: you don't have to beat the bear, you just have to outrun the guy next to you. I was coming off a respectable 1994 season. Not great, but respectable—that's the low bar I was setting for myself here. And I'd made a home for myself in the Oakland area. I was active in the local community. The fans seemed to respond well to me. I got along with a lot of the players, especially Dennis Eckersley, the only true star on a crappy team that was going nowhere in a pretty decent hurry. I'd helped pitch three different teams into the postseason (the 1986 Mets, the 1988 Mets, and the 1992 A's)—altogether, a respectable baseball résumé. If I had a bad start or two, I didn't think that would be enough to bounce me from the pitching staff.

I thought I'd put enough distance between me and the bear to keep running for the next while. Let him bite some other pitcher in the ass and leave me alone to do my thing—even if my *thing* wasn't quite what it used to be. Basically, I was mired knee-deep in complacency, and at the end of the day (at the end of a career!) complacency only shows you the door. You can't keep toiling at the professional level in any endeavor without stepping it up from time to time, only here I couldn't quite step it up. My last start—August 15, against Kansas City—produced the following dispiriting stat line:

	IP	H	R	ER	BB	SO	HR	ERA
R DARLING, L (4–7)	5.1	6	5	5	3	4	1	6.23

It wasn't spectacularly awful, just awful, and it came at a time of year when last-place teams start to think about the future. September call-ups were just a couple weeks away, and it might have occurred to me that it was somewhat ironic, for a guy who'd earned his stripes as a late-season call-up, pushing aside an established starter for a last-place team, to be the established starter pushed aside by another young gun.

But, alas, such is life. Such is baseball. And such are the woes and worries of a starting pitcher when the bottom falls out of his game.

Tony La Russa called me into his office to give me the news. He said, "Ronnie, we're gonna start this kid, Doug Johns."

Doug Johns. (Doug Johns?) It was a passing of the torch no one would remember except me—and, perhaps, Doug Johns, a cup-of-coffee left-hander who'd go on to pitch in parts of four seasons before disappearing into the baseball archives. I've since looked back on this moment and thought, Gee, wouldn't it have been nice to have been replaced by a future All-Star? Then I could say, "At least I lost my job to Mark Mulder."

Tony played it as respectfully as he could. He was extraordinarily decent about it. He said, "I'm sorry, Ronnie, but we're gonna shut you down for the rest of the year. We want to see what this kid can do."

It was a conversation I should have seen coming, and now that I was in its middle, it was like it was happening to some other veteran who could no longer get hitters out.

Tony laid out my options. He said I was welcome to stick around and travel with the team. He knew I was tight with Dennis. He knew I could be an asset in the clubhouse, even if I couldn't contribute on the field. He knew how much I loved being around the game, and he hated like hell to take that from me with just six weeks left in the season. However, in order for me to stay around, the A's would have to put me on the disabled list, because major league rosters wouldn't expand for another few weeks. The decision to go with Doug Johns required a roster move of some sort. I understood that. There would be no job for me in the bullpen, no chance to spot-start until the other September call-ups joined the roster. I understood that, too.

A word or two on Tony La Russa—the man gave me the single best piece of advice I ever received from a manager. It was 1992. We were in Detroit. The A's had picked me up the previous summer in a trade with the Montreal Expos, for Matt Grott and Russell Cormier (two other guys who never made much of a dent in baseball history), two weeks after the Mets had traded me to the Expos for Tim Burke. And now here I was, in the first month or so of my first full season with Oakland, off to a disappointing start. We had early batting practice, and I was out in center field at Tiger Stadium. That's how I used to get my running in. I would shag my ass off for an hour.

Tony ran out to meet me. He said, "Hey, Load. Got a minute?"

He called me Load. He called everyone else Skip. Me, he called Load. I still don't know why.

I said, "Hey, Load. What's up?"

I figured if he could call me Load, I could return the favor.

He said, "What's going on?"

I said, "What do you mean?"

He said, "How are you feeling?"

I said, "Physically, I feel fine."

He said, "Is something going on at home?"

There was, actually. There was the usual strife and strain. My wife and I would end up getting divorced a couple of years later, and I guess this was the beginning of the troubles between us.

I explained it to Tony, best I could.

He listened, best he could.

It wasn't an easy conversation to have, because ballplayers didn't usually talk about this kind of stuff with their managers, but we got through it. Finally, Tony said, "Listen to me, Load. As a human being, I care. But as your manager, you've got to start winning some fucking games. This is ridiculous."

I'd lost a game to Cleveland the night before, giving up five runs in four innings. The outing before that, against Minnesota, I'd given up five runs in four and a third. I couldn't find the plate. I couldn't locate my pitches. I couldn't do shit. Tony was right to call me on it, and he really got to me. He came right out and said what needed saying, and then he went back to the batting cage while I stayed in the outfield. Running. Thinking. Feeling sorry for myself. The more I ran and thought and felt sorry for myself, the more I realized Tony was on to something. Normal people get to live their normal lives. They get to come home at night and work through their problems. Being a professional means doing your job. A surgeon doesn't get to have an off day just because he's not getting along with his wife. A machinist can't afford to miss a beat on the assembly line. Doesn't matter what your job is: air traffic controller, tax attorney, peanut vendor—just suck it up and get it done. You can slog through your shit on your own time.

It sounds simple to me now in the retelling, but at the time this was the biggest lightbulb-over-the-head moment of my career—probably because it found me in one of the first trouble spots in my marriage. It was a key lesson, and it turned my season around. I wound up going 15–10 that year, and pitched well enough to convince the A's to sign me to the biggest contract of my career—a three-year deal for $7.5 million.

Now here we were, at the tail end of that big contract, in the middle of another difficult conversation. As Tony spoke, I started to feel bad for him. I thought, This can't be easy. I thought, What a shitty job. I thought, How many times has this poor guy had to tell a ballplayer he's through?

It was August 19—and the reason I remember the date is that it was my birthday.

I said, "Two things, Tony. First, thank you for wanting to keep me around, but today's my birthday, and you didn't wish me a happy birthday. And second, I've never been on the disabled list in my entire career."

He said, "Tell me the first thing and the second thing are both wrong."

I said, "Afraid not."

Tony had been around ballplayers long enough to know that a guy who'd played thirteen seasons in the bigs without a trip to the disabled list wasn't about to "volunteer" for such a designation. It'd be one thing if I was actually hurt, but I didn't want that kind of blemish on my record for no real reason.

He said, "Can't tell you how sorry I am about this, Load. I know it's not much, but happy birthday."

I said, "Yeah, thanks."

We talked briefly about my other options. I could retire—which meant I wouldn't get paid for the balance of the season.

(At my salary, that meant a sacrifice of about $500,000.) I could get released—which meant I would get paid, but I'd have to suffer the indignity of being released. It also meant my dignity now came with a price tag: $500,000.

Tony said, "Take your time, Ronnie. Think about it. Just tell me what you want to do."

THE END OF MY MET CAREER had been a whole other indignity. It found me one late afternoon in August 1990 at Dodger Stadium, in the fourteenth inning of a must-win game—for the Mets as a team, and for me as a contributing member.

For a pitcher, it's rarely a good sign when you're working the fourteenth inning. It usually means something is not going right with your career. Either you're fighting to make an impression or you're scrambling to return to form. About the best you can hope for is to not screw up—never a sure recipe for success. This particular extra-inning affair presented itself as a kind of final proving ground, and by the twelfth inning manager Bud Harrelson had already used four pitchers. I got the call in the bullpen, and as I stood to get warm I tried to put myself in a positive frame of mind. That's one of the toughest things for a reliever, I was quickly learning—especially a hardly used long-relief guy who was called on only as a last resort. Keeping sharp between mop-up and extra-inning appearances, when all that's expected of you is to eat up some innings in a laugher or to keep the game close later on, is a difficult assignment. I'd started against San Diego just four days earlier, going six nothing-special innings and allowing five earned runs in a 7–0 loss to Ed Whitson. That start dropped my record to 5–8 for the season and inflated my ERA to a hardly respectable 4.60, so I was clearly struggling.

Still, I was a competitor, and every time they handed me

the ball I wanted to justify the decision. This time was no different. In fact, I remember warming up out in the bullpen and feeling an extra-special something on my pitches. It might have been wishful thinking, but I don't think so: my fastball was hopping. It felt to me like I was throwing harder than I had in two or three years. Maybe it was because I hadn't gotten a lot of work that season, so my arm was unusually fresh and lively for late August. Or maybe it was because I had something to prove. I looked around that beautiful old stadium, which back then wasn't quite so old as it is today, and I took a deep breath of the cool, dry southern California air, and I began to fill myself with a quiet, certain confidence. I'd always liked pitching in Dodger Stadium. I was excited to get the call to warm up, but don't read too much into my enthusiasm: I hated pitching out of the bullpen, but only a little less than I hated the idea of not pitching at all.

A utility outfielder named José Gonzalez had come on to pinch-run for my old friend Hubie Brooks in the bottom of the ninth, and he was due up first in the twelfth inning. I wasn't too worried about him. He was mostly a pinch hitter and a pinch runner, an occasional late-inning defensive replacement. The book on him was that I didn't really have a book on him, but I got him to fly meekly to Kevin McReynolds in left. Then Dodger catcher Rick Dempsey surprised the hell out of almost everyone in the stadium by laying down a bunt to try to get something going. Before he even got the bat on the ball I thought, What the hell is a forty-year-old veteran catcher doing trying to bunt his way on? But, all credit to Rick, he managed to do just that, after which Dodger manager Tommy Lasorda promptly inserted a pinch runner, replacing Rick with fleet-footed José Offerman. I was so momentarily flustered by this unexpected turn that I hit Juan Samuel, who had briefly been our Met teammate the season before. That put runners on first and second, with only one out, and as Mike Scioscia came to the plate to pinch-hit for light-hitting shortstop Alfredo Griffin I thought, Okay, Ronnie, you've got yourself a situation.

This was a meaningful late-August game for us. The first-place Pirates had already lost to the Reds that afternoon, so we knew we had a chance to climb to two games back in the standings and one game back in the loss column. There was a lot more on the line than my flagging career prospects.

Scioscia was one of the last position players on Lasorda's bench, and he would almost certainly remain in the game at catcher to replace Dempsey, so I tried to overpower him with my fastball, on the thin hope that he might be a little distracted by the prospect of getting behind the plate the next inning when he'd been expecting a day off. I finally struck him out looking, and I hung on until the bottom of the fourteenth, slogging through the Dodger lineup along the way. Eddie Murray led off the inning—the ninth man I'd face. I never liked pitching to Murray. He was a little too disciplined for my taste; for a home-run hitter, he didn't strike out all that often, so I knew I'd have to pitch him carefully. Plus, he'd go on to hit .330 that year, so he was really seeing the ball well. I worked the count to 1–2, then got Eddie to pull the ball on the ground toward first base for the first out.

That brought José Gonzalez back to the plate, and I immediately dug myself a small hole. I missed my spots on the first couple pitches and got behind in the count—a development visiting pitchers like to avoid in these sudden-death, extra-inning games, when every base runner can put an abrupt end to your workday. Then, on a full count, I came in a shade too high with my fastball, and Gonzalez sent it down the left-field line for a home run to end the game.

I'd given up a ton of home runs in my career—but that

was the first and only time I'd served up a game-ending, walk-off home run. It was crushing.

Just like that, we were done. More to the point, *I* was done. I knew the ball was gone as soon as Gonzalez hit it, but as it cleared the fence there was time for every doubt, every uncertainty to play itself out in my head. I had time to think, What the hell happened to my career? Where did it all go wrong? Why am I even in this game, in the bottom of the fourteenth inning? And then, as I started to walk off the field, the questions continued: What am I still doing here, in a New York Mets uniform? Why have I not been traded? Why are they embarrassing me like this? And why am I embarrassing myself?

I had no answers, just questions. I had always been a durable pitcher. I'd never been on the disabled list; I'd missed only those few starts that followed my thumb injury in that 1987 game against the Cardinals. I'd always been the guy who wanted the ball in a big game, but now I wasn't so sure. I'd allowed all this doubt and uncertainty to creep into my head, to where my rallying cry was no longer "Give me the damn ball!"

Now it was more like "Me? Really?"

I never made it out to the team bus after the game. I was in no hurry to get back to the hotel. I had some friends I was planning to meet for dinner, but I asked the clubhouse kid to get a message to them that I wouldn't make it. One by one, my teammates filtered out of the clubhouse toward the bus. I grabbed a couple beers and sat by myself. (Back then, there was always beer in the clubhouse—most of us reached for a cold one right after the last out and drank it in front of our locker. If we were facing in, toward the wall, it meant we'd had a bad game; if we were facing out, toward the room, it meant we'd done our part.) I was determined to get to the bottom of all those questions that had started bouncing through my head the moment José Gonzalez pounced on that hanging fastball—and until I did, I wasn't going anywhere.

After the locker area had cleared, I wandered over to a small storage room adjacent to the clubhouse. I grabbed another couple beers and sat down on a giant equipment box. There was no one around. The team bus was long gone. By this point, I was about a half dozen beers into my introspection. The clubhouse personnel had all been sent home. There might have been one or two stadium workers still lingering in the bowels of Dodger Stadium, but nobody bothered me. For the longest time, nobody bothered me. I don't think anybody had any idea I was still in that storage room. A part of me wondered if anybody even cared.

I sat and sipped and sank into one of the deepest funks I've ever known. I thought through every damn thing that had gone wrong that season, every pitch I shouldn't have thrown, every pitch I should have thrown instead. I thought about how much the game meant to me—not this particular game, although it meant a lot and it represented a whole lot more, but the game in general. It was all I knew, basically. It occurred to me that I might have to learn how to do something else. This was the first time since I'd earned my spot in the big club that I allowed myself to doubt my abilities or to question my future in a baseball uniform. Let me tell you, it's not a place you want to go in your thinking as a young athlete. I'd just turned thirty. By today's standards, I'd have had another ten years or so to worry about stuff like this, if I stayed healthy. Even by the standards of the day, it seemed premature.

I thought, How can you win fourteen games one season and feel like you're done the next? It shouldn't happen that way. It doesn't happen that way in any other sport. LeBron James doesn't average thirty points a game one season and single digits the next. Even in baseball, at other positions, it doesn't happen that way. You don't go from being a .300 hitter to batting .165. You don't go from a forty–home run year to a ten–home run year. Today's game was a full-in-the-face reminder of how fleeting success can be for a major league pitcher. One day you've got it, the next day you don't. At the same time I didn't feel like anything had slipped away. I still felt like I could get hitters out consistently, like I could help my team, like I deserved a spot in the rotation. Heck, I'd been throwing bullets that afternoon in the bullpen.

When I finally looked at a clock it was nine-thirty in the evening—about four hours since I'd given up that home run to end the game. I wondered where the time had gone. Some empties were on the equipment box alongside me, and I wondered where all that beer had gone, too. I thought, This can't be good, me sitting here all night, wallowing in my own gloom, so I hopped down from my perch and made for the exit. I left thinking I had something to prove. To my teammates, who really hadn't seen me pitch at all that year, at least not to my ability. To my manager and coaches and the front-office guys, who seemed ready to write me off. To the scouts in the stands with the radar guns, who were deciding if I might be able to help their teams. (I hadn't heard of any specific deals being discussed that might have involved me, but the scouts are always out there, checking you out, seeing if you've still got it.) And, mostly, to myself. I wasn't ready to stop pitching just yet, but I had to find some way to claw myself back from the Siberia of long relief and spot starting and into a major league rotation. And soon.

EX-BALLPLAYERS TALK A LOT about their retirement, and I've yet to come across anyone who walked away from the game with serious money on the table—the choice Tony La Russa laid out for me on my thirty-fifth birthday. Most guys I know believe that at the end of their careers they still deserve whatever was negotiated when they signed their last contract. That's the direction I was leaning in, with this endgame scenario.

So what did I do? I took a shower—thinking it was probably my last shower as a professional ballplayer. Certainly my last as an Oakland A. As I stood there under the water, I felt a strange sense of euphoria. It was like this great weight had been lifted. I was giddy. It was an irrational sort of giddiness, an unsettling sort of giddiness, but it was very definitely a giddiness. This thing, this uncertainty that had been dogging me all season, was now upon me. I didn't have to come to the ballpark anymore, half-wondering if I'd be pulled aside and told I was through. I didn't have to roam the outfield before games, feeling like shit because I hadn't been doing my part. I didn't have to take the mound when it was my turn to start and know in my bones I was about to get the crap kicked out of me. I didn't have to deal with any of that anymore.

I toweled off, dressed, and grabbed a can of beer. I didn't tell anyone what had passed between me and my manager. I didn't call my wife. I didn't call my dad. I didn't tell any of my teammates. I thought, This is how I'll celebrate. I'd always considered myself a blue-collar guy, and this was a blue-collar move. There'd be no champagne for me at the end of the road, just a can of domestic beer.

We were living in a town called Danville at the time, just outside Oakland. Our two boys were pretty young. I had this fantasy in my head that my wife and kids would spill out of the house and welcome me home like some long-lost soldier, but that's not exactly how it went down. Not even close. I walked in the door at six-thirty that evening. I hadn't been home at six-thirty in fifteen years, not during baseball season. I walked in expecting a big greeting. I wanted to shout it out: *I'm home, guys! For good! For real!* I wanted my kids to trip over each other, scrambling to reach me for a hug. I wanted to tell them I'd be around to drive them to their practices, to take them to school each morning. I wanted to tell my wife I'd work at being a better husband. We'd take vacations together, go on outings together, be a full-time, full-fledged, year-round family . . . at long last. All those things you think you'll do, when you finally get the time, that's what I was going to do. Whatever had been going wrong, I'd now have a chance to set right. But as I walked in the door and started to download the story, my wife had something else she was trying to do. My boys looked at me like I had two heads. Everyone was busy. The boys were heading out for sleepovers that night. My wife was heading out to a tennis tournament. On my birthday, no less!

Here I'd always thought I was the one gumming up the works at home. I had this picture in my head of my wife and kids holding down the fort in my absence, waiting by the door for me to return, but of course that was just a fantasy. (And not even a *healthy* fantasy at that.) The reality was that they were living busy lives of their own. I had nothing to do with anything. If I'd come home just a few minutes later, the house would have been empty.

As a ballplayer, I'd always held myself to two standards, in terms of performance: when the hitters told me I was done, I'd listen; and when I couldn't take my turn on the mound and give my team an equal or better chance to win, it would be time to go. Here, at long last, I'd sunk to both lows. I didn't need Tony La Russa to tell me what I already knew, deep down.

It's especially tough for a pitcher to come to the realization that he's done. A position player with declining skills might still be able to contribute in the field, or on the base paths, at least from time to time. He might go 0 for 4 one day at the plate, then get a couple seeing-eye hits the next day to help his team win a ball game. But when a starting pitcher has the equivalent of 0 for 4 days every time out, there's no shrinking from it. There's no setting it aside and hoping it goes away. There's no catching a break, no seeing-eye singles to shake you out of it. Pitchers are made to feel like a smaller part of the club to begin with, and as your performance declines you start to feel ever smaller. Even your role as a veteran sage, offering advice to younger pitchers, is reduced, because who wants to get advice from someone who can't get anybody out?

Is there a magic number in your stat line that tells you when you're through? No, not really. Not for me, anyway. For some pitchers, maybe it's an earned run average over 5.00 or 6.00—two big numbers I'd shot past a long time ago. Maybe it's a number on the radar gun. Maybe it's knowing your manager and your teammates no longer trust you to pitch them out of a tough spot, and so you no longer trust yourself.

For me it was the crack of the bat. There are some batters that get a hit off you, and then you look over at first base and think, How can I give up a hit to *him*? That's when I knew. I could hear it in the solid *thwack* of the bats of the opposing hitters, like I was throwing batting practice. Like I had nothing. I started to think, I don't belong on this field. I could get someone hurt, that's how bad I was throwing. In my case, my arm was shot. It wasn't a mental thing. It wasn't a mechanical thing. It wasn't a shift in my approach. I just couldn't throw hard enough. I could still execute the perfect pitch, and place it just where I wanted it, and some utility infielder would still smoke it down the third-base line because he could wait on it long enough to drive it into left field.

It gets to where you try everything and nothing works. Even your uniform starts to feel like it doesn't fit. Not because you've put on weight but because it doesn't feel *right*. Like it belongs to someone else. Like you're playing at being a ballplayer. Your shoes are a little tight. Your hat, in the second week of August, is not your typical August hat. It's more like a May hat, because you haven't been pitching deep enough in games to get that nice August feel, where it's stained and it doesn't smell so good and it's a wonderful, beautiful badge because it represents how hard you've worked all season long.

I called Tony La Russa the next day and told him the A's would have to release me. I wouldn't go on the disabled list. I wouldn't retire and leave all that money on the table. I was as proud as the next ballplayer, but stupid pride is just that— stupid. A couple days later, I went down to the clubhouse to clean out my few things, and as I sorted through my gear and the assorted odds and ends that tend to accumulate in an athlete's locker over the course of a long season, it occurred to me that very few of us get to leave at the top of our game, on our own terms. Sandy Koufax, certainly. Joe DiMaggio, nearly. Cal Ripken Jr., sort of.

Me, I wasn't on top of anything. It wasn't how I would have scripted it—but the truth is, I would have put off scripting it, because I didn't want it to end. It's a good life, a baseball life. It's rich and rewarding and endlessly fascinating. And then, before you know it, it's gone.

Acknowledgments

Writing, like baseball, is a team sport. You can make the perfect pitch, but if there's no one behind the plate to catch it or no one behind you to field the ball once the batter puts it in play, you're just going through the motions.

To Andrew Miller, my editor, a special thank-you for keeping this project in the strike zone. I led the National League in walks in 1985, but you would not allow a free pass here. Also, thank you for your keen baseball insights and your knowledge and love of the game, all of which proved essential as we put this book together.

To Dan Paisner, my co-writer. I have spent the vast majority of my athletic life trying to be a good teammate, to put forth a true collaborative effort on and off the field. Here I'm afraid I've come up woefully short. Your patience, dogged determination, and eleventh-hour trips to the mound were endlessly admired and appreciated, and the experience of writing this book was like none other. My friends think I am a complex man, but you simplified a life. You helped to harness my *stuff* and place my memories and analysis in context. Your friendship throughout this process was invaluable. Now

I know how Ernie Banks must have felt: after working with you on *The Complete Game,* I'm ready to play two!

To Mel Berger, my literary agent, thank you for getting this project off the ground, for finding something to admire in my loose notes and rambling thoughts, and for being our biggest cheerleader as we slogged our way to deadline.

To everyone at Knopf, thank you for believing a baseball book was worthy of your most distinguished house. A special thank you to Paul Bogaards, Sara Sherbill, Maria Massey, Claudia Martinez, and Bonnie Thompson for your various extra efforts and enthusiasms.

To all the teammates, coaches, and front-office folks who had a hand in my baseball career. You are too many to mention, but no one has lived a more charmed life than me, and it is because of all of you. Bus trips, plane rides, and long road trips did nothing to dissuade my love of the game. In the end, it is the people you play with who give the game life. I am forever indebted to all of you.

JOANNA   TYLER   JORDAN

Index

A Note About the Authors

Ron Darling was a starting pitcher for the New York Mets from 1983 into 1991 and was the first Mets pitcher to be awarded a Gold Glove. He ended his career with the Oakland A's in 1995. Since 2006 he has been a game and studio analyst for SNY, covering the New York Mets; since 2007 he has also been a game and studio analyst for TBS, for that network's game-of-the-week and postseason broadcasts. Darling won an Emmy Award for best sports analyst in 2006. He was born in Honolulu, Hawaii, raised in Millbury, Massachusetts, and attended Yale University, where he was a two-time All-American. He currently lives with his family in Manhattan.

Daniel Paisner has collaborated with dozens of athletes, actors, politicians, and business leaders on their autobiographies and memoirs. He is coauthor of *Last Man Down: A Firefighter's Story of Survival and Escape from the World Trade Center* with FDNY battalion commander Richard Picciotto, and *The Girl in the Green Sweater: A Life in Holocaust's Shadow* with Krystyna Chiger.

A Note on the Type

This book was set in Granjon, a type named in compliment to Robert Granjon, a type cutter and printer active in Antwerp, Lyons, Rome, and Paris from 1523 to 1590. Granjon, the boldest and most original designer of his time, was one of the first to practice the trade of typefounder apart from that of printer.

Composed by
North Market Street Graphics, Lancaster, Pennsylvania

Printed and bound by
R. R. Donnelly, Harrisonburg, Virginia

Designed by Claudia Martinez